Archaeology beyond Dialogue

Foundations of Archaeological Inquiry

James M. Skibo, series editor

Expanding Archaeology
James M. Skibo, William H. Walker, and Axel E. Nielsen

Behavioral Archaeology: First Principles
Michael Brian Schiffer

Evolutionary Archaeology: Theory and Application
Michael J. O'Brien, editor

Unit Issues in Archaeology: Measuring Time, Space, and Material
Ann F. Ramenofsky and Anastasia Steffen, editors

Pottery Ethnoarchaeology in the Central Maya Highlands
Michael Deal

Pottery and People: A Dynamic Interaction
James M. Skibo and Gary M. Feinman, editors

Material Meanings: Critical Approaches to the Interpretation of Material Culture
Elizabeth S. Chilton, editor

Social Theory in Archaeology
Michael Brian Schiffer, editor

Race and the Archaeology of Identity
Charles E. Orser Jr., editor

Style, Function, Transmission: Evolutionary Archaeological Perspectives
Michael J. O'Brien and R. Lee Lyman, editors

The Archaeology of Settlement Abandonment in Middle America
Takeshi Inomata and Ronald W. Webb, editors

Complex Systems and Archaeology: Empirical and Theoretical Applications
R. Alexander Bentley and Herbert D.G. Maschner, editors

Essential Tensions in Archaeological Method and Theory
Todd L. and Christine S. VanPool

Archaeological Perspectives on Political Economies
Gary Feinman and Linda Nicholas, editors

Archaeology beyond Dialogue
Ian Hodder

Archaeology beyond Dialogue

Ian Hodder

THE UNIVERSITY OF UTAH PRESS
SALT LAKE CITY

FOUNDATIONS OF ARCHAEOLOGICAL INQUIRY
James M. Skibo, editor

Printed on acid-free paper

 The Defiance House Man colophon is a registered trademark of the University of Utah
Press. It is based upon a four-foot-tall, Ancient Puebloan pictograph (late PIII) near
Glen Canyon, Utah.

04   05   06   07   08   09   10
5   4   3   2   1

LIBRARY OF CONGRESS CATALOGING-IN-PUBLICATION DATA

Hodder, Ian.
   Archaeology beyond dialogue / Ian Hodder.
      p. cm. — (Foundations of archaeological inquiry)
Includes bibliographical references (p.   ) and index.
   ISBN 0-87480-779-4 (hardcover : alk. paper) — ISBN 0-87480-780-8
(pbk. : alk. paper)
   1. Archaeology—Philosophy. 2. Archaeology—Methodology.
I. Title. II. Series.
   CC72.H615 2004
   930.1—dc22   2003021962

Contents

Contents

I

Dialogical Archaeology and its Implications

It is now widely accepted that archaeologists and conservation and heritage managers need to engage in dialogue with interested parties. There has been a massive increase in international charters for the management of archaeological sites over recent decades, and many of these have turned their attention to the processes of collaboration with local communities around sites and monuments. For example, the General Assembly of ICOMOS in 1987 adopted the Charter for the Conservation of Historic Towns and Urban Areas which includes guidelines for the participation of residents. The Charter for Sustainable Tourism that emerged from the World Conference on Sustainable Tourism in 1995 stated that tourism must be "ethically and socially equitable for local communities." The Australian chapter of ICOMOS (the International Council on Monuments and Sites) has produced the Burra Charter, which moves away from defining sites and monuments in objectivist terms, and towards the description of cultural landscapes as understood and perceived by indigenous peoples (Australia ICOMOS 1981). The Corinth Workshop on Archaeological Site Management in May 2000, organized by the Getty Conservation Institute, refers to the importance of collaboration with local community members. Indeed, the Getty Conservation Institute has modified and developed the planning framework outlined in the Burra Charter (Avrami et al. 2000; see also de la Torre 1997). Specific examples of collaborative work include that at the Nevada test site (Stoffle et al. 2001) and at the Barunga rock art site in Australia (Smith et al. 1995; see also Smith and Ward 2000).

Most archaeological sites attract multiple stakeholders, many of whom may be interested in the types of narrative that are being constructed about the site. There has been much involvement of local communities in the construction of visitor centers and site interpretation, and there have been reflexive attempts to open the "site tour" to groups of different background (e.g., Handler and Gable 1997; Leone et al. 1987). The training of indigenous archaeologists allows a fuller degree of participation, though usually within the methods set by the academy. When indigenous archaeologists (Watkins 2000) are fully trained within the academy, it might be argued that their potential for expressing alternative voices is compromised. But in many collaborative examples, close integration has occurred between archaeologists and Native Americans (Swidler et al. 1997).

Experiments in using the internet to involve more communities in the process of interpretation have been at least partially successful. For example, McDavid (1997, 2000) has used a website about the Levi Jordan Plantation in Brazoria, Texas, to mediate relations between archaeologists, local community members, and descendents of both slaves and slave owners.

The wider context for these moves toward greater leveling and participation and democratization are social and economic changes including those termed globalization, post-industrialization, high capitalism, and even the cultural changes grouped under the heading of post-modernism (Hodder 1999a). The importance of diaspora and the internet also needs consideration. This book accepts that the contemporary global context of archaeology demands a whittling away of the centrality of "the academy" and an involvement in greater dialogue and participation, not as a "dumbing down," but as a real engagement with multiple perspectives. But the book also tries to move on to a consideration of what the implications of adopting such a position are. It is argued that dialogue and collaboration and multivocality on their own are not enough. Many discussions of dialogue assume that we just carry on as normal but add a bit of collaboration—add collaboration and stir. Rather, changes are needed in the ways in which we work as archaeologists.

DIALOGUE

There is a need at the start to distinguish dialogue from debate. Archaeology has always involved debate. Indeed, the discipline is partly defined by the "great debates" regarding "antiquity of man," or more recently the date of the first spread of humans into the Americas, or the relevance of evolutionary principles for cultural change. The emphasis on dialogue includes such debates but it moves on subtly from "debating archaeology" (Binford 1989).

In order to understand this shift it is helpful to look at some of the ways in which power and influence in archaeology have to some extent moved away from the white, male, Western "academy." I so clearly remember, indeed it probably still happens, that after a lecture to the Society of Antiquaries in London, the Chair would ask Professor so-and-so to make his comments on the paper just given. In contrast to the controlled debates in the cloistered halls of the British Academy or the UISPP (Union International des Sciences Prehistoriques et Protohistor-

iques), we have in recent decades seen the focus of debate shift to other fora such as the World Archaeological Congress (Ucko 1987). The increased influence of the young and less established is seen in the highly successful TAG (Theoretical Archaeology Group) conferences in Britain. There has been increased acceptance of the need to collaborate with "fringe archaeologists" such as metal detector users. There has been an acceptance and incorporation of feminist debates and women's issues. Even the rise in contract archaeology has created a center of influence outside the universities.

These shifts have meant that debate in archaeology is no longer mainly within the academy and it can no longer claim to be solely academic. There is a fuller acceptance of multiple views including from sources outside the Western academy, and there is a fuller acceptance of the ways in which the past and present depend on each other. The acceptance of this interdependence implies that adequate scientific research involves a continual awareness of the relationships between past and present. Indeed, I would argue that while several decades ago many archaeologists would have defined their discipline as "the study of the past through its material remains," or some such phrase dealing only with the scientific study of the past, today many more would accept a definition that included the present—such as "a mode of enquiry into the relationship between people and their material pasts."

The focus on dialogue in this book partly involves the search for dialectical arguments, by which I mean those that recognize the unity of opposites, that seek tensions in social processes, that see societies as both structured and contingent, and that recognize the role of agency as well as unacknowledged conditions and unintended consequences. But the focus on dialogue more specifically relates to the contention that scientific knowledge does, and should, proceed through debate, both within and beyond the boundaries of the discipline, and including reflexive critique of the assumptions and taken-for-granteds of the academy.

At one level, such a conviction could be said to be an example of the excesses of post-modernism. The latter is often associated with the erosion of the boundaries between high and low culture and the embrace of multiculturalism and multivocality. But at another level, it derives from specific social contexts in which the long-term use of archaeology to marginalize the interests of nondominant groups has been contested. Over recent decades there have been many examples of minority groups mobilizing social concern through claims on the archaeological past.

Claims for critical dialogue and inclusivity often have a moral tone, and certainly one of the underlying themes motivating the emphasis on dialogue is ethical. A recent focus on ethics in archaeology (e.g., Wylie and Lynott 1995) responds to tensions in the relationships between archaeologists, and between archaeologists and non-archaeologists (clients, visitors, contractors, indigenous communities, etc.). Ethics are discussed in this volume in relation to the employment of unskilled archaeologists (Chapter 7), and in relation to interactions between archaeologists and indigenous archaeologists (Chapter 16). Widely accepted in archaeology and anthropology today is an ethical responsibility to engage in contemporary debate—as in the 9/11 focus in *American Anthropologist* 104(3) in September 2002, and in the archaeological response to the same debate (Meskell 2002b; Rathje 2001).

In general terms there is increasing conviction in archaeology that past and present are constructed in relation to each other in a dialectical fashion. Thus it can be argued that "Çatalhöyük and I, we bring each other into existence" (Hodder 1990). Archaeologists have increasingly begun to explore the ways in which monuments and artifacts are caught up in identity formation and in the construction of memories (Alcock et al. 2003; Rowlands 1993; and see Chapter 2, this volume). But the dialectical emphasis takes us away from the idea that we, as subjects, simply manipulate an objective past in our own interests. The notion that "Çatalhöyük and I, we bring each other into existence" tries to escape from subject/object, mind/body, mind/matter oppositions. Rather, our identities are caught up in a very direct way in monuments and materials, both at group and individual levels. As archaeologists we play an active part in constructing people's relationships with their pasts, and so with themselves. As archaeologists we also have a duty to be more aware of this process than most, and to tease apart the construction of the past/present self relationship.

Material culture can be argued to be mute, but the claim is contradicted by the meaningfulness with which we experience the world. It is impossible for humans to perceive or explore a material world without telling stories about it, without reading some tale into the way things happen or are arranged. In this way, material culture is never mute—its patterning always immediately motivates interpretation. There is always immediately a dialectical unity of opposites between past material culture and present social interest. The past always appears "for" someone, some group, some social interest.

It is the role of the archaeologist to be centrally located in this two-sided unity between object and subject, past and present. Particularly when it comes to the distant past, the past is immediately constructed as an inverse of "us," located as a mirror image "other," located in an other time (Fabian 1983). And yet the material appears material, objective, there, unavailable for argument and critique. The role of the archaeologist is to transform the otherness of the past, to make its material immaterial, to make transparent the apparent objectivity of the past in its relations to the present.

The distant, especially the prehistoric, past has a special ability to be involved in the construction of our deeper taken-for-granteds. The greater distances in time allow us to explore what it is to be human at the most fundamental of levels. Indeed, the distances in time allow us to perceive some characteristics as fundamental. I do not mean by this a pseudo-Freudian view that layers of consciousness equate with depths of time. Rather, I mean that exploration of human societies over millennia gives the impression that we can consider questions such as (in addition to the more specific and small-scale) whether we are "basically" competitive or cooperative, whether male dominance is "natural," why certain parts of the world are "more developed," and so on. Dialogues involving prehistory often lead to questions concerning "basic" characteristics of what it means to be human. What is culture, what is society. In this way, prehistory has an important role in education and in the critique of everyday assumptions.

The dangers in such dialogue are perhaps most severe when they are linked to notions of regional identity, as when prehistory is enlisted in the support of claims regarding the "essential" nature of being German, or of being European or American. It is precisely the historical awareness of such misuses that motivates current moves towards transparency and dialogue. The wide acceptance of the view that dialogue, participation, and multivocality are simply "best practice" in archaeology, heritage management, and conservation responds to awareness of a history of misuse of privileged relationships with the past.

But too often, in my view, this recognition of the need for dialogue and critique has just been an add-on: business as usual except the need for some "consultation with stakeholders." This is inadequate for a number of reasons. A serious commitment to dialogue involves changes in method and theory, and in archaeological practice.

BEYOND DIALOGUE

One of the main reasons for the need to move on beyond dialogue is that the methods and theories we use themselves provide the terms of dialogue. The methods and theories can thus include assumptions and perspectives that can silence alternative voices. They often involve assumptions that themselves contradict other interests. At one level there is the question of whether the voice of the subaltern can ever be heard within a conversation that takes place in the language of the dominant. Chapter 3 asks the question whether the sub-altern can ever "speak." Is the subaltern always destined to be caught within a debate defined in the interests of the dominant group? At another level, the problem is to change methods and assumptions in such a way as to allow alternative agendas to be set and alternative perspectives to be explored.

One of the changes that has begun to be recognized in archaeology concerns the way we write. These new forms of writing seek to dissolve the appearance of neutral objectivity (e.g., Edmonds 1999; Joyce 1994; Tilley 1994; Tringham 1994). Such intellectual moves have been made in response to feminist and post-structuralist critiques. But the new forms of writing so far attempted in archaeology have largely been synthetic accounts, and have had little impact on the process of archaeological writing in the field (though see Bender et al. 1997). In this volume new forms of writing are discussed in Chapter 13 and a form of thick description is tried in Chapter 2. But a more radical shift in the practices of archaeology involves the direct use of indigenous voices. The "gazing back" by "native" anthropologists can lead to new forms of ethnographic text (Jacobs-Huey 2002). In archaeology, involvement of a native Madagascan voice in the interpretation of Stonehenge has led to new insight (Parker Pearson and Ramilisonina 1998). Local community members are involved in the post-excavation process of analysis and interpretation at the prehistoric site of Çatalhöyük (see Chapter 7) and direct quotes from them are used in the synthetic publications of the site (Chapter 16).

In writing in this way, it becomes more clearly apparent that writing is a form of doing—a form of social intervention in the world. Indeed, one might say more generally that the move beyond dialogue involves a shift from representing and writing "for," to a social doing "with." Even if, as archaeologists or curators, we mainly write and represent, we have to take an active responsibility for what we write. We have to participate and be part of the social process. Some of the issues resulting from such engagement are discussed in Chapter 6. In particular, the archaeologist cannot engage in dialogue and critique only from the outside. To have an effect, archaeologists need to both be within relations of power and work against dominant unreflective interest.

But ultimately, the notion that the move beyond dialogue to a socially responsive archaeology largely involves new forms of writing probably results from the nature of such debates within cultural studies and ethnography. In archaeology, on the other hand, the move beyond dialogue involves changes in the way archaeologists work (Ludlow Collective 2001). In particular, field methods are implicated. Such moves have come to be termed reflexive in both anthropology and archaeology. Reflexivity here refers to both collaboration and critique.

There have recently been a number of attempts to develop reflexive field methods in archaeology (e.g., Andrews et al. 2000; Bender et al. 1997; Chadwick 1998; Faulkner 2002; Fotiadis 1993; Gero 1996; Hodder 1999a, 2000; Lucas 2001a; Politis 2001). It might be argued that this turn to the reflexive in archaeology is ironic. After all, social and cultural anthropology has recently seen a sustained critique of the concept of reflexive ethnographic method (e.g., Lynch 2000; Robertson 2002; Salzman 2002). At the very least, the archaeological move might seem delayed, given what Robertson (2002) describes as a 20-year history of reflexive discussion in anthropology (e.g., Clifford and Marcus 1986; Gupta and Ferguson 1997) and given the indications of even earlier beginnings (Robertson 2002).

I wish to argue, however, that the development of reflexive field methods in archaeology is neither delayed nor ironic. Rather it results from specific issues and problems which are of a rather different nature from those found in ethnography. Archaeology as a discipline grew in the eighteenth and nineteenth centuries as an integral part of the projects of nationalism and colonialism (e.g., Trigger 1984). For many European countries, for example, the archaeological past still has a self-evident relationship with the state. The protection of ancient monuments is a function of national governments, however much local and diverse voices might be raised against them.

A closely related issue is that the distant past in many parts of the world may have no present communities which can stake a direct claim. Even though, as recognized above, we always immediately weave stories around artifacts and monuments of the past, there is no one today, for example, who can speak for, or represent the interests of, the "Beaker people" of the third millennium B.C. in Europe, and the same is true for countless other cultural groupings identified by archaeologists in the deep past. In much of archaeology, the fieldworker may have little interaction with "other," "indigenous" voices of "informants."

It is precisely when the past *is* claimed by present communities, that a reflexivity has been forced on archaeology. Post-colonial processes, global interactions, and the massive rise in the destruction of archaeological sites and monuments around the world have together created an awareness of divergent opinions about how the past should be managed. While there have been parallel intellectual debates in archaeology over the last 20 years (Shanks and Tilley 1987), the main impulse toward reflexive concerns in archaeology has been the increased use of the past in identity formation and land-rights claims (Gathercole and Lowenthal 1989; Kohl and Fawcett 1995; Layton 1989. For a recent review see Meskell 2002a). While reburial issues in the United States have led to some objectivist retrenchment, they have also led to greater consultation (in NAGPRA and Section 106 of the National Historic Preservation Act) and to anti-objectivist calls for the full integration of oral histories and indigenous knowledge (e.g., Anyon et al. 1996; Stoffle et al. 2001; Watkins 2000).

Excavation methods have been largely untouched by the issue of reflexivity until recently. This may be partly because of the link between excavation and the idea of "keeping a record" that is held in guardianship by the state. State and government institutions in many countries have the responsibility for making sure that sufficient records are kept of what is found, and that the material finds and monuments are properly curated. This "primary" role is seen as separate from the interpretations that archaeologists are then allowed to make, usually with less state supervision. There has thus been little room or motivation for the introduction of reflexive methods in excavation methods themselves.

Another reason for the rather different position of archaeological fieldwork in comparison to ethnography, is that it often uses a wide range of techniques adopted and adapted from the natural and physical sciences. Most archaeologists spend much of their time in the field worrying about radiocarbon dating, geophysical prospection surveys, DNA sampling, Munsell color charts, Harris matrices, micromorphology, phytolith analyses, and so on. Much of their work is carried out in on- or off-site laboratories devoted to archaeozoology or archaeobotany and the like. Such work seems a long way from observer participation with local communities. It has the aura of laboratory science, and empirical description seems straightforward. Of course, many archaeologists are aware of the post-positivist critique of value–neutrality in such contexts, and they may have read works such as those by Latour and Woolgar (1979) on the social factors involved in laboratory life. But such deconstructions rarely provide clear guidelines about how a reflexive scientific archaeology should proceed.

For most archaeology, there can be no easy import of the reflexive methods used in ethnography. Archaeology sits between the natural sciences and the social issues and conflicts that make reflexivity so essential. It is necessary to develop specifically archaeological ways of being reflexive that respond to this particular context.

As Lynch (2000) has noted, there are numerous ways of defining reflexivity. I do not use the term here in ways that refer to behavioral reflexivity, or to systems feedback. Neither do I equate reflexivity simply with the examination of self. I have argued elsewhere (1999a, 1999b, and see Chapter 13) that some reflexive writing in archaeology verges on the egocentric and self indulgent (cf. Robertson 2002). I accept the criticism (Salzman 2002) that accounts of the self are not, in some privileged way, outside bias and critique. Rather, reflexivity as used here refers to a recognition of "positionality"—that one's position or standpoint affect one's perspective (Rosaldo 2000)—and thus reflexivity involves recognizing the value of multiple positions, and multivocality. It also involves a critique of one's own taken-for-granted assumptions, not as an egocentric display, but as an historical enquiry into the foundations of one's claims to knowledge.

CONCLUSION

In this volume, the mechanics and implications of a reflexive archaeology that moves beyond dialogue are discussed in Section II. The move beyond dialogue takes seriously the incorporation of dialogue and critique, as many have done and as is discussed in Section I, but it also involves changing the ways in which we work as archaeologists. In Section II, one set of approaches to changes in methods is described. In addition, some of the difficulties and challenges that are opened up are discussed, partly as a result of critique from other authors (Fekri Hassan in Chapter 5 and Yannis Hamilakis in Chapter 6). One of the implications of following a reflexive approach is that major changes are needed in the way that archaeology is organized. In particular, the low value assigned to field archaeologists themselves can be related to the assumption that the data are just objective. This unreflective, nondialogical perspective has underpinned the overall separation of universities from field and contract archaeology. The conditions of work of field archaeologists and their lack of involvement in the interpretive process both impede the development of scientific archaeology.

It is important too that the theoretical content of archaeological interpretation responds to the moves beyond dialogue. In Section III, general discussions of contemporary theoretical debate in archaeology contrast approaches which are underpinned by a separation of subject and object with those that accept the social nature of knowledge. Trends such as post-structuralism, agency, and embodiment are discussed, and there is a brief critique of behavioral and cognitive processual archaeology. In general terms new theoretical trends in social archaeology foreground a dialectical relationship between past and present, an indeterminacy and a focus on power/knowledge systems. In addition, in this section, consideration is given to practical issues to do with the location of archaeology within anthropology and the social sciences. It is argued that for archaeology to play a fully active role in theoretical debate, it needs to be located outside, if closely allied to, anthropology, and in flexible relationships with a variety of disciplines.

Finally, in Section IV, the impact of incorporating dialogue and reflection in constructions of the past is discussed, with particular reference to case studies in Europe and the Near East. These studies contain accounts of the past in which change comes about through dialectical processes (contradictions and tensions within a unity of opposites) and in which social meaning and social practice are thoroughly embedded. These accounts also include dialogues with some British prehistorians who have, in my view, uncritically accepted aspects of a nostalgic nationalist agenda. But finally, and most important for this volume as a whole, these specific accounts culminate in a concluding chapter in which the research directions are embedded within various contemporary social issues. Here, in this conclusion, the move beyond dialogue has resulted in attempts to situate archaeological knowledge within practical interests of divergent groups such as politicians, local residents, Goddess followers, and artists. Here the questions we ask, and the answers we give are situated. The accounts in this concluding piece do not "provide what people want," but they do engage in real-world debates by using specialist archaeological knowledge to challenge and critique and move forward. There is a recognition that archaeologists need to take a stand as members of global and local societies. In this way, archaeology becomes a memory machine that acts and intervenes to build people's worlds.

I. The Globalization of Archaeology

This first group of papers sets the scene by exploring ways in which archaeology is becoming diversified and globalized. It looks at how archaeological sites are being opened up to contested perspectives and at how new forms of tourism and global exchange are leading to engagements with the past in which multiple perspectives need to be taken into account.

In Chapter 2, which describes recent work at Çatalhöyük in Turkey, there is an account of interactions between archaeologists and a variety of local and global groups. The chapter opposes a globalized post-modern pastiche "past for fun" with a past that matters, that has depth and passion. More specifically it identifies a number of stakeholders in the site such as those derived from a local traditional Islam, those associated with globalized commercial interests, and those engaged in goddess worship. The subtle negotiations and tensions between these groups, and the need for the archaeologist to "take a stand" rather than attempt to be a disinterested mediator, are described. The chapter also situates work on the Neolithic of the Near East within a long tradition of "Orientalism," whereby the Near East has been constructed as an "other" to Europe. So one question that results is whether we can as archaeologists ever step outside our own discourse and engage in a two-way dialogue with diverse communities. Chapter 3 notes how this issue has been raised by writers such as Foucault, Spivak, and Bhabha. While it is important for archaeologists to work with "the locals," the construction of "the local" as yet another "other," an inverse mirror image of ourselves, has to be questioned and problematized. This chapter argues, however, that "the subaltern can speak" despite the tendency to be overwhelmed in Western science and discourse.

2

The Past as Passion and Play
Çatalhöyük as a Site of Conflict in the Construction of Multiple Pasts

INTRODUCTION

This article will include "thick descriptions" of the site at Çatalhöyük as viewed from different perspectives. Recent work at the site has quickly become embroiled in a maelstrom of conflicting interpretations. "The past matters," but to different people in different ways. The past can be erased or it can be forgotten, later to be picked up and reused with new meanings. The variety of currents in the Near East make this a complex and highly charged process. But it is all too easy to take a distanced stance which is itself part of the appropriation of the past for intellectual gain. Any analysis of the sociopolitics of the past in the Eastern Mediterranean is itself a construction, an intellectualization, an appropriation. This chapter attempts to counter this process by attempting to describe thickly the processes through which a particular site has become engaged in a practical struggle.

An underlying theme is that the kaleidoscope of interests that have converged on Çatalhöyük can be grouped into two broad categories, themselves a product of an underlying tension between, on the one hand, a global and multinational commercialism and homogenization which views cultural difference as play and pastiche and, on the other hand, an increasingly fragmented world of competing identities, ethnicities, and nationalisms within which the past *matters* very directly. "Hotel Çatalhöyük" may be a long

way from "Hotel Auschwitz," but it raises some of the same concerns about the clash between, on the one hand, the past as play, post-modern façade, commodity, and resource, and on the other hand, the past as passion, depth, history, and ownership. It is argued that these two dimensions of experience of the past in the Near East interact in complex ways and that the past as commodity and as Oriental theme park does not undermine the use of the past in political engagement when local communities, as at Çatalhöyük, become re-engaged in their history.

THE ARCHAEOLOGICAL DISCOURSE

It is too easy, and at least to some extent incorrect, to say that archaeologists have excavated in the Near East in order to elucidate the prehistory and history of that region. Archaeological interpretation of the Near East has also been embedded within a Western construction which opposes the East or Orient as "other." The prehistory of the Near East has been constructed in a "play of difference" within academic discourse.

As Said (1978) has shown more generally, the Orient has been constructed as the Other of Europe. Especially in the nineteenth and twentieth centuries the Orient came to be seen as stagnant and despotic in order to define the democratic dynamism of Europe. In the writing of the prehistory of Europe and the Near East these are not abstract ideas. In a very concrete way they came to define the dominant discourse of European prehistory as exemplified in its most important practitioner, V. G. Childe. In the preface to the first edition of the *Dawn of European Civilisation* (1925), Childe said that his theme was the "foundation of European civilisation as a peculiar and individual manifestation of the human spirit." In Europe "we can recognise already these very qualities of energy, independence and inventiveness which distinguish the western world from Egypt, India and China." To Childe, the opposition between Europe and the Orient was especially clear in the Bronze Age because, unlike the Orient, "European metalworkers were free. They were not tied to any one patron or even to a single tribal society. They were producing for an intertribal if not an international market."

To exemplify the opposition in the Bronze Age, Childe compared Crete with Egypt and despotic Mesopotamia. He described

the modern naturalism, the truly occidental feeling for life and nature that distinguish Minoan vase paintings and frescoes. Beholding these charming scenes of games and processions, animals and fishes, flowers and trees, we breathe already a European atmosphere. Likewise in industry the absence of the unlimited labour-power at the disposal of a despot necessitated a concentration on the invention and elaboration of tools and weapons that foreshadows the most distinctive feature of European civilisation.

Thus, the Near East was seen as the cradle from which agriculture and civilization initially spread. But the main developments that laid the foundations for a dynamic, and ultimately capitalist, society took place in Europe during the Bronze Age. The Near East may have been the "cradle" from which the "birth" took place, but the Orient never "grew up." In Childe's view it became stagnant and despotic—it became the "Other" of Europe, its inverse.

Anatolia has been placed in a difficult position in the traditions of research influenced by Childean Orientalism. Anatolia is not within the cradle but neither is it in the European center of regrowth. As Özdoğan (1995: 27) points out, "areas to the north of the Taurus range, the high plateau of Anatolia, are regarded as still being outside of the 'nuclear zone.'" One clear consequence of this has been the lack of theoretical discussion about the development of Neolithic societies in Anatolia. Equally, there has been a lack of serious attempt to look for sites in Anatolia and known site densities remain low for many areas and periods. Further, "it is of interest to note that even after the recovery of Hacilar, Çatal Höyük and Aşıklı in central Anatolia, these sites were considered for some time as trading posts for obsidian and salt trade, and not as indicators of a developing Neolithic culture on the Anatolian plateau" (Özdoğan 1995:28). There were similar implications of this Anatolian "blindness" for the chronologies of Anatolia and Southeastern Europe. 3000 B.C. had been set as the start of sedentary life in both areas. But with the large-scale application of ^{14}C dates in Europe, the dates of Southeastern early Neolithic sites were pushed back 2,000 to 3,000 years. "However no one considered the impact of the change in datings on the chronology of central Anatolian cultures" (Özdoğan 1995:28). Renfrew's (1973a) discussion of calibrated ^{14}C dates created a "faultline" between Europe and Asia. The effect was to focus attention on developments in Europe at the expense of those in Anatolia. The latter remained caught uncomfortably between the emergent developments in Southeastern Europe and the long sequence of cultural developments in the Near East.

More recently Özdoğan (1995) has argued for a different Neolithic sequence in central Anatolia and for strong links between central Anatolia and Europe in the Chalcolithic. In the work by Turkish archaeologists such as Ufuk Esin (1991) at Aşıklı Höyük and Refik Duru (1992) in the Burdur areas we begin to obtain a clear picture of a central Anatolian sequence which belies a simple Orient/Occident opposition. "Central Anatolia should neither be considered as a nuclear nor as a marginal zone to the low lands of the Near East, but as a distinct cultural formation zone, developing on different lines from the Near East" (Özdoğan 1995:54).

THE GLOBAL AND THE LOCAL

Research at Çatalhöyük and other work in central Turkey can help to counteract the Europe/Orient set of differences. But these archaeological examples are part of a wider movement which now challenges that opposition. The new discourse is globalism. "Globalization has rendered much of the discussion of East and West in orientalism redundant" (Turner 1994:183). The Orient was constructed as "other." With globalization "others" have become less strange and have been imported into all societies as a result of human mobility, migration, and tourism. "Otherness has been domesticated" (Turner 1994:183). With the collapse of communism and the traditional oppositions of cold-war politics of the post-war era, Islam may function as a substitute for the dangers of communism. But Islam is increasingly part of the "inside" of the Western world. For example, the Rushdie affair in Britain forced a debate about the recognition that Britain was now a multicultural society. In Germany, Turkish migrants now pose a significant social issue. Globalization has created a variety of traditions within a given community.

Turner sets up a very clear contrast between Islamic fundamentalism and the commercial processes of late capitalism. He argues that Islamic fundamentalism rejects modernist secularism because of its lack of coherent values and because of its gross inequalities of wealth and power (Turner 1994:88). Fundamentalism has created an anticonsumerist ethic of moral purity based upon classical Islamic doctrine (Turner 1994:92). The corruption of pristine faith is going to be brought about by Tina Turner, Coca-Cola, and Ford (Turner 1994:10). This erosion of faith "has to be understood in terms of how the diversity of commodities and their global character transform in covert and indirect fashion the everyday beliefs of the mass of the population" (Turner 1994:17).

Certainly, to the extent that Çatalhöyük has been threatened by antiquities dealing, there are grounds for an opposition between commercialism and fundamentalist and nationalist concerns. The excavations in the early 1960s were closed by the Turkish state for a number of reasons, including problems with the conservation of wall paintings and sculpture. But at least some of the reasons for the closure concerned the purported disappearance of artifacts from the site and the involvement of James Mellaart in the "Dorak Affair." The latter involved the disappearance of a claimed "treasure" of Bronze Age artifacts from northwest Anatolia. Recently the Turkish state has been successful in gaining the return of the Lydian treasure from the Metropolitan Museum in New York. Attempts are being made to return the Schliemann treasure to Troy. All these instances foster a sense of national heritage and an assertion of Turkish identity in the face of the colonial encounter and in reaction against the pillaging of the extraordinarily rich and diverse antiquities of Turkey.

There are other ways in which commercialism might be thought to confront and erode Islamic fundamentalism. The site at Çatalhöyük is located in a traditionally conservative area, largely rural, and with minimal technological development. More recently, massive irrigation schemes funded by international agencies have led to the rapid development of large-scale agro-industry. Yet the local population around the site tends to be traditional, conservative, and strongly religious. The renewed work at the site and the project's plans for the future might be seen as opening up this local world to new commercial interests. The site guard, Sadettin, has applied for official permission to build a shop at the site to serve the increasing numbers of tourists. There are plans for T-shirts and a range of products. Several artists have asked to be given the right to make "tasteful" objects derived from, but not replicating, the prehistoric finds for sale at the site, in Turkey, and in the USA. Travel agencies in Istanbul, Britain, and USA vie with each other to organize special-interest tours. Plans are being developed for a museum and visitor center at the site, and for international traveling exhibits of the art. Carpet dealers in Konya use designs from Çatalhöyük, or legitimated by books concerning Çatalhöyük (e.g., Mellaart et al. 1989), in order to enhance their sales. In Istanbul, a Turkish designer, Rifat Özbek, shows clothes modeled by Linda Evangelista and which incorporate the Çatalhöyük "Mother Goddess" image. These clothes appear in *Hello* Magazine (January 1991) and demonstrate the ways in which the site can become involved in a global commercial market. These commercial opportunities are certainly taken up locally and nationally in Turkey and they have the potential to transform Islamic fundamentalist belief.

But other experiences suggest that such an opposition between a global commercialism and Islamic fundamentalism are overly simplistic. The relationships between the Çatalhöyük project and the local mayor (Çumra belediye baskanı), especially with regard to the 1996 local agricultural festival, illustrate the complexities well.

The mayor in Çumra is at present (since 1995) a member of the MHP party—Islamic but primarily nationalist. The rhetoric of the party is at times anti-Europe, anti-foreign involvement, and anti-secular. At times it was difficult working with local officials who might be members of the MHP or the religious Refah party (banned in 1997). Some would very pointedly not shake hands with female members of the team, especially on Fridays, since such contact would mean washing again in preparation for the mosque. Our English-speaking Eurocentric friends in Istanbul were always surprised that we got on so well with the mayor. In our early years at the site he helped us with accommodation in Çumra, with equipment and materials.

He always embraced me and showed the greatest of respect. In 1995 he asked us for some photographs, especially of the naked "Mother Goddess" to put in the foyers of all the hotels in Çumra and in neighboring districts. The *belediye* had

its own hotel in Çumra. Inside it was full of Islamic religious references in its décor. Guests had to remove their shoes at the door. In such a context large images of the "Mother Goddess" seemed so inappropriate, especially in a town in which all women always remained covered in public. Why did the mayor want to do this?

The contradictions increased. In 1996 the mayor made a formal proposal to the authorities in Ankara to set up a Çatalhöyük museum in Çumra itself. In the same year he announced to us that he wanted to call his annual agricultural festival the Çumra Çatalhöyük Festival. We were to provide a film and slide show, which we did, to a large and attentive audience. After the slide show the mayor started handing out prizes for the best tomatoes and melons. I was embarrassed suddenly to be called on to the stage to be honored and embraced in my turn, and presented with a plaque.

Why this public endorsement? What was the public advantage? After all, here is a foreign team digging a pre-Islamic site which confronts Islamic teaching both in its use of images and in its specific representations of women. Certainly the naked images are only acceptable because of their non-Islamic context. But the project clearly introduces commercialism and Western attitudes. Why should it be so overtly embraced by an Islamic nationalist from a political party on the far right? Part of the answer is simply that our work brings money into the region, it increases employment, and it encourages tourism. It contributes to economic development and helps to gain a popular vote. It was for these reasons that the mayor finds himself, as a result of the project, the center of media attention and the host to political figures who visit the site from Konya and Ankara. His wider political ambitions are served.

The mayor's rhetoric at public occasions involving the site deals with the contradictions in subtle ways. Çatalhöyük, he says, is a site of great national significance. It is the source of Anatolian civilization. And yet it belongs to the world. Its knowledge is for everyone, without boundaries. We wish to give it to the world. The international scientific interest shows the importance of Anatolian civilization.

The mayor continues, "Çatalhöyük is for all humanity." When I tell my Turkish friends in Istanbul about this they gasp, "Did he really say that?" And in many ways his strategy is risky. There is all the reason in the world for him to be distrustful of us. There are many local people in the Çumra area who remember what happened in the 1960s, who blame the archaeologists, and who are suspicious of renewed foreign contacts. The site and its imagery might be seen as confronting Islamic traditionalists. And yet, overall, he has decided, at least for the moment, that it is in his interests to support, embrace and even promote the project.

In the above instance, rather than a simple opposition between Islamic groups and religion and the international and commercial components of the project, we see subtle ways in which adjustments are made in order to achieve specific aims, such as increased employment and political status. At least in Turkey some accommodation between the global and the Islamic is clearly possible. The same is true in the following example.

Women, their heads covered, their shoulders weighed from a long day's labor in the fields, are driven past the site at high speed in the backs of the trucks of their menfolk. Some of their sons and husbands are working as laborers on the new excavations. I asked for some women to work at the site but the menfolk refused to let them go. The younger women have been taught in school that Çatalhöyük is the origin of Anatolian civilization, the origin of Cybele, the Earth Mother. The posters of the bare-breasted Mother Goddess seem very alien. "The site is full of images, our menfolk say. It must be pre-Islamic."

The women from the village confide in some of the women from the foreign team in their midst. In fact there is a remarkable and immediate rapport between the women—an embracing and incorporating of women, just because they are women. They confide that their men are very hard; they give the women little freedom, little money. It is a hard life. But in the end, after two years of negotiating, the men say the wives and daughters can work at the site after all. Perhaps they have grown to trust the foreigners. But, most likely, the men, the families, want the money. When the local people are paid, some of the women find it difficult even to sign their name, and they refuse to take the money—their husbands take it from them.

So, in this local case, men gradually accept the need to allow change in the actions of and attitudes toward the women in the community. Women and men locally turn a blind eye to the naked "Mother Goddess." If it brings tourists and jobs so much the better (say some men); if it brings us wages so much the better (say the women). Indeed, local attitudes seem to change in a number of ways.

Local attitudes to the past in the Çatalhöyük area are being studied by David Shankland (1996). Folk knowledge sees the mounds as liminal. They are the landmarks that define the boundaries between communities. They are also the dwelling places of the spirits of the dead. At night the lights of the spirits can sometimes be seen as they travel from one mound to another. There is archaeological evidence that the Çatalhöyük mound was used as a cemetery from the Hellenistic period onwards. We excavated Byzantine graves on the East mound. And yet this tradition associating the mounds with the dead does not prevent the excavation by local communities of soil and clay from the mounds for building materials. Indeed the walls of the buildings on the local villages are full of sherds deriving from the mounds. Perhaps this practical use and the tradition of digging help to explain the acceptance of our own archaeological work at the mounds.

Shankland argues that this local folk

knowledge is not matched by an in-depth historical understanding of the site. Although the site is mentioned in primary schools in connection with the origins of Anatolian civilization, there is little knowledge of historical sequences beyond a simple pre-Islamic–Islamic opposition. He argues that it is for this reason that there has been little response to the Open Days organized for the local communities during our digging seasons.

On the other hand, I have been struck by the degree of fascination and interest when I have organized tours of the site for our workers. Their eyes wide at the images, and bubbling with questions, comments, and parallels with their own lives, houses, and artifacts, they are excited by ideas about interpretations of the site. Far from being alienated from their past by this engagement within a global system of universal scientific knowledge, their sense of local identity and community seems enlivened and strengthened.

> There are deep cuts across both East and West mounds at Çatalhöyük, paths worn by centuries of feet toiling from village to village in the Konya Plain. And there is a lone Islamic gravestone on the East mound, marking the burial place of a fallen woman, so the story goes. These mounds had a local meaning, a 'fork' (çatal) in their daily pathways. But now these routes and graves are cut off by a fence, locked gate, and guards. The site has been taken over by the state and is being excavated by foreign teams with lasers and computers. Busloads of Goddess tourists from California engage in debates with the foreign archaeologists about matriarchies.

But is it quite so confrontational? The notion of a simple opposition between local and global knowledge is undermined by the complexity of social and cultural currents at all levels in Turkish life. One such complexity derives from the division within Turkish politics between those who favor closer links with Europe and who welcome the recent Customs Union, and those who are suspicious of such links. The latter views are associated with fundamentalist and nationalist currents of thought. But the Turkish groups who have become most involved in the Çatalhöyük project tend to be very Eurocentric. The individuals involved tend to live in Istanbul, have often had an elite English-speaking education, and have often spent part of their lives in Europe or the USA. The Istanbul "Friends of Çatalhöyük" organization, which has been successful in raising funds for the project, comes largely from this group. Those people from Istanbul who come to the site include highly articulate, professional and well-to-do Turks, fascinated by our work and by its implications. They like the idea that in prehistory there were many cultural links between Anatolia and Europe. They are enthralled by the project's use of new scientific techniques and of the Web. Some organize and take part in the Goddess Tours. They are part of a global community.

> The first time it happened we were all very much taken aback. We did not know what was happening. A message had come to the dig house that the leader of the Istanbul Friends was bringing a group of people to the site, as part of a tour of Turkey. Would we meet them in the local restaurant in Çumra that evening?

> Most of the team went—about twenty of us at that time. We were ushered into a room with a long table around which about thirty middle-aged women, and a few men, were sitting. We were arranged amongst them. Alcohol is not allowed in public places in Çumra. But they provided a cocktail of cherry juice hiding vodka. The questions began. Why were we digging the site? Did we believe that men had been allowed into Çatalhöyük? Had we found evidence of the Goddess? Did we not realize that the bull's heads represented Her reproductive organs? What did the female members of the team think about my androcentric interpretations? How were their voices heard?

> The following day they came to the site. They were interested in our work, but they also stood in a circle and held hands and prayed. Afterwards they

seemed genuinely moved. They said the presence of the Goddess was very strong. You could feel Her coming up through the earth.

The Goddess Tours have become regular since then, although often occurring at times when we are not at the site. The participants are largely professional women from the USA, but they include women from Europe. And it is into this world that some of the Istanbul Friends easily fit. Indeed, some of the Friends from Istanbul were instrumental in tabling a motion at the Beijing UN Conference on Women which named Çatalhöyük as the spiritual center of the Goddess Movement in Turkey and in the world.

The global character of these New Age Mother Goddess, Ecofeminist, and Gaia movements may confront traditional Islamic attitudes to women, but there are undoubtedly significant sections of elite Istanbul society that welcome such links outside Turkey and use them for their own purposes. Since Atatürk, the commitment to secularism has been a central, if recently diminishing, focus of political life in Turkey. Istanbul in particular is a social and cultural metropolis of enormous size and diversity. There are many shades of accommodation between secularism and fundamentalism. The old intellectual elite is global in perspective and contributes to a political debate which is complex and multistranded.

When a group of the Istanbul "Friends" association came to the site I could see they were angry, despite their politeness and support. They disliked the new dig house. It was unimaginative, dull, functional, not appropriate to such an important site. And worst of all, it was painted bright green! They decided they would not help fund the construction of the dig house. I was disappointed. I needed their help.

The dig house, an ambitious version of an architectural genre found on many sites in the Near East, had been designed by an architect in the local museum service in Konya. Most of his previous work had dealt with the restoration of the wonderful Seljuk architecture in and around that city. The design was approved by the local ancient monuments board. I had contracted a builder from Konya who was strongly recommended by the local museums service. He turned out to be a great pleasure to work with. I respected and liked him enormously and trusted him completely. He chose green because the color is identified with Islam. He and his family, like many in Konya, were strongly religious.

It was anathema to some of the Istanbul visitors that the dig house should be painted green. It seemed inappropriate. But I decided not to bow to their demands that we repaint the building. It seemed important to respect local Islamic sensitivities in this case.

In other examples, too, it is possible to show local resistance to the global interests of Istanbul Turks or international commercial or New Age movements. For instance, the Istanbul Friends have started a clever and very successful campaign to "Lend a Hand to Çatalhöyük," which involves giving handprint certificates (based on a Çatalhöyük wall painting) to donors. One proposal is that a long wall be built at the site on which donors can make their handprints. For the moment, this move has been resisted because of local concerns about site preservation. Perhaps the clearest example of the interaction between these different currents of interest in the site is the following:

One of the commercial sponsors of the project is an international credit card company. With its Istanbul-based PR firm, this company is genuinely interested in supporting the project while at the same time making use of its commercial potential. For example, during press visits we all wear hats with the company logo, and a replica of the "Mother Goddess" with the company name is handed out to clients at receptions in Istanbul. The company sees a particular link to Çatalhöyük because I argued that obsidian could be seen as the first "credit card." Members of the team laughed when I told them and the obsidian specialist was embarrassed. Perhaps I was embarrassed, too, but I justified my compliance by arguing that obsidian was exchanged widely (like credit cards) and that ethnographically, artifacts such as obsidian can come to act as media for exchange, and exchange involves setting up debt (and thus credit) between the giver and receiver.

In the end this global commercializing process would have an impact locally. The company wanted to set up an exhibit in the museum which showed the development of "credit cards" from the first obsidian to the latest credit cards with microchips. I could not help but see the, probably unintended, outcome of this. Turkey is seeing a massively expanding market for credit cards, but the main take-up is in the urban centers. In rural areas there has been less impact. The exhibit and the message about prehistoric credit cards might not only legitimate the modern company's claim to be concerned with Turkish culture but also might encourage local interest and take-up.

Nevertheless, the support of the company was genuine and very much needed if the project was going to be able to continue and have any long-term benefit for local identity, tourism, employment, and social change.

I wanted to hold a ceremony at the site to open the dig house. I invited the Minister of Culture as well as local and national politicians. The Minister of Culture had recently changed to be a member of Refah, the religious fundamentalist party. I wanted our sponsors to come to thank them. Indeed, the Minister of Culture would unveil a plaque listing their support. This "photo opportunity" was rejected by the credit card company which decided it did not want to be associated in this way with the Refah party. Here, commerce and Islam confronted each other and the former stood down.

In the end the minister did not attend and sent his Director General of Monu-

ments and Museums. The European Ambassador also came. West and East, secular and religious, met and talked at a podium decked out in a Turkish flag by the mayor. The speeches described the importance of the project and I presented the buildings to the Turkish state. But the currents of differing meanings, strategies, and interpretations were rife.

In all the political maneuvering, the site and the local concerns seemed to play little role. They seemed overrun by global processes and oppositions. But on the other hand, the mayor and other local officials made their speeches too and there was considerable coverage in the local press. Black Mercedes, flags flapping at high speed, swept in clouds of dust. Armed guards surrounded the mound, and out got the national officials. They came and went, involved in their own strategies. Local people had to be bussed in to create a crowd at the ceremony—a true "rent-a-crowd." The local people seemed to understand the motives behind the show for what it was. They tolerated the event as long as it meant they could continue to work, make money, and follow their own strategies. The ceremony, and the national, fundamentalist, and global strategies in which it was enmeshed, was necessary if their own lives were to continue to change in ways they, from different points of view, wanted.

Thus, there is no simple opposition between global knowledge and interests and a local and fundamentalist Islam. New Age Women's Movements are received differently in different communities, national and local, in Turkey. In the local villages around Çatalhöyük and in Çumra, people participate differentially and purposefully. They are not simply duped into being "globalized." People have to be bussed to the opening ceremony. A blind eye is turned to the naked Goddess in the visitor center at the site. Locally, women may obtain their own wages and the mayor follows his political ambitions. Locally, men and women use the past in their own ways. They may be drawn into a global process but they use the past in their own ways. They may be drawn into a global process but they use that process locally in complex ways, rejecting some aspects and emphasizing others. Change occurs, but in a complex and diverse way. It is no longer an issue of monolithic blocks, as in Europe versus the Orient, secular versus fundamentalist religion. Rather, there is a diversity of global and local experiences and responses within which Çatalhöyük is embroiled.

A REFLEXIVE MOMENT

So far I have written in terms of an overall argument about the shift from East versus West to global versus local and I have made the point that local interests are not entirely taken over by global processes. All this, even my use of narrative "thick descriptions," is situated within an academic discourse which might seem to be far removed from the events I am describing. I have constructed the events in a particular way because of my own interests. Indeed any analysis of heritage in the East Mediterranean is "at a remove"; a past appropriated for intellectual gain. There are two points I wish to make about this process. The first deals with disjunction between the controlled and structured description or text and the contingent process. The second deals with the need to recognize that the archaeologist is not a disinterested observer but part of the process.

Our own emphasis on "discourse" within the "discipline" underlies the account I have given. I have written as if the processes I have been describing could be observed, channeled, controlled. Any attempt to write about how the Çatalhöyük past is used, and any attempt to write about how the past matters in the East Mediterranean cannot help but reduce historical processes to an organized scheme or flow. In the following account I want to demonstrate the limitations of this view.

It ranks as one of the worst days in my life. I ended up stunned, bitter, angry and deeply depressed about whether the project would continue.

The day had started so well. The credit

card company had arranged an elaborate and expensive press trip to the site. In the morning between fifty and sixty newspaper and TV reporters turned up at the site. During the day the tours all went extremely well. Members of the team were dutifully wearing their promotional hats. The project was coming over as exciting and important. It was getting great coverage. The sponsors and the PR firm were happy. After all, this press day was to be the main return on their investment this year. There had to be a lot of good press coverage and it looked as if there would be.

A few reporters had left and I was relaxing for a moment before the rest departed, when a member of the team came to say that a small bead had disappeared from one of our laboratories. It was one of the objects that had been on display and despite the continual presence of three team members the object had disappeared. The government representatives were told. They called the police. The reporters were searched and held at the site for three hours before being allowed to leave.

Rumors started flying, but so many people could have taken it. There had been so many people there that day. I suddenly saw that in this one event, this one instant, the whole project could flounder. Despite all the planning, all the effort over five years could be undone in one brief act. After all, the site had been closed in the 1960s partly because of incidents in which artifacts disappeared. Would this event play into the hands of local or national groups who objected to the international or foreign character of the project? Even if a permit did continue to be granted, would we be able to gain sponsorship again? Indeed, in the following days the national press printed stories with headlines such as "Scandal at dig of the century." How could we ever get sponsorship again? I began to feel that, for one reason or another, the project might have difficulty continuing.

As it turned out, the press coverage during and after the event was very supportive. The papers started carrying positive accounts of the project which did not mention the theft of the bead. The sponsors continued their support and the central government authorities did their best to recover the bead. The damage seems to have been, at the time of writing, marginal. But in that moment and in the days immediately afterwards I feared the worst and I saw how fragile was the negotiated position for all players in the Çatalhöyük project. Everything happened so quickly and in such a variety of directions that the outcome was unpredictable. Structure met conjuncture (Sahlins 1981) and no amount of discursive understanding of East–West, global–local, or even structure–conjuncture could determine or control the way in which things would go.

Such a critique of academic discourse in the context of archaeology and heritage in the East Mediterranean does not imply that the archaeologist should stand at a distance from the processes in which she or he is involved. Indeed this is the second point I wish to make about the need to be reflexive when gazing at, and encapsulating in theoretical discourse, the role of the past in the East Mediterranean. Since the writing and the discourse have effects, there is a need for positive engagement. In the events just described, I did write letters, get on the phone, make visits, increase security in the stores and laboratories, and so on. While such activities could not control the way things went, they perhaps contributed, from a particular standpoint, to what was, is, and will be an ongoing negotiation between different and changing interests.

As other examples of the need to move beyond the passive gaze to positive engagement, decisions had to be made, and choices had to be taken about whether to remove the green paint on the dig house. Equally, complex as the issues are, I felt it was important to push for the employment of women at the site. It was necessary, in these examples, to "take sides." The same has to be said even in the most "open" and multivocal discourses.

The results of the project are being placed on the Web and resources are being channeled into a variety of interactive and presentation media. These include hypertext (Thomas 1996; Tringham 1996). The aim here is to open the data from the site to multiple audiences, to allow different experiences of the site, to allow discovery in a range of different channels. But it is clear that there is no such thing as open multivocality. A certain level of knowledge is required to participate in hypertext presentations. And certainly the links and nodes are created by the producer of the hypertext. One has to make choices about what audiences are aimed at and what messages are to be given. As much as the Web and hypertext allow a greater diversity and openness of communication, the onus remains on the producer and writer to be reflexive about the impact of "the text" in the world.

The same point can be extended to the writing of the present article. It could be argued that at least some of what I have written here might offend the groups involved in an ongoing archaeological and heritage project. I have taken the decision to say some things here because I believe that the issues are important and that our experience at Çatalhöyük might help to draw attention to the need for debate about the role of archaeology in a Near East which is involved in processes of globalization. I have not said other things here because of the need to respect the perspectives of some of the groups and individuals involved. As noted above, I cannot predict the outcome of this intervention in what is a complex process. But I do assert the need to monitor the results of statements and to engage actively from a particular standpoint.

CONCLUSION

Both in the academic debate about the prehistory of Anatolia and Çatalhöyük and in the practices of public engagement with the site, the old oppositions between Europe and the Orient or between secularism and religious fundamentalism are transcended by the processes of globalism and fragmentation. Çatalhöyük is caught in a maelstrom of perspectives and special interests. These are global in scale. But they are also highly diverse and fragmented, extending from carpet dealers in Konya and New York, to ecofeminists in San Francisco, to women in the local village near Çatalhöyük. Some of these engagements are highly commercial and disinterested—the past as play, the Orient as theme park. Others are motivated by specific highly charged interests. But passion and play are not opposed in some simple opposition. In the global process they interact and feed off each other in myriad ways, equally emboldening and undermining the other.

I have talked in this chapter of the "team" working at Çatalhöyük. It may not be too much to say that I am no longer sure what the team is. The boundaries of those who do or do not work on the project are difficult to define. Certainly there are the named individuals who have permits to excavate at the site. But some specialists on the project do not visit the site. And many I have asked to contribute from around the world in order to, for example, help interpret the art have no close involvement with the core "team." And then what should I make of a psychoanalyst from California with a particular perspective on the art who publishes an article about the site in the *New Scientist*? Or what should I make of an aboriginal artist from South Africa who wishes to come and work at the site to model her female sculptures? She also wants to contribute to our work. And since the site data are on the Web, what should I make of all those who write in and make their suggestions, or who write their own articles about the site based on our data, and contribute to

"our" understanding of the site? And what should I make of it if people take our data from the Web and change them and create a new alternative database of their own? Such things are at least potentially feasible. Rather than there being a well-bounded "team" working on the project, Çatalhöyük is involved in a global process of interpretation. The "team" is global. And I would argue it has to be if the divergent special interests are to be given access to the site. It is not possible to deny that contemporary information technologies allow an enormous dispersal of information so that numerous special interest groups can form and define themselves through an engagement. But so, too, there are many groups who do not have access to the technologies or to the knowledge necessary to use them. The fragmentation within and across the globalization processes needs to be reflexively engaged.

As much as those involved in the project may try to foster plurality and multivocality, the communication does not take place on a level playing field. The techniques used on the site, from virtual reality to the sieving of microresidues, promote a particular vision within the kaleidoscope. There is no solution to the paradoxes. Any attempt to "make sense of it all," including the opposition between "play" and "passion," is itself a construct. It is for this reason that I have included so many "thick descriptive" narratives in this chapter. It is only in the concrete moments of engagement that the sociopolitics of Çatalhöyük take their form.

3

Who to Listen To?
Integrating Many Voices in
an Archaeological Project

The idea of confession in contemporary archaeology resonates with calls for reflexivity and critique. We are supposed to become transparent in our discussions of research and its results. We are supposed to open up, and quit the safe haven and comfort of the positivist opposition of fact and interpretation. We are supposed to leave the clean testing of hypotheses, and sully ourselves in the messiness of multivocality, fluidity, back and forth probing, and social critique.

At one level there is a loss of control in this process. It is less easy to control the interpretive process when it is opened up to debate and critique. The opening up involves a social dispersal of authority. But at another level, the notion of the confession recalls Foucault's account in his *History of Sexuality* (Foucault 1981) where the confessional is a bridge that leads into a disciplinary society. In baring all we open ourselves up to disciplinary sanctioning. One sees this in reflexive archaeology in questions such as "are you being pc enough?" or "how closely do you work with the locals?" or "how many women do you have on your project?" In these critical questions a normativity is imposed. The confession is an opportunity to probe and critique and bring into line. New standards of behavior are imposed—even new standards of thought. The thought police, that is all of us, probe ever deeper into the private recesses of the archaeological life, forcing a disciplinary normativity.

But as Foucault argued, power is not only oppressive. It is also productive. At one level the move to the confessional allows greater monitoring of archaeological work and a greater disciplining of archaeological research. On another level, such disciplining is needed in order to protect the interests of disadvantaged groups. In the old hypothesis-testing mode, the people involved could be of little interest. For example, it was, and still is sadly, possible for US or European-based projects to work abroad with little concern for local issues. Funding from NSF (despite recent changes in guidelines) and the British Academy makes few or no requirements regarding assessments of the local social impact of archaeological projects. While the situation is fast changing in practice, it is still possible to gain funding to carry out research abroad or among indigenous communities with no concern whatsoever for the impact of the work on local communities. The hypotheses can be tested, dealing with questions asked in the colonial centers. These questions may concern issues such as social complexity or trade networks or specialization of production—questions which may have little resonance among indigenous groups. The testing of theory against data is seen as separate from the social process surrounding excavation and fieldwork.

So the new form of confessional disciplining is necessary in order to begin to move towards a climate of opinion in which such behavior is unacceptable. Hopefully the confessional process will open fieldwork and research up to scrutiny. In doing so the iniquities of the present system will be opened to critique. And perhaps even, ultimately, the funding agencies themselves may be pressured to change. If this is the prize of greater disciplinarity then I, for one, am willing to pay it.

And yet, does not this new openness also seclude and exclude? Spivak (1999) is relentlessly critical of the well meaning postcolonial discourse that, under the banner of liberalism, seeks to engage in auto-critique and deconstruction. This metropolitan discourse continues a colonial impulse. It tries to engage the subaltern in a Western discourse that is not only elitist but also difficult, specialized, and abstract. The Western metropolitan discourse also, because of its emphasis on language and representation, undermines the concrete grounds for the struggle against oppression. By engaging the subaltern or "the native informant" in dialogue, are we not simply forcing a new form of representation on "the other"? When "they" speak, is their voice only "our" voice echoing back? How can "they" hope to engage in dialogue on such unequal terms?

I want to argue in this paper that it is possible to engage in dialogue, while taking these criticisms into account. Aware of the difficulties it remains possible, in my view, to engage other voices in the interpretation of the past in ways that create a real hybrid archaeology. By use of the term "hybrid" I refer to Homi Bhabha (1994) and to the notion that the blends, fusions and mixes that occur in the process of dialogue go beyond a simple syncretism or incorporation by one of the other. Rather, something new is created that owes a debt to more than one side in the dialogue. But I also want to show that this process is a difficult one, because of the concerns discussed already. The discourse in which we work is highly specialized. I have already in this paper referred to Spivak and Bhabha, both notoriously difficult authors. This is the background or baggage which I bring with me when I come to Küçükköy, the small rural

village near Çatalhöyük, the mound site where I work in Turkey. Most people in this village have had little or no formal education beyond fifth to eighth grade. I come with my post-structuralist gobbledygook. And I bring with me people with PhDs in micromorphology, isotopic analysis, phytolith and lipid analysis. And I want to have a dialogue on equal terms? As one of the women in the village said "we collect dung and burn it in our fires; you collect dung and study it under the microscope." The worlds are far apart; and yet I want to show that dialogue can be achieved and hybrid results attained.

MULTIVOCALITY AT ÇATALHÖYÜK
There are many communities or stakeholders to whom we listen at Çatalhöyük. These include government officials at national and regional levels, Turkish archaeologists, sponsors, carpet sellers, Turkish students, other international archaeologists, Goddess worshippers, artists and musicians, and so on. I have tried to engage in dialogue with most or all these groups, and one of the difficulties is certainly the conflicts and differences between their interests and agendas. But in this context I have only time to discuss one particular group—the local community. I am aware of the difficulties in using this term and the critique of the "local" is well developed (e.g., Appadurai 1996). I do not take the local for granted—while it has material dimensions it is also the case that archaeology is often complicit in the construction of the "local" (as in local museums, working with the locals, etc.). It is certainly the case that our work at Çatalhöyük helps to construct the nearby village of Küçükköy as local. Indeed, one of the dangers in engaging the community around the site in dialogue is that we construct them as "native informants." I will return to this issue later.

From the start of our excavations at Çatalhöyük in 1993 we have employed workmen on the excavation as unskilled laborers and craftsmen. Initially we were discouraged from employing women but after a time women came to work for us as sorters of micro-residues. We also have a house staff of men and women. Through time some of the men and women have become skilled in specific tasks. Twenty to forty people from Küçük-köy and neighboring villages and towns work for us for two to four months a year. At other times of the year they mainly work as farming families. A few are employed all year round as guards and tour guides at the site. Some degree of income has been received from taxi trips to the site and from a small tourist shop and cafe that someone from the village has built by the site.

There are various ways in which the local community has been involved in our work, although contact is limited by language differences. There is very little ability to speak English and only a portion of the dig team speaks Turkish. And so engagement has been specifically arranged—by holding tours of the excavation for the Turkish staff for example. There are two anthropologists who work on the team and in Küçükköy. They study aspects of the impact of the project on the local community. Ayfer Bartu has given slide shows in the village about the research of the project, both for groups of men and women. She has also enabled the women of the village to produce an exhibit about the site in their own words and using their own photography. This exhibit is in the on-site Visitor Center. She and Can Candan have also trained one of the women from the village to use a camcorder and to make her own film of the project.

And so on. There are many ways in which the people who live (spend most of the year) in the villages and towns near the site are involved in the project. But it could be objected that they are being excluded from the work of excavation and analysis itself. The project provides scholarships for Turkish students, including people from the regional university, to gain training in archaeology in Turkey or abroad. It tries to train Turkish students to be fully fledged excavators and researchers at the site. But most of the excavation undertaken by the Cambridge–Stanford team is done by fully trained or professional archaeologists. Excavation and recording at Çatalhöyük are difficult. Even professional archaeologists find it difficult. In my view, ex-cavation should be carried out by trained professionals. No members of the local community have gained sufficient training to be involved in excavation and research, although they have been trained to carry out less skilled tasks such as sieving, residue sorting, flotation, etc.

I confess that I am uncomfortable about this; but I do not see an alternative. There are other communities to protect, and in my view professional excavators comprise one such community that does a job that should be properly paid and recognized. The project has a duty to train Turkish, including local, students. In that way ultimately the situation may change. But I cannot avoid the fact that excavation at Çatalhöyük involves a host of skills—understanding of Harris matrices, some knowledge of sampling procedures for DNA, isotope, micromorphology, phytolith analysis, and some understanding of the circumstances in which one should take such samples, etc. It would be wrong in my view to claim that such skills could quickly be gained by nonarchaeologists.

But this does not mean that members of the local community cannot be involved in the interpretive process. In fact we ask their advice all the time. They live in an environment very alien to us—with harsh winters and hot dry summers on a high plateau. They are used to building houses and tending animals and cooking in ovens in this particular environment. To some degree they live in houses not dissimilar from those at Çatalhöyük, in that they are made of sun-dried mudbrick and the walls are plastered with local muds and clays. Of course, there is absolutely no assumption of any continuity between the present and 9,000-year-old Çatalhöyük. But there remains a danger that the local community is indeed being constructed as local—in the sense of nonmodern, traditional, lost in time. The critique of Fabian (1983) seems relevant: we are placing the local community not in our time, but in some other more traditional, lost, past time. After all, they have fridges and TVs and cellular phones too, and many spend time as migrant laborers in Germany. Why emphasize their lives as traditional and local (see also Castañeda 1996)?

While the discourse of the traditional and local and "native" is undoubtedly colonial in impulse, it can be reformatted to allow entry into dialogue and debate. As far as possible in our discussions with the local communities I have tried to focus on aspects of their lives that are linked to the possibilities and constraints offered by the physical environment of the Konya Plain. I have tried to focus on the material properties of ovens, hearths, bricks, and so on. The local specialized knowledge in these areas does not need to be seen as traditional or prehistoric, as a hangover from the past. Rather it is a form of modern knowledge that can engage with our own knowledge—another form of specialization.

And so the local community has shown us how ovens of the type excavated at Çatalhöyük could have been used. They have helped us build a replica Çatalhöyük house for partly experimental reasons. They have given endless useful advice on the uses of plants found at the site and ways of processing them. We have discussed ways of cooking and storage, and the ways of making mudbricks and getting plaster onto walls. They have advised us on different forms of refuse and decay or organic materials. On the day-to-day level this advice is continual and invaluable. They bring a form of specialized knowledge that the professional archaeologists simply do not have.

Such discussion is, I am sure, common on archaeological projects. And yet the dialogue is often erased from the final publication, except perhaps for passing notes and anecdotes. Certainly at Çatalhöyük these rich voices were not getting into the publications and research designs. And so it seemed important to try and find a way in which this recursive, nonlinear dialogue could be incorporated into the final texts.

In 2000 and 2001 the Cambridge–Stanford project moved into a major phase of post-excavation analysis and writing. Most of the team spent months at the site analyzing, discussing, and writing. How could we

prevent this becoming a process that excluded the local voices? We decided to involve those local people who had been working on the site in the post-excavation production. In particular, in 2001 we paid four members from the village to work with us. Some people have been shocked that we paid them. I think this shock comes from the view that these people were our "local or native informants." They were not. They had jobs in the fields to go to. In working for us instead, they had to be paid—as co-members of the team.

Our first tries were disasters. In one of the labs, about twenty of us sat facing the four people from the village, with a translator by their side. The questions came thick and fast. What are your attitudes to rubbish? Why do you keep some types of rubbish separate? In what season do you plaster the walls? What different types of plaster do you use? We were trying to do a vicarious ethnography, treating them as "native informants." This was our confrontation with "the other," an exoticized local. We were fascinated with the "otherness," falling over ourselves to ask more and more questions—to revel in their difference.

For their part, I think they were taken aback, rather overwhelmed. It was certainly a one-sided dialogue. We were doing all the asking. They responded, but they could only do so within a frame set by us. We held all the cards. We knew where we were coming from. They could only defend against the onslaught. This was precisely the one-sided, dominating discourse against which I warned at the beginning. The fact that it led to little new knowledge is by the way. This is not the way to do an ethnography. But the main problem was their inability to contribute on their own terms.

And so we changed tack. Future meetings were smaller in scale. The group from the village met with a small number of archaeologists working on a specific topic such as burning, seasonality, rebuilding of houses, and landscape, and in the first part of the meeting, or in the first of two meetings we explained the evidence we had come up with and the methods we had used. We then outlined specific interpretive problems that we had met and asked their advice. The response was very different. *They* were now able to ask questions. They often thought and discussed among themselves and came up with their own interpretations. They pushed us to think of things differently. All of those involved in these discussions came away with new ideas and with a feeling of having been pushed in new directions.

All the encounters were recorded on video, and the texts transcribed from these tapes will be reported in the final publications. Thus the voices of the villagers will be reported directly as quotes in the volumes and websites produced as a result of the post-excavation seasons.

I would like to give some more detailed examples of this process. The chapter that I was writing myself for the final volumes is on memory. There is much evidence from Çatal-höyük of re-use of sculptures, skulls, and buildings (see Chapters 14 and 16). This re-use is often elaborate and sustained, even involving Neolithic excavation—a digging down to obtain earlier buried items and bringing them into the present. But there were a number of things that puzzled me and so I discussed them with the group.

In the houses at Çatalhöyük there is an enormous emphasis on scouring out storage bins, filling in ovens, cleaning floors, dismantling timbers, and filling in rooms at the time of abandonment. This all suggests elaborate abandonment processes which I had presumed were ritual in nature. I assumed, based on ethnographic analogies and on parallels from the Neolithic in Europe, that the elaborate abandonment procedures were part of the construction of memory. The house was ritually closed, cleansed, and restarted with ritual foundation deposits. I explained all the evidence of digging out construction posts or timbers, scouring and cleaning out plaster to the group from Küçükköy. But they had a very different take on the evidence. For them, plaster and timber were scarce resources. It was difficult, they said, to find the right muds and clays to make a form of plaster that was

easy to spread and which did not crack. These are their (translated) words: *the posts were probably removed so that they could be reused in a later house. Scouring of bin floors, house floors, and mouldings may have occurred so that the fine plaster could be reused in later houses, especially if some forms of lime-rich muds and clays were difficult to obtain. Even the removal of hands, feet, and heads from relief sculptures prior to infill may have had the same purpose—to provide high quality plaster for the next phase of building. The intentional filling of an oven (rather than knocking it down) may have occurred because the fired oven helped to provide a firm base for the building which ensued.* I felt suitably admonished. They were taking a resolutely processual archaeology line. Everything had a practical optimizing rationale. There was no need to invoke ritual.

I had a similar experience in another case. I pointed to the evidence that the houses were usually organized so that the entrance and the oven were in the south part of the building. I thought this implied some habituated memory. People 9,000 years ago at Çatal-höyük must have been brought up within a habitus which organized internal space into south–north oppositions. Once again, the villagers wanted to emphasize the practical logic of these patterns within houses. This is what they said about the ovens on the south side of the rooms: *It is obvious that if placed on the north wall, the strong prevailing winds from the north would push smoke back into the house. The location of the oven on the south side of the house ensures that more smoke will be taken away from the house.* So, again, they seemed to be natural processual archaeologists!

In the end, in these examples and countless others, I changed my mind and changed the argument. While I did not abandon the notion that the houses were organized through habituated practices and memories, I also found it helpful to recognize that the embedding of habituated practices within a practical logic serves to reinforce and sustain them. In our discussions we reached a hybrid compromise—something new that both sides had contributed to. I dropped the emphasis on ritual, agreed to the practical logic, but that seemed to reinforce the argument about the reproduction of habituated practices.

CONCLUSION

I would like to argue that we can answer in the affirmative to Spivak's question "can the subaltern speak?" I hope the examples I have given demonstrate that it is possible for other voices to be heard and incorporated into a dominant discourse. Of course, it could be argued in return that this example simply shows the incorporation and silencing of the subaltern into a colonial regime of truth. One of the ethnographers working in the village near Çatalhöyük argues that before the arrival of archaeologists the villagers had a very different idea of the mounds and of their past. The archaeology has changed this indigenous view and the four villagers working with us have been incorporated into our discourse. They are learning our techniques and ways of reconstructing the past. But it is not the case that the way we construct the past at Çatalhöyük is unchanged by our interactions with the villagers. I have shown how the dominant discourse has been challenged and changed. The result is a hybrid to which the villagers and we have contributed.

But the incorporation of the local voice, its contribution to the science that we pursue, is only possible because we open up to listen and include. This is where the confession-alplays its role. Confessions may be self-indulgent and self-serving. They appear to be individual. And yet they provide the mechanism for disciplining and creating normativity in the individual self. If that normativity involves a duty to listen and include, it can only be of value in breaking down barriers between "us" and "them," even if there is a danger that it creates new ones.

II. The Impact on Method—
Interpretation at the Trowel's Edge

A second group of papers examines the impact of a more global and multivocal archaeology on the methods used by archaeologists in the field and in the laboratory. A wide range of new techniques are considered with particular reference to their experimental application at Çatalhöyük. The section includes my responses to various criticisms of the approach.

Chapter 4 critiques the separation of data and interpretation in field method (looking especially at the methods proposed by Barker). The notion that one can just describe and record without interpretation is insufficiently dialogical and is internally contradictory. In order to remove these inconsistencies, and in order to be more responsive to diverse stakeholders, a reflexive approach is needed. Four components of a reflexive approach are defined—reflexive, relational or contextual, interactive, and multivocal. As an example, a series of practical steps taken at Çatalhöyük is described—all involving interpretation at the trowel's edge, i.e., a closer and more dialogical unity of data and theory. When published, this paper led to a response from Fekri Hassan, which in turn led to a counter argument that is here reproduced as Chapter 5. This chapter reinforces the critique of dichotomous separations of fact from interpretation, and science from society, and low-level from high-level interpretation. In making these claims for a dialogical rather than a dichotomous perspective, an underlying contention is that everything we do as archaeologists has a social and political dimension. Our rationality has to be adjusted or argued for in a social arena.

In similar vein, Chapter 6 was written as a response to an article by Yannis Hamilakis which also contained a critique of the reflexive approaches being developed at Çatalhöyük. This chapter deals with the issue of the role of the intellectual in society, and in doing so it faces up to some of the problems and contradictions that are produced by reflexivity and social responsiveness. In particular the chapter critiques the idea of an autonomous intellectual, and argues that to have influence the archaeologist needs to use structures of power while critiquing them. Thus it is necessary, in dialogical fashion, to be at the same time inside and outside structures of power.

These various arguments result in a longer and more developed argument in Chapter 7. This looks back at the history of field archaeology and argues that the development of excavation field methods in archaeology was closely tied to the social position of fieldworkers. In other words, field archaeology was never just scientific description—it was always embedded within specific labor relations. The chapter also notes disaffection in field contract archaeology today resulting from a wide range of factors, including the separation of excavation from interpretation. The chapter argues that this separation and the notion that archaeological excavation can be seen as unskilled undermine the scientific basis of archaeology. A reflexive archaeology is discussed that empowers field archaeology by (a) focusing interpretation at the trowel's edge, (b) bringing multiple perspectives close to the moment of excavation, and (c) documenting the documentation process. These arguments extend those already found in Chapter 4, partly as a result of the critiques reported in Chapters 5 and 6. In addition, the reflexive experiments at Çatalhöyük are put into the wider context of similar shifts in method being explored at other sites.

4

"Always Momentary, Fluid, and Flexible"
Toward a Reflexive Excavation Methodology

Although processual and post-processual archaeologists conceive of "data" in different ways (Patrik 1985), there has been little discussion of a post-processual methodology (but see Carver 1989; Tilley 1989). This is understandable; any notion of a general methodology separate from the context of the production of knowledge could conflict with approaches which emphasize critique, interpretation, and multivocality.

Most excavation record forms still separate description and interpretation in the way advocated by Barker (1977, 1982). Carver (1989:669) argues that this tradition in Britain extends back to Pitt-Rivers, such that "English excavators, particularly, believe that there ought to be a science of retrieving archaeological evidence which has nothing to do with the interpretations that are subsequently made." The general emphasis on "objective" recording found in field contexts in many parts of the world would suggest that the postprocessual debate has had little impact in this arena.

I wish to argue that there are two reasons for a reconsideration of archaeological "data collection" techniques. The first—"internal" or logical—concerns a contradiction that lies at the heart of the empiricist and objectivist approaches to "data." The second—"external"—concerns the wider world within which archaeology today operates. I will illustrate the impact of this global context with

reference to renewed work at Çatalhöyük (Hodder 1996).

DIGGING CONTRADICTORILY

Consider the following two statements from Joukowsky's *A Complete Manual of Field Archaeology* (1980:218–219, 175):

> In addition to day-by-day notes, the square supervisor is responsible for a subjective interpretation of the meaning of his or her excavation. This subjective analysis is submitted at the conclusion of his/her work in a particular area and is physically kept separate from the objective facts, so that assumptions are kept distinct from field notes.
>
> If the earth is from a sterile layer, it can be dumped, but if it comes from an occupation level, the earth should be carried to the screen, spread on it, and sifted so that no telltale signs will be overlooked.

The first statement argues that interpretation should be kept separate from objective fact; it should occur only after data have been collected. The second statement contradicts this by arguing that the methods used depend on prior interpretation. The excavator has to interpret a deposit in terms of whether it is an occupation level before screening (sieving) is used. How is one supposed to know whether a layer is sterile before it has been screened?

Interpretation occurs at many levels in archaeological research, and in the example just given, it cannot be confined to a higher level. How we excavate a site is generally determined by our prior interpretation of the site. The screening and point-proveniencing of all artifacts common on excavations of Palaeolithic cave sites are minimal on historic urban sites. Even within a site, decisions about whether to screen are frequently made on the basis of interpretation. A "floor" context is excavated more intensively than one interpreted as "fill," with 100 percent water-screening only being used in the "floor" context. In such cases, whether an artifact exists at all within the archaeological view depends on interpretation. Microartifacts may only be recovered because of full water-screening of "floor" contexts. The same artifact from a "fill" would not be searched for or recovered; it might simply "not exist." The objective existence of an artifact as "data" depends on the interpretation made prior to and during excavation. How can it be maintained that subjective data interpretation should only occur after objective data description and collection?

Archaeologists have typically dealt with the problem of needing to know what is being excavated before it is excavated by sampling different parts of deposits or sites in different ways, or by taking initial trial soundings *(sondages)* before full excavation. The assumption in such cases is that any mistake made in the exploration of a deposit or site can be rectified in digging other parts of the "same" deposit or site, or even other sites in the same region or class of site. The problem with this approach is that we cannot assume that all the sampled parts of cultural deposits, sites, or groups of sites are similar. In laboratory-based archaeological research or in experimental archaeology it may be possible to repeat experiments, varying conditions in a controlled way, so that different instances of the "same" phenomenon can be examined. In excavation, whether different parts of a deposit or different deposits or sites are the "same" is itself an interpretation. That interpretation might be best made after excavation—but it has to be made prior to excava-

tion if trial soundings of an entity such as a pit or site or of a category such as a class of pit or site are to be made.

This contradiction, which lies behind both empiricist and problem-oriented research designs, is again clearly illustrated by Philip Barker's *Techniques of Archaeological Excavation* (1977, 1982), which describes methods which have become common in British field archaeology. On the one hand, Barker accepts that "interpretation...inevitably begins as features are seen, dissected and removed" (Barker 1982:145). Since recording begins during excavation, and since "the interpretive element in the recording can never be completely isolated," the archaeologist has a great responsibility to interpret immediately, as layers are uncovered (Barker 1982: 145). Since recording begins during excavation, and since "the interpretive element in the recording can never be completely isolated," the archaeologist has a great responsibility to interpret immediately, as layers are uncovered (Barker 1982:146). For Barker, recording is always an interpretation; a section or profile drawing records what the excavator sees rather than simply what is there.

So, for Barker interpretation is prior to or at least embedded within recording and excavation. But it is a very different strain in Barker's account which has come to dominate British field archaeology; the contradictory view that this interpretive component should be minimized by separating evidence from interpretation. "Immediate on-site recovery...should be as objective as it can be" (Barker 1982:147); "in order to minimize the interpretive element in the record" (1982: 145) neutral terms such as "feature" and "context" should be used. Barker argues for formalized cards and coding sheets—indeed for the whole system of "objective" data description that has become routine. Subjectivity and speculation become central only at higher levels of interpretation (Barker 1982: 147).

Why was it possible to side-step the centrality of interpretation within "data description"? Partly because of the prevalence of the empiricist and positivist traditions within the discipline. Partly because of the need to handle increasingly large amounts of data and the codification implied by computer-aided techniques. Barker (1982:206) expresses this latter need in suggesting that the excavator may start off with doubt about whether a posthole might be a root hole, or whether a floor might be a random scatter of pebbles. Although Barker feels that this interpretive doubt should be retained in the excavation report, he accepts that it often is not; if all such interpretive issues were included in the report it would become too dull because there would be *too much information*. The handling of large amounts of data has led to highly codified and rigid computerized recording systems, systems that require data gathering to be separated from and be prior to interpretation.

The key point is that excavation method, data collection, and data recording all depend on interpretation. Interpretation occurs at the trowel's edge. And yet, perhaps because of the technologies available to deal with very large sets of data, we have as archaeologists separated excavation methods out and seen them as prior to interpretation. Modern data-management systems perhaps allow some resolution of the contradiction. At any rate, it is time it was faced and dealt with.

It is not sufficient to respond by saying that hypothesis testing procedures or the promotion by government agencies of site evaluation and research programs foreground interpretation. By these means, method is related to theory (Carver 1990). But the internal contradiction is not resolved because, whatever the prior knowledge and theories about a site, we do not find exactly what we predict. In addition, the testing of prior knowledge still involves the evaluation of whether a particular feature in the ground is an example of a general category (pit, hearth, etc.). In these ways, the moment of interpretation in the field is not wholly determined by prior views. Thus the methods employed have to be fluid and flexible rather than pre-determined. In practice, the adoption of hypothesis testing or site evaluation procedures has been accompanied by a continued separation of data description and interpretation in most excavations and reports.

THE WIDER CONTEXT

The second reason for reconsidering archaeological "data collection" techniques derives from the global context within which archaeologists increasingly work. Are archaeologists adequately fulfilling their responsibilities to the societies within which they work by arguing for a separation between data and interpretation? Is it ethical to deal with the contradiction between the need to describe large amounts of data and interpretive uncertainty by arguing that description occurs before or separately from interpretation? Is this the best way to fulfill our public duties?

I will argue not, because a clear movement within archaeology and heritage has brought multivocality and interactivity central stage. Reburial issues and the need to cooperate with indigenous Australian or American groups, land rights issues throughout the world, the impact of feminist archaeology—all these are examples of the opening-up of archaeology to a wider set of interests. Within museums and heritage centers the need has increasingly been felt to respond to multiple voices and to engage in a wide range of issues.

As one small example of these globalizing tendencies I mention our recent renewed work at Çatalhöyük (Hodder 1996). As archaeologists we bring our universal and specialized terms and codes, our disciplinary discourse. We bring our technologies and our interest in comparative evolutionary schemes and our global questions dealing with, for example, the origins of agriculture or of complex society. The Turkish state quite properly has other concerns in mind, to do with historic preservation. And at the site itself we are visited by busloads of people on "Goddess Tours" who are interested in a spiritual connection with the site, who may come to pray, or who are part of New Age, Ecofeminist, or Gaia movements (cf. Conkey and Tringham

1995; Meskell 1995). We see that Linda Evangelista is wearing a large image of the Çatalhöyük "Mother Goddess" on the front of clothes she is modeling for the Turkish designer Rifat Özbek (*Hello* magazine, January 1991). And yet the local women in the area in which we work remain covered, and the men seem confronted by but willing to make advertising use of the naked "Mother Goddess" (Shankland 1996). There is a whole field of carpet studies and carpet dealing which looks to Çatalhöyük for the origins of kilim designs (Eiland 1993; Mellaart et al. 1989). The site and its imagery seem to exist in a whirlwind of competing and conflicting special interests.

How can we impose our specific archaeological perspective on this diversity of local and global interests? The stock answer is for the project to become involved in heritage and museums, to provide information on the World Wide Web, etc. These directions are certainly being taken at Çatalhöyük; display panels and buildings have been provided and there are plans for a museum or interpretive center. The project has its Web home page. But the fact that these answers are insufficient was made clear in discussions with the New Age women's movements. When we told them that we would provide the data so that they could make their own less androcentric interpretations of the site, they complained that this was not enough—"because when you hand over the data to us, they have already been interpreted by you."

That statement challenges the objectivity, distance, and neutrality that archaeological method has built up for itself. In response, we need to go beyond a method which excludes and dominates, which separates description and interpretation as if description was mere data that could be objectively handed out to people to interpret subjectively. The challenge is to accept the central role of interpretation in the very process of the construction of data. The challenge is to introduce interpretation at the primary level.

Çatalhöyük is a peculiar case, it could be argued, and most archaeology takes place within a less diverse context. But, in fact, few archaeologists work today in an environment

in which there are not multiple voices and conflicting interests. This is not just post-processual dogma; the post-processual debate has to be set within the wider context of globalism. Diversity in archaeology, heritage, and museums is parallel to and part of changes in the economies and societies within which we live. Whether one calls these changes "high," "late," or "post-modernism" is less important than their undoubted widespread impact.

The key linking concept behind the varied aspects of these high/late/post-modern trends is globalism. Globalism—which can be defined in a number of ways (e.g., Featherstone 1991; Featherstone et al. 1995)—involves closer integration caused by new trends in economies (especially global scales of production and global markets), the new information technologies, and other global issues such as the protection of the environment. But at the same time as creating homogenization and the "global village," these processes and their technologies lead to fragmentation and individualization, in a counter-trend partly the product of niche marketing and the new fragmentation of work practices. But it also marks the reaction against globalizing and homogenizing tendencies by groups seeking new and diverse identities, new meanings and senses of self.

In this new world—in which information is widely disseminated but in which there is also a diversity of educated, informed, and active special-interest groups—it becomes increasingly difficult for archaeologists to live with the contradiction in their "data collection" techniques. The public role of the archaeologist in a global and diverse, fragmented world is increasingly to cooperate and to integrate. As in the reburial debate, it is necessary to temper universal science with a sensitivity to local interests. It cannot be acceptable to attempt to close debate by saying, "This is objective and descriptive," when what we really mean is, "This is our interpretation." The issue of scientific objectivity is no longer simply theoretical. In a recent *Society for American Archaeology Bulletin*, groups within archaeology seeking to work together with Native Americans and integrate the use of oral traditions in archaeological interpretation argue that "scientific knowledge does not constitute a privileged view of the past... it is simply another way of knowing the past" (Anyon et al. 1996:15).

TOWARD A REFLEXIVE METHODOLOGY AT ÇATALHÖYÜK

Introducing a methodology at Çatalhöyük which foregrounds interpretation at the trowel's edge has involved dealing with four issues. The first is the need to be critical of assumptions and taken-for-granteds (Leone et al. 1987), to be *reflexive* about the effects of archaeological assumptions and work on the different communities within the public domain. The second is the need to be *relational* or *contextual*. Meaning is relational; the interpretation of a pit depends on the dating of the ceramics, but the dating of the ceramics depends on the stratigraphical relations of the pit, which are themselves uncertain and partly dependent on the ceramics, and so on. Understanding the pit involves also knowing about seeds and bones and lithics, etc. Everything depends on everything else. So to interpret involves creating a circuitry between participants in the project and between different types of data. One implication is that conclusions are always momentary, fluid, and flexible as new relations are considered. The third issue involves being *interactive* in the sense of providing information that can be questioned and approached from different angles. The fourth involves being *multivocal*, plural, open or transparent so that a diversity of people can participate in the discourse about the archaeological process.

The practical steps taken to achieve these at Çatalhöyük are these. As on many "excavations abroad," it is necessary for many of the nonfield project specialists to be present on site. But it is possible to turn this necessity-into a virtue, with ceramic, faunal, lithic, archaeobotanical, micromorphological, etc., specialists present within excavation trenches and taking part in the primary interpretive process. This interaction is achieved by daily or twice-daily tours and individual visits, and

it is now planned to have primary processing of faunal remains and perhaps other artifact categories in the excavation area rather than in the field laboratory. The aim here is twofold. The first purpose is to contextualize specialist information within the particular characteristics of the site; rather than assuming what burned bone looks like universally, the identification of burned bone can be informed by the interpretation of context. If the bone comes from a deposit which is, on other evidence, heavily burned, then it, too, is more likely to have been burned. In this way, general knowledge about what burned bone looks like can be accommodated to specific evidence for burning at Çatalhöyük. The second purpose of the tours is to empower and inform members of the excavation team by surrounding them with information; the more that is known about the artifacts as they come out of the ground, the more is immediate interpretation facilitated. In this way methods and recording techniques can be adjusted. This type of interaction may often be difficult because it breaks down barriers and boundaries between field and laboratory expertise; it may involve conflict between field professionals and academic or laboratory personnel. The end result is beneficial in that excavation and sampling strategies can be enhanced by an informed interpretation of what is being excavated and sampled.

On smaller-scale projects, similar integrative effects may be obtained by merging the roles of nonfield and field specialists. For example, faunal specialists may be involved in field excavation, at least on a part-time basis; and increasingly field staff seek training in other areas of professional training. The regional or local availability of nonfield specialists becomes a priority. Another integrative strategy relevant to projects of all sizes involves escaping from the self-evident nature of archaeological "objects" (Conolly, pers. comm. 1996). These empiricist and objectivist approaches have always been underpinned by the apparently self-evident nature of the objects archaeologists study—bones, ceramics, seeds, lithics, and layers. The fragmentation of archaeological research is founded on the apparent objectivity of these differences among objects. Much of the field research at Çatalhöyük involves microscopic analysis (for example, micromorphology or study of lithic microdebitage). At this microscale, the self-evident boundaries of objects disappear in that, for example, the distinctions between layers become blurred when viewed in terms of the deposition of mineral particles, or the distinctions between pots and lithics are undermined by traces of obsidian flakes used as pottery temper. If the object categories on which archaeological research is founded can be seen to be the product of the conventional lenses used in analysis, the door is opened for constructing new "objects" of study which partition the object-world in different and multiscalar ways. "Objects," such as "burning," or "decoration," or "rubbish," cut across the lower-level domains based on conventional artifact categories and allow fuller integrative work. A "rubbish" specialist, for example, would need to use general information about the effects of depositional and post-depositional processes as well as field observations and information from a wide range of artifact categories.

Getting information back to the excavator as quickly as possible is essential. This may be assisted by new technologies; immediate digital data input may allow the quick production of artifact distributions and plans. At Çatalhöyük we have invested in a local, on-site computer network; all the terminals of the laboratory and field staff are linked by a hub so that data sheets and plans can immediately be accessed and linked to artifact-based information. Indeed it increasingly seems necessary to have a dedicated "data-analyst" present with the time and resources to search for relationships between different types of data.

As noted, a reason for the highly codified recording systems developed in archaeology has been the need to deal with large data sets. A major challenge at Çatalhöyük has been to construct a database which allows the maximum amount of flexibility, change, and inter-

action. The system, initially designed by Tim Ritchey and now by Anja Wolle, is a standard relational database (initially Microsoft Access running on a Windows NT server machine) in which all aspects of the project are entered; excavation unit sheets as well as the faunal specialist records are on the same database so that querying between artifact data and context data is facilitated. The aim here is to allow artifact categories (e.g., burned bone) to be evaluated against context information (e.g., whether a deposit or house is burned), and simultaneously to allow context categories (e.g., burned deposit) to be evaluated against artifact information (e.g., whether a bone appears burned). Within a nonlinear, circular process such as this, categories and definitions change on the basis of multiple strands of information. It becomes necessary to tie codes and definitions of categories to dates and explanations. It may also be helpful to allow comparison and retrieval at different levels of abstraction. Contexts might be described both abstractly in terms of positive (e.g., layer) or negative ("cut") events, or in terms of more specific alternatives and probabilities (e.g., floor 70 percent; midden lens 30 percent).

While flexibility and the erosion of the notion of fixed objective categories can perhaps be engendered by these means, placing large amounts of information into a database in a way that allows efficient retrieval and comparison will always require considerable codification and fixity. Our aim is to embed the database within other information which contextualizes its own production. This reflexivity helps us to be critical of the assumptions we make, and it means that at future dates we or others can look back and understand why we made this or that interpretation, why we used this category or that context definition. It facilitates use of the site archive by later generations.

The contextualizing information includes more than coded forms and texts. The construction of a multimedia database is essential if a full range of information is to be provided to a wide variety of audiences. Access

Figure 4.1. Interpretation at the primary level: social interaction in the Çatalhöyük trench, 1996. On the right, James and Arlette Mellaart, excavators of the site in the 1960s, help the conservator Connie Silver understand what happened then. Director Ian Hodder is listening in. This group is being filmed by the Karlsruhe team. Watching that is the project's social anthropologist Carolyn Hamilton. The whole is being photographed from the top left by Shahina Farid.

provides the ability to point to different types of data through OLE (Object Linking and Embedding). When designing the database, the field type (e.g., video field or autocad field) can be set as OLE object, which then gives the flexibility of including data from any OLE-aware application.

One of the contextualizing types of data placed on the database at Çatalhöyük is the diary kept by the site and trench directors. With more computer terminals at the site it is hoped to have wider participation in diary-writing by members of the project. Keeping some form of diary or running account of an excavation used to be the prime method of recording information. The site or trench notebook is still advocated by, for example, Joukowsky (1980). But in British contract archaeology at least, most excavations have moved to some form of single-context recording with codified forms and prompts, and a version of this system is used at Çatalhöyük.

Barker (1982:147) argued against notebooks of "prose whose loose format invites the writer to confuse the stages of recording, deduction, interpretation and speculation." Since these stages are, in truth, inseparable (Carver 1990:299) it becomes essential, both scientifically and ethically, to record what was being *thought* when records were being made and methods chosen. We have found at Çatalhöyük that writing a diary in the pseudo-privacy of typing at a terminal leads to highly personal and revealing accounts (even though the entries, as it turned out, are immediately and avidly read by others on the network). The entries in the diary can be linked on the basis of unit and feature number searches to the codified information so the latter can be set within the context of the production of knowledge. At the very least, the process enhances information exchange and debate within the project.

One important aspect to the context of

production of knowledge on an archaeological site is visual. At Çatalhöyük, daily video documentation takes place of group discussion in trenches, individual accounts of excavation progress, and laboratory work. In this way team members can point to information they consider relevant, debates can be recorded, and illustration provided. These videos are digitized, edited into short clips and stored on the database with attached keywords. From the database can be retrieved not only field descriptions, Autocad drawings, artifact locations and dietary information for any particular unit, but also video about that unit, its discovery, and interpretation. The editing process is of course selective, but the visual documentation always includes more "peripheral" information than texts or forms, and it includes more of the surrounding context within which team members are working and interpretations are made. Indeed, the video documentation at Çatalhöyük, achieved with the collaboration of the Center for Art and Media-Technology at Karlsruhe, has become very central to our methodology. Not only do the videos allow later critique and evaluation of the construction of data on site, but they also lead to greater information flow about interpretation (as people listen to each other live or on playback in the laboratory) and a greater readiness to submit one's own assumptions to scrutiny. As members of the team pointed out, the ever-present eye of the camera means that thought-processes are much more out in the open.

The destabilization of taken-for-granted assumptions and the critique of universal codes is also encouraged by the presence in the field team of an anthropologist whose concern is to study the context of production of knowledge. Carolyn Hamilton worked with us during the 1996 field season, using participation techniques and, for example, the diary to try to expose some of the assumptions we were making, some of the contradictions we were not facing, and some of the potential for alternative interpretation. An ethnomethodological study of an archaeological excavation has been conducted by Gero (1996). Rather than making the Çatalhöyük excavation the object of study, Hamilton's aim has been to participate in and contribute to the excavation process. As with the video work, Hamilton's presence quickly came to be far from marginal. Her work interdigitated with ours so completely that very many of our interpretive and methodological ideas derived from discussion with her. The presence of a team member dedicated to questioning leads to a greater understanding of the processes in which we are engaged. The anthropological work not only makes the account of the production of knowledge (for example, on video or in diaries) by team members more complete, it also means that the knowledge itself is informed by a greater awareness of alternative interpretations. Hamilton also had privileged access into our thoughts through individual interviews; she was able to point out for us parallels and comparisons between team members. Again, communication and interactivity were enhanced. The benefits to the project are tangible both in terms of results and working relations.

One example of many in the 1996 season at Çatalhöyük was Hamilton's observation that we were still being very descriptive in our field recording. As an anthropologist she felt that we did not get beyond the static. We did not think through in the field how artifacts had become incorporated into the archaeological record. Our primary data description did not include consideration of the agency behind the broken pot on the house floor. This critique helped us to see that interpretation had to become a routine part of primary recording if relevant questions were to be asked of the data during their discovery.

So far I have described the site as being interpreted by "team members." On any project there will be differential participation by members in the construction of knowledge. One of Hamilton's aims is to explore some relations of production of archaeological knowledge at the site. This is certainly necessary since differences in education, gender, country-of-origin, and so on limit any ideal of open communication (Gero 1996). But in the global heritage market identified earlier in this paper, even the idea of a well-bounded "team" is increasingly difficult. What qualifies for membership of "the team"? While a core group undertakes the fieldwork, research, and publication, many people in the global community may wish to have direct access to the site data and to participate in its interpretation. For this reason, the entire raw database is being placed on the Web, including drawings and diaries, but excluding, for the moment, the video clips which require too much storage space for the Internet. The presence of contextualizing information in the database allows others to understand the process of the construction of the coded information and to be in a position to criticize and reevaluate from alternative perspectives. The "data" are thus not hoarded by "the team" until publication; they are immediately part of a public interpretation.

We are also developing the use of hypertext in ways parallel to Ruth Tringham's (1994) "Chimera Web" for the Balkan Neolithic site of Opovo. It can be argued (e.g., S. Thomas 1996) that the use of hypertext and nonlinear multimedia datastructures allows some decentering of the author and some "writerliness" of texts for which some theoretical statements have been called (Bapty and Yates 1990; Joyce 1994; Spector 1993). Since it is possible for each "reader" of the "text" to move through it in different ways, there is a greater openness to a wide range of interests and greater opportunities for interactivity and engagement. It is possible in this way to embed a narrative about the site in links to the database, to visual material, reconstructions, and so on at various levels of specialist knowledge. Care must be exercised here, as J. Thomas (1996) has indicated. A certain level of archaeological knowledge may be required before the user of hypertext or hypermedia can effectively interact with it. It may be necessary to ensure that part of the hypertext deals with explaining terms and assumptions, so that the tools necessary for interaction are made available and easily accessible.

Virtual reality, as applied by the Karlsruhe team working at Çatalhöyük, has already been important in providing a deeper understanding of what it could have been like to move around within and between the buildings at the site (Forte and Siliotti 1997). This has been achieved by video-length computer animation, but also using Quick-Time VR, VRML, and Real-Time computers (some of which is accessible at the project's Web address). A phenomenological or experiential approach has been championed by a current generation of British prehistorians (e.g., Barrett 1994; J. Thomas 1996; Tilley 1994). In situations of less or minimal monument survival, or where there has been substantial landscape change, virtual techniques may allow experimenting with alternative forms of interaction between people and the worlds they have constructed around them. The intention at Çatalhöyük is also to use virtual reality to provide a nonspecialist "front end" to the database. Users will be able to "fly" into the site, into individual buildings, "click" on paintings or artifacts and so move gradually, if desired, into all the scientific information available in the database. Potentially, users will be able to move through the site, exploring information, and coming to their own decisions about the "data" at different levels. One problem we have at Çatalhöyük is in deciding whether a building is in some sense a "house"; rather than accepting "our" conclusions on this, users will be able to access the data, as far as that is possible, and can come to their own conclusions about the definition of a "house" at Çatalhöyük.

CONCLUSION

The aim of introducing a discussion of methodology at Çatalhöyük was to move toward the four goals of reflexivity, contextuality, interactivity, and multivocality. These same concerns, in varied guises, reappear in many areas of the post- or high-modern world (Lyotard 1984, 1991). They are themselves linked to, and perhaps produced by, new information technologies (Castells 1996; Porter 1997); it is to be expected that in trying to operationalize these concerns in archaeology, the technologies themselves come to play a central role. It would have been appropriate to couple this text with a video debate among participants in the project. Conventional academic publishing by single authors is only part of an overall process and it is limited in its ability to further the fourfold aims.

But simply to introduce the new technologies is clearly insufficient. While high-speed processors on-site, hypertext, multimedia, and virtual reality may all foster some of the reflexivity, contextuality, interactivity, and multivocality that is required, they have to be aligned with broader changes in approach and work practices. The technologies perhaps provide an opportunity rather than a solution.

Placing so much emphasis on the point of excavation may lead to a re-empowering or recentering of the field excavator. It may also involve retraining and reskilling individuals so that they can handle the increased amount and complexity of knowledge made available to them during the excavation process. Alternatives might involve breaking the distinction between field and laboratory staff, and providing opportunities for field staff to be trained also as specialists in other areas and levels of research. More generally, the separation between field professional, university academic, and laboratory scientist within the discipline do not provide a good context for the necessary degree of interpretive interaction. If interpretation is not to be seen as secondary but as primary to data collection, then so will the institutional divides between data collection, analysis, and interpretation be further eroded.

As a further example of the relationship between methodological change and the need for wider accompanying changes in approach, it is possible to consider the impact of widespread data accessibility on the careers of project researchers and field staff. It will often be the case that some aspect of their career development is linked to publication; if primary data about the project are immediately widely available, the ability to publish original information may be undermined.

Some safeguards and controls on information dissemination may be deemed necessary at certain points in the circuitry.

Despite these problems and implications, the end result of a reflexive methodology is an approach with scientific advantages. If more information is available at the point of excavation, choice of sampling and excavation method will be more appropriate to the questions being asked and the problems being studied (Carver 1989, 1990); fuller recording of relevant information will also be possible. If more contextual information is available to those working on materials from the site, there is less danger of inappropriate codes and categories being imposed from outside. If those conducting excavations are open to a wide range of perspectives, they may be more willing to adjust general views to the particularities of the information being discovered. A final scientific advantage might be claimed in the production of archives with sufficient contextual information to make them more usable than those archives based on highly objectified and codified data systems.

Whether or not these claims for scientific advantages come to be met, there are also ethical considerations. Day by day it becomes more difficult to argue for a past controlled by the academy. The proliferation of special interests on the "fringe" increasingly challenges or spreads to the dominant discourse itself. As part of the global heritage economy there is a massive dissemination of cultural information. Rather than leading to a simple homogenization, this process has involved a decentering and a burgeoning of special-interest groups. These communities, however dispersed and virtual they might appear to be, and however they depend on a technological system, have created for themselves new, varied, and independent identities. Many are extremely well informed. Within this unstable kaleidoscope it is no longer so easy to see who is "in" the academy and who is "outside," in the same way post-modernism blurs the distinction between "high" and "low" culture. Within the global communities fascinated by some aspect or other of Çatalhöyük, where does one draw the line between those within or outside the "team"? Is there a need to draw a line? Is not the better solution to make the line as permeable as possible while being responsible for the protection of certain rights? Is it not better to accept openly that even in the construction of archaeological data, interpretation is required?

Note: The Web address for Çatalhöyük is: http://catal.arch.cam.ac.uk/catal/catal/html

Acknowledgments

Many of the ideas expressed here derive from discussion with members of the various communities with an interest in Çatalhöyük. To them all I am greatly indebted, and in particular to Louise Martin, I.R.S. Russell, Tim Ritchey, and James Colony. Thanks also to the reviewers and editor. The project is sponsored by Visa, Koçbank (main sponsors), Merko (long-term sponsor), British Airways, Shell, and Glaxo-Wellcome.

5

Whose Rationality?

In the context of discussing the need to bring "unity and harmony to a world afflicted by ethnic, sectarian and nationalist conflicts," Hassan (1997:1021) talks of "upholding the mandate of reason." Whose reason? It is clear that Hassan refers to the reason of a world community of trained archaeological experts (1997:1024). Trained by whom? He talks (1997:1021) of archaeology as a "scientific discipline within the academy." Which academy and defined by whom? The academy Hassan refers to guards against any usurpation of the concept of "fact" (1997:1024) and upholds canons of knowledge against the abandonment of reason (1997:1021). Again, concepts of "fact" defined by whom, and whose reason?

In reading Hassan's critique I sensed echoes of eighteenth-century Enlightenment thought and nineteenth-century colonialism—an uncritical Western belief in universal rationality. This spirited defense of empiricism and positivism takes us back at least to pre-TAG days, and certainly to before the accommodations made on both sides of the processual/post-processual debate (e.g., Hodder 1992; Renfrew and Bahn 1991). Apart from the nostalgic pleasure of revisiting old battlefields, I respond to Hassan because I believe fervently that he is profoundly, even dangerously misguided.

I answer this way because of the conviction that even archaeologists should heed some of the abiding lessons of the twentieth century (e.g., Hobsbawm 1994). Hassan writes as if science or scientific anthropology will protect us from all sorts of evils. This may well be true in the example he provides, but it is surely only half the story. After the horrors of the Great War, the Holocaust, and Hiroshima, how can we put our faith in the mandate of reason, meaning the mandate of Western reason? For many of my generation, those who grew up experiencing the insanity of Vietnam, it is difficult to have much faith in Western rationality. Another great movement of the twentieth century has been the decline of many colonial powers and the resurgence of ex-colonial nations and indigenous groups. In this post-colonial world, the notion that the Western voice is only one of many has been reinforced. How, in such a world, can authority derive from self-appointed "experts" in "the academy"?

The awareness of difference and of the need to listen to other voices has taken on a particular urgency at the end of the twentieth century in the context of globalism. In my view, the type of universal rationality espoused by Hassan plays into the hands of the homogenizing tendencies promoted by those who control the new information technologies. We are wrong to dismiss the new technologies as "razzle-dazzle" (Hassan 1997: 1024). They have the power to transform our lives, to homogenize, to limit debate and diversity, to create a true "end of history." But these same technologies can be used, not to

Table 5.1

mandate of reason	prejudice, emotion, dogmatic belief
epistemological canons of veracity, plausibility and accuracy	political, moral agendas
canons of knowledge, accuracy	subjective error
methods of science	dogmatism, chauvinism, demagoguery, idiosyncratic beliefs, revelations
scientific domain	ethics (and aesthetics, history, poetics, novels)
scientific discipline within the academy	a priori beliefs about the mother goddess, etc.
"fact" and the expert	public, popular

promote universality, but to guard against the erasure of history. The new information technologies can be used to promote difference, and it is for this reason that I suggest their use to encourage reflexivity, relationality, interactivity, and multivocality.

TOWARDS NONDICHOTOMOUS THINKING

Throughout Hassan's critique he reasserts old dichotomies. These can be set out as follows:

Thus reason is opposed to beliefs based on fear, self-importance, authority, prejudices, superstitions, and mental disturbances. The competence of trained scholars using standards and canons of description is opposed to superstition, dogmatism, obscurantism. Hassan (1997:1021) is incorrect to argue that archaeological science, or any science, is not driven by belief. It is belief, often passionately held, that generates questions, hypotheses, and research pathways. It is belief, often dogmatic in tone, that leads to innovative lines of enquiry. It is belief, in the guise of theory, through which we make sense of the data so that they are, to some degree, theory-laden, as even processual archaeologists now accept (e.g., Renfrew and Bahn 1991).

It is difficult to define science in the dichotomous way described by Hassan. Many philosophers of science would accept (e.g., Hesse 1995) that many of the characteristics which Hassan describes as nonscientific are an essential part of science. Certainly it is clear that the success of theories does not rely solely on correspondence to data; other factors such as coherence, rhetoric, story-line, authority, reputation and social network undoubtedly play a role (e.g., Latour and Woolgar 1979). Hassan tries to make his point by twice (1997:1021, 1024) using the analogy of the medical doctor who provides the patient with an expert opinion. But even a competent physician may listen to the public and incorporate other voices. Having just been to a doctor who passed on advice influenced by alternative medicine, Hassan's analogy seems inappropriate. More generally, we can recognize today that the doing of science is a complex, socially embedded process. Within the field of anthropological science there has been an extensive debate about the need to incorporate other voices, leading to wonderful (but still "scientific") narrative ethnographies such as that of Humphrey and Onon (1996). A discussion of the need to introduce qualitative methods has taken place in the social sciences more generally (Denzin and Lincoln 1994). We need to think about science, including archaeological science, in nondichotomous ways.

INTERPRETATION AT THE TROWEL'S EDGE

One of the clearest dichotomies identified by Hassan is that fact and theory can be separated from each other at primary levels of interpretation, though he also provides examples of an empiricist and positivist rhetoric according to which facts are seen as theory-laden. For empiricists in archaeology, this rhetoric translated into the practice of sticking as close to the facts as possible. For positivists and processual archaeologists the great leap forward was to argue that we need to be explicit about the theories brought to the facts. This more critical attitude to the relationship between theory and data has been construed in a number of ways by processual archaeologists over the last three decades. Some have asserted the scientific objectivity of the facts; others have said that we can only test hypotheses in the present (Binford and Sabloff 1982); others have placed their belief in the independence of arguments (Binford 1989). This is not the place to rehearse why these responses are flawed (see Hodder 1992). The concern in my paper (Hodder 1997) was to demonstrate that whatever the rhetoric about how to deal with the theory-ladenness of data, in practice archaeologists have developed a field method which routinely separates "description" of data from interpretation. Most excavation forms that I have seen do this. In the same way, Hassan (1997) describes the separation of low-level description from high-level interpretation. Archaeologists have developed approaches such as "problem-oriented research design" in which theories are stated a priori and tested against data. In particular, they have developed highly codified systems of categorization, measurement, and description. To codify and standardize must be to assume that systems of observation can be separated from the specific character of the site or data being studied. Theory is separated from data but imposed on the data. This is neither a critical nor a coherent response to the theory-ladenness of facts.

Hassan (1997:1022) describes levels of interpretation and argues that the levels are significantly different. He appears to suggest that some levels of identification are less controversial, and that at these levels measurement uses standards—presumably those set by an academy which does not cater to "particularist world views" (1997:1023). However, Gero (1996) has demonstrated that even the most basic aspects of archaeological excavation and field recording may be infused with gender bias. Hassan (1997:1022) gives the example of the identification of a "hearth." At Çatalhöyük we prefer the term "fire installation" precisely because we recognize the difficulties of "identification" of such features, including the gender biases involved. Hassan (1997:1023) also unfortunately argues that ethical grounds provide no basis for determining whether a skeleton in a grave is a male or a female. In fact, it is now widely recognized that sexes are defined differently in different cultures and that biological differences between the sexes are partly culturally and socially constructed (e.g., Knapp and Meskell 1997; Yates 1993).

As another example of the presence of interpretive processes at the primary level, I have been struck by the use in Japanese archaeology of painted white lines to define the edges of features on sections (profiles) or on excavation surfaces. I point this out not to argue that such painting does not clarify features in photography, but to emphasize the contrast between different archaeological traditions. I was taught, and I teach my students, never to draw lines on the ground or on sections because such lines bias interpretation. It is anathema to me to obscure soil interfaces with white paint. In these two traditions, the primary data are being constructed in very different ways depending on "particularist world views."

Hassan (1997:1023) is simply incorrect to assert that no archaeological discourse on the role of Çatalhöyük in agricultural origins can at the same time assert that agriculture was good or evil. Since the writing of Rousseau, Western discourse on agricultural origins has been underlain by a debate about the origins of inequality, the "fall of man," and the emergence of property. Whether we see the adoption of agriculture as driven by a harnessing of the environment or by social competition and the emergence of dominating and exploiting groups, we are engaging in a debate that has ethical dimensions.

It is futile to attempt an absolute separation of levels. The highest levels insert themselves into the lowest. As we dig we are engaged in a bewildering array of social issues, many of them constructed within Western discourse. The trowel's edge, as it scrapes across the soil surfaces, is not somehow suddenly unsocial, mystically placed outside society.

ETHICS AND EPISTEMOLOGY

Another dichotomy to which Hassan returns is that between ethics and epistemology. He asks (1997:1023) "What has *ethics* here to do with an epistemological question?" I have already given examples of how high-level and ethical issues do insert themselves into primary data identification and interpretation. But I want to emphasize that the supposed separation of ethics from any level of archaeological enquiry is not only an incorrect description of archaeological practice but is also dangerous.

Positivism, for example, can be used as an epistemological position to foster emancipatory processes. It is not surprising that positivist and processualist archaeology was initially seen as attractive in the recent post-dictatorship worlds of, for example, Spain and Chile. In these countries, at particular historical moments, a positivist approach (allied to either Marxism or processualism) offered neutral, unbiased, rigorous, democratic methods in a social and academic context which had lacked such characteristics. It is this dimension of positivism that Hassan describes when he talks of using "standards that can be followed by anybody" (1997: 1023). But exactly the same positivism can seem itself biased and authoritarian when used by dominant groups against minority interests. When used by North American archaeologists against the "particularist world view" of Native North Americans, as in the reburial debate, positivism and science are used to close off debate rather than to open it up. This point has been well made by those working with Native American archaeological groups (Anyon et al. 1996).

Thus, it is dangerous to trust in the separation of ethics and epistemology. To do so is to lose sight of the manipulation of epistemology and the construction of ethics for social purposes. Both are embroiled in the daily practices of archaeology. We have to remain alert as to how epistemologies are used within

the discipline and to what the effects are on society. This is why I advocate a reflexive approach, one that monitors the social effects of archaeological practices on a wide range of different communities. The safeguard against misuse is not some unflinching belief in one epistemology, whether it be empiricism, positivism, or dialectical hermeneutics. Rather, the safeguard resides in the reflexive application of epistemologies in a changing social world. This is why there is a need to incorporate multivocality, relationality, and interactivity into archaeological practices.

Similarly, there is nothing inherent in the use of the new information technologies which would lead to a particular social use of archaeology. The standardization and potential for centralized control of the Internet can lead to a universalization of Western and dominant attitudes. The un-networked can be further excluded and marginalized. But the same technologies can be used in a very different way—to promote diversity and access to information by minorities. Once again, the safeguard for a diverse world and for diverse rights of access to the past is a commitment to reflexivity, and a critical examination of the uses to which the technologies are put.

CONCLUSION: BEYOND THE SURFACE

Hassan (1997:1025) objects that the first major publication of the new Çatalhöyük research program (Hodder 1996) looks like "any processualist excavation report"—except that it is not an account of any excavations. This point is important because the limiting of that report to surface survey also limits the amount of "depth interpretation" that can occur. The artifacts recovered on the surface of the Çatalhöyük mounds (as well as those badly provenanced artifacts recovered from museum stores) do not have sufficient contextual information to allow any more than the imposition of a priori assumptions. Thus, a fully relational or contextual account could not be built, and there was little we felt we could do in the way of transforming our survey techniques. The emphasis on reflexive methodology became much clearer as we began excavation. Here there is sufficient contextual data to engage in not the testing, but the fitting of theory and data in a reflexive, relational, interactive, and multivocal way. Perhaps there is a potential now to return to a reconsideration of surface methods and to introduce reflexive approaches.

As already noted, I agree with Hassan (1997:1024) that many communities may be unable to participate in global flows of information such as at the Çatalhöyük Web site. Some communities can gain access to the site in this way and so produce their own "sites" (for a New Age version of Çatalhöyük see http://www.wordweb.org/sacredjo/may.html). But Hassan is quite right that local communities may be excluded from or alienated by such technologies. This is why a broad range of communicative media needs to be tried. The Çatalhöyük project makes use of sponsorship and media to support the education and training of schoolchildren and students at all levels, including at the site, and we have produced bilingual panels for display at the site and at other locations locally and nationally in Turkey. Funds have successfully been raised for a museum which will be built by the site in 1998 and which will include an exhibit produced by the local community.

It seems anachronistic that we should today sit in Cambridge or London defining a mandate of reason, adjudicating on the usurpation of facts and on which epistemologies are ethical. In a post-colonial world, every aspect of our work and all our assumptions as archaeologists need to be open to critique and evaluation by a wide range of different communities in different ways. We cannot assume an authority, we have to argue for it. We cannot simply police the boundaries of the academy and of the discipline against particularist world views. We have increasingly to argue our case in the temporal flows of a diverse global community.

6

Archaeological Practice as Intellectual Activity

There is very little in the article ("La trahison des archéologues? Archaeological Practice as Intellectual Activity in Postmodernity," *JMA* 12(1) [1999]:60–79) with which I disagree. It seems to me to be a mature and careful analysis of some important areas of concern in current intellectual debates. What indeed is to be the role of the archaeologist as intellectual in a world in which "academic freedom" is increasingly compromised by funding bodies, individual donors, special-interest groups, lobbyists, and a general climate in England and the United States of "accountability"?

So I agree entirely when Hamilakis states in his conclusion that the archaeologist should accept the responsibilities to

> interrogate and challenge institutional regimes for the "production of truths," illuminate and expose the links of knowledges with power, and adopt a critical stance in the current global battlefields of cultural production and consumption (Hamilakis 1999:74).

I also fully agree with the conclusion that an archaeologist as intellectual should be aware that "a multivocality that fails to address the structures of power and authority is at the very least a chimera, and at worst an appeasement of the manufacturing of consent" (1999:75).

If we are agreed on aims, perhaps problems emerge in the choice of methods to achieve those aims. But again, I agree with the image of archaeologists as intellectuals who use specialist knowledge to take an active stance in the social and political fields. They have a privileged position in relation to this production and dissemination, and a special responsibility regarding the uses and abuses of that knowledge in society.

But who among us would claim to be autonomous? Hamilakis at times conjures up the image of an intellectual able to comment and critique without the need to be concerned with consequences. The image of the autonomous intellectual is difficult outside the confines of the independently wealthy. Most of us who have worked as university academics are aware of examples of colleagues whose ideas have strayed too far beyond the acceptable canon, and who have suffered as a result. Our freedom to critique is bracketed.

While a lack of full autonomy must be present in any state-funded or private university system, social dependency is still more evident in archaeological field projects. We all realize, indeed we teach students, that research designs need to be tailored to suit the interests of potential sources of funding. One writes a very different proposal for the National Geographic Society, the NSF, or the British Academy. Different approaches and accounts of one's work are needed for funders, local government officials, colleagues, and so on. Corporate and private sponsors have yet further, different perspectives which need to be catered to.

In reality, the image of the autonomous intellectual archaeologist is false. We all have to make compromises when it comes to a practical engagement such as a field project. If no compromises were made, and if no collaboration with companies like Visa and Shell took place, there would be no ability to act in the world, to open up a moment and a space for critique. If we simply confronted all the structures of power, as Hamilakis at times verges on proposing, then there would be no power with which to confront power. The only possibility open to us intellectuals is to engage in a process of negotiation, debate, and critique, both within and against the structures that empower us.

As Hamilakis I think recognizes, this process of engagement and critique is extremely difficult and delicate. Indeed, Hamilakis's recognition of this need to compromise and adjust to practical contexts is evident in his introduction to his own article. Realization of who the commentators would be influenced the writing of the final paper. At Çatalhöyük we have all become increasingly aware that the conflicting interests in the site and project are finely and dangerously balanced. If it all collapsed, our utter powerlessness would be unveiled. To be able to act, to be heard as archaeologists, we need to be able to negotiate between the conflicting interests, using them with a sensitivity in order to achieve some aims of our own.

What social aims do I/we have at Çatalhöyük? In the asking of this question, the initial problem emerges. The various members of the Çatal teams do not have an agreed political agenda, and their reasons for participating are diverse. But I agree with Hamilakis that a sufficient aim cannot be simply the promotion of archaeological work or securing jobs for archaeologists. From my own perspective, the aim of combating Orientalism is only one of many. One important strategy for me, especially in the context of Turkey, is to demonstrate that cultural heritage can make a difference. By this I mean that there is an enormous need to counter the widely held view at all levels in local, national, and international bodies that cultural heritage is marginal and has little economic and social value. I hope to show that cultural heritage management at a site such as Çatalhöyük can lead to a wide range of benefits including: sustainable economic development through tourism; greater awareness of identities that empower social groups at local, regional, national, and international levels; increased understanding of the interests and rights of groups divided on gender, class, ethnic, religious lines, and so on. These may well seem inflated aims, but in a longer piece I would hope to demonstrate ways in which the project acts politically in all these areas and in relation to all these groups. Of course mistakes are made and consequences can be unexpected and unwanted. The ability to control outcomes is limited. But at least we can be critically engaged in a variety of local processes at multiple scales.

I have space here only to address some of the specific issues raised by Hamilakas. First the question of nationalism. The situation regarding this matter in Turkey is far more complex than Hamilakis describes. Certainly "the state" has used Çatalhöyük to emphasize nation, and currently uses the project for a variety of ends. But the whole idea of "nation" is highly contested already in Turkey. The state includes conflicting political parties and institutions in endless coalitions, continually renegotiating terms. State and nation are riven by conflict between secular and religious views, between fundamentalist and nationalist, and between those that look to Europe and those that look East. At the local level in the Konya and Çumra areas where we work, it is necessary to take a position in relation to nationalist and opposing fundamentalist groups. We make some compromises certainly. And those compromises enable our work. But they need not be uncritical and unconditional compromises. My own view is that experience of the project's work at Çatalhöyük has had an impact on the rhetoric and strategies of local nationalist politicians. There may be too much optimism in this claim, but we have seen changes of attitude as nationalists acknowledge and accept the need to incorporate a project dealing with a pre-Islamic and pre-Turkic past which attracts international interest and increases local employment. In struggling to make sense of these contradictions, we, including the nationalist politicians, adjust our views. It is possible to work alongside a nationalist politics while influencing it. It is possible to compromise and critique.

And so with Shell and Visa, and with our other major sponsors including now Boeing, Fiat, and a Turkish bank—Koçbank. Of course, major international companies may have policies with which project members disagree, and there has been tense debate within the project about collaboration with some international agencies. Personally, it is again a matter of evaluating particular companies and agencies and deciding at particular moments on the right strategy. Sometimes bans and boycotts are appropriate. For example, I was an active supporter of the 1986 ban on South African participation at WAC in Southampton. I still feel that was the right thing to have done. Despite the attraction of funds much larger than any so far obtained for Çatalhöyük, I have always refused potential sponsorship of the project from tobacco companies. But in other cases, compromise and collaboration are in my view more effective. For example, I was impressed by the wide range of measures being taken by Shell Turkey to support environmental and cultural causes. It seemed to me that it was right to support such changes in policy and to encourage it—I write articles in the Shell Turkey magazine *Ilgi* and give talks to staff. I believe, again perhaps naively, that it is possible to influence this corporate management culture in positive directions.

The notion of political correctness is fraught with its own problems. Who decides what is correct? How is correctness policed? I agree with Hamilakis that it is necessary to take a stand. But the armchair intellectual lives in an unreal and impossible world. If archaeology contributes to intellectual debate and social and political issues, it does so through mechanisms of power and authority. The power to act comes from society. Certainly an autonomy is available to archaeologists based on specialist knowledge, but it is only a partial autonomy, enabled by structures of power within which we all must work.

7

Social Practice, Method, and Some Problems of Field Archaeology

Åsa Berggren and Ian Hodder

We wish to argue in this paper that the development of excavation field methods in archaeology is closely tied to the social position of fieldworkers. We also note disaffection in field contract archaeology today resulting from a wide range of factors, including a lack of fit between method and social and career aspirations. The social practices associated with reflexive archaeology are described. We recognize that other factors, such as economic and theoretical, have influenced the development of field methods and we will refer to them here, but we focus especially on social factors.

EXCAVATION AS LOW-SKILLED, LOW-PAID LABOR

In our view some of the problems in contract archaeology today in Europe and the United States are the culmination of a long-term trend in which the practice of excavation is seen as low skilled, capable of being carried out by low-paid workers, volunteers, prison inmates, or the unemployed. We will argue that this conception of excavation led to the adoption of particular methods which are inappropriate in the changed social context of archaeological excavators today.

Archaeological fieldwork in Europe and the Americas has a long trajectory (Hamann 2002; Schnapp 1996) but by the eighteenth and early nineteenth centuries it was often an elite pastime. As stricter archaeological legis-

lation emerged in the nineteenth and early twentieth centuries, fieldwork became more systematic. In Britain Pitt-Rivers was the first official government Inspector of Ancient Monuments, and the first "scientific archaeologist" (Clark 1934; Daniel 1962). He used careful recording methods and large-scale excavation. He visited excavations at least three times a day, and had a superintendent on site to control the work when he was not there (Pitt-Rivers 1887:xvii). In the USA, too, the collection of data was often performed by others than the excavation directors themselves (Fagette 1996:xvii).

A similar situation pertained in British colonial contexts. Important for the development of archaeological techniques in Britain was Sir Mortimer Wheeler's experience in India as head of the Archaeological Survey of India. Here he developed and refined his famous "box method" before presenting it for general consumption in his *Archaeology from the Earth* (1954). One of Wheeler's aims was to teach Indians about their past—to help them discover the richness of the Indus civilization. His colonial attitude to the Indian and the Indian worker on his excavations has been well documented by Chadha (2002). Wheeler worked with an "army" of "local" workers that had to be disciplined in military style. While he and trained assistants did the recording, the workmen dug and moved earth.

It is possible to see the Wheeler box method as ideally suited to this colonial context. The grid of baulks provided a control. As long as the location of finds in layers was recorded, and as long as the sections/profiles around each box or square trench were drawn, it was possible to put the evidence back together again. Whatever mistakes had been made in the digging, and however unskilled the workers, as long as these rules were followed, control could be maintained. It was the trained archaeologist who drew the sections/profiles and made sense of whatever had taken place in the trench. The system allowed the unskilled to be controlled by the skilled colonial master.

Similar methods were used widely in colonial contexts. The great excavations of the Near East often involved huge numbers of "local" laborers, many unskilled in archaeology. When employed over many years, and in some cases families were employed over generations, as in Egypt, the local laborers amassed an immense empirical and practical knowledge, although this information rarely found its way into scholarly publications. Even in the cases of highly skilled laborers, the recording of finds and sections by Western-trained archaeologists allowed a control (Kenyon 1953). At the end of each day, Sir Leonard Woolley would tour the excavations noting down finds and the finders. At the end of each week he would tot up the finds made by each person and pay him accordingly.

In the twentieth century in Europe and the USA, unskilled workmen performed the excavation, sometimes without supervision (Rahtz 1974b). In some places convicts were ordered to do the work. The workmen were replaceable tools in the machinery and their work was systematized in certain ways that controlled the workers and assured that the data were recorded in the correct position. In different parts of Europe and the USA, different methods were more popular. For example, the Wheeler box method was more prevalent in the UK than elsewhere. But whether the box method was used, or sec-

tions and baulks and arbitrary levels, the procedures allowed a distanced control of the unskilled. Another factor influencing the choice of excavation method was the culture-historical framework. This object-centered historical approach led to a focus on general stratigraphies and depths, and to the recovery of artifacts with little emphasis on detailed contextual relationships. This was another reason why it was thought acceptable for excavation itself to be performed by supposed unskilled workers.

Rescue or salvage archaeology started to be more common as early as the 1930s and 1940s in the United States, mainly as part of labor relief programs (Fagette 1996) and by the 1950s there were a number of archaeologists engaged in rescue archaeology in Britain (Rahtz 1974a). Schemes to assist the unemployed were again common. As the scale of salvage archaeology increased, there was a move toward a greater professionalization of field archaeology. In Europe and the USA this has to varying degree been associated with the emergence of private contract archaeology. Contract resource management firms began to appear in the United States and in Britain in the 1970s (Hunter and Ralston 1993). Some form of contract archaeology, although often more tightly controlled by the state, has emerged in many European countries over recent decades (Cleere 1989). While many early salvage and contract archaeologists would have concurred that excavation was a skilled process that depended on the expertise of the excavator, the widespread use of supposed unskilled labor suggests a limited commitment to this view.

Whether salvage archaeology came to be seen as open to the market or not, the overall rise in the scale of archaeology led to larger numbers of field archaeologists, and larger numbers of them working all year round. Conditions of work, career structures, codes of ethics, accreditation, and qualifications all became of central concern, but slowly. For many, older ways persisted. There is mention of "foremen" and the professional archaeologist is said to have to watch "his raw labor and direct them personally" (Rahtz 1974a: 62; see also Estabrook and Newman 1996: 179; Kiln 1974; Lucas 2001a:55). But amateurs and also volunteers and unpaid students were increasingly barred from contract excavations, as they were not to compete with the professional archaeologists. Archaeology had become a job market, and there was a need to secure a standard of professional ethics and to be accountable in the eyes of the public. These demands were partly met by the founding of the Institute of Field Archaeologists (IFA) in Britain in the early 1980s (Hunter and Ralston 1993:40) as well as the Society of Professional Archaeology (SOPA) in 1976 in the United States (Hester et al. 1997:17). This organization changed in 1997 into what is now the Register of Professional Archaeologists (ROPA) (McGimsey et al. 1995).

But, at least partly as a result of the long history of field archaeology as involving low (or no) pay and low qualifications, the conditions for the full-time professional field archaeologist were poor (Paynter 1983). In the United States, many still have low pay and poor working conditions. In a recent survey of the CRM industry, Wilson (2001:37–38) noted that field technician wages were low, there was a lack of medical benefits and adequate safety provision. The United Archaeological Field Technicians (UAFT) was formed in the United States in 1991 as a reaction to work conditions in private firms. Their own website reports a recent national survey in which 70 percent were found to have no home to return to at weekends or in periods between work (homeless), 90 percent had no health insurance or retirement plan, and 50 percent relied on unemployment on an annual basis (http://members.aol.com/UAFT/fieldtec.htm). There has been much discussion of the term technician, and recently there have been attempts to have archaeological field technicians legally classed as unskilled labor (McGuire and Walker 1999). In this paper we argue that field excavation is or should be a highly skilled task. But the current low status of field "technicians," in the

United States and in many other countries, results from a long history, and from a current market-oriented approach to field archaeology which maintains wages at a low level.

In order to understand the social relations of production of archaeological knowledge (Patterson 1995), it is important to consider the relations between contract archaeology and the universities in Europe and the USA. In the USA, student labor was always a large part of contract archaeology. Here there was more of an influence from the universities on the way that contract archaeology was conducted. The scientific ideals of the 1960s with a positivist agenda of hypothesis testing and the systematic description of objective data greatly influenced the archaeology of the time. Just to collect and describe data without a clear sense of problem orientation seemed inadequate and unscientific.

But in both Britain and America, as the numbers of contract archaeologists increased, and as the rewards out-stripped those available in universities, a clearer split began to emerge between contract archaeology and the universities. In Britain a clear separation gradually emerged as rescue and contract units increased in size and professionalism, and as it became clear that the developer would not pay for large post-excavation budgets. In a survey of the "American archaeologist," Zeder (1997:208) noted "strong and growing tensions in American archaeology" between the archaeology practiced in academia and museums and that of archaeologists in the private and public sectors. Despite often higher salaries in the private sector, those working in private and public CRM feel that the training of students in academia does not prepare them well for their careers (Wilson 2001:30).

If we look at the way archaeological data were perceived during the rise and growth of contract archaeology, we see a social divide between the people who produced the data by excavating it and those who were to interpret it. This point is made extensively by Wilson (2001) and McGuire and Walker (1999).

In her survey, Wilson (2001:30) notes "a gulf between industry managers and field technicians that has made it increasingly difficult to comply with legislative goals and to contribute to our understanding of the past." Of the many problems, she records "a general lack of nonmanual labor responsibilities (including interpretation) assigned to field technicians." To be called a "Professional Archaeologist" in the USA one must meet standards set forth by the US Secretary of the Interior and respective State Historic Preservation Officers. "Archaeological Technicians" need not have such requirements, and cannot take jobs as "Principal Investigators," or "Professional Archaeologists" (http://members.aol.com/UAFT/fieldtech.htm).

The fact that the more archaeological knowledge one had, the further away from the actual excavation one was placed in the hierarchy, was considered problematic by some. The result was that the actual digging was performed by the ones with the least archaeological knowledge, and the least capability of seeing the "potential meaning in a wider context" (Musson 1974:82).

One response to this situation was to argue, at least in Britain, that there should be some flattening of hierarchical structures so that more recording was put in the hands of the field excavators. This tendency was closely connected with the need to excavate very large urban sites, but it was also linked to the professionalization of the field archaeologist. Rather than excavating in trenches, or in Wheeler's box grids, open area excavation came to be widely used (Lucas 2001a: 52). Each excavator was given responsibility for excavating and recording a bounded unit (context/locus) of deposit, or of groups of units. Stratigraphic relationships would be recorded for each unit and then put in relation to each other on a Harris Matrix (Harris 1989; Harris et al. 1993). This procedure meant that greater control and a wider range of functions could be delegated to the field excavator. The emphasis on excavating units (contexts) in plan rather than with box sections and baulks gave greater responsibility to the excavator as no sections remained to

provide a control over what had been removed. One had to trust the excavator.

This shift in method is intimately linked to a shift in social practices—and in particular to increased professionalization, especially in Europe where there is less dependence on student labor. However, the use of single-context recording quickly became a routine that could be so codified that relatively unskilled excavators could use it. Despite the initial aims of some practitioners such as Musson (1974), the method became routinized and associated with the description of data—the level of interpretation allowed was minimal.

PROBLEMS TODAY

Recent reviews of field archaeology present a normative view with some sense of change (e.g., Hester et al 1997; Purdy 1996; Roskams 2001; Thomas 1998 [1979]) whereas others call for radical change (Chadwick 2003; Lucas 2001a; Shanks and McGuire 1996). But in many arenas the sense of disquiet is palpable. Steve Roskams (2001) notes two negative developments in the professionalization of field archaeology. The first is what he calls "a manual-worship" in which the archaeologists do everything "by the book," not adjusting to the site in question. In this way the site manual and the research design always remain unquestioned. The second is the categorization of excavators as nonthinking "shovels," a situation in which field archaeologists are regarded as simple technicians without any influence on how work is carried out. Decisions and priorities are left to the site director, and the people with direct contact with the archaeology have little input (Roskams 2001:68). This viewpoint repeats the warning of one of the architects of processual archaeology who pointed out that standardized scientific approaches to field archaeology needed "the constant intervention of thinking human beings" (Redman 1987:249–251).

Gavin Lucas (2001a:12) sees the danger of the separation of the excavator from interpretation in the organization of contract archaeology. The separation leaves the excavators with no voice: "there is a very large group of anonymous and silent archaeologists engaging in fieldwork in Britain and elsewhere today, who have no voice" (Lucas 2001a:12). He suggests that the organization itself creates silent excavators who are also unseen, not shown in photographs etc. Today in the United States "there is a low morale among field technicians" (Wilson 2001:31). There are calls for a more visible field archaeologist, and there is evidence of much frustration, both among field archaeologists and amongst laboratory specialists (Blinkhorn and Cumberpatch 1998). In the United States CRM archaeologists have been labeled "almost proletariat" (Watson 1991:273) and despite the large volume of CRM practice "its interpretive potential has yet to be realized" (Hester et al. 1997:17). Watson (1991:273) discusses the problem of communication in which the CRM archaeologists in the United States are shut out from theoretical debate. The journal *The Digger* is a forum for the field archaeologists themselves in Britain where much of the frustration and disillusion in the field are articulated. The journal can be read on line at http://www.archaeo.freeserve. co.uk/DiggerFrame.html. There is a glass ceiling perceived in the hierarchy that stops people without university degrees both in Britain and the United States.

A rather different or "stadial" view can be adopted, in which it is argued that the field technician role is an apprentice stage in the development of an archaeological career. In the United States, many students have traditionally funded their studies by working in CRM firms. Those that continue in private and public CRM work move on to be crew chiefs and later to be managers. There are two problems with this perspective. First, it leaves the field technician working in poor conditions and separated from the interpretive process. Second, it is a model that may reflect the experience of many who entered the CRM world in the boom years of the 1970s. But McGuire and Walker (1999) argue that most of those that entered CRM since the end of the 1970s have had a very different experience in which advance to su-

pervisory positions is difficult without the requisite degrees and in which the costs of education have increased dramatically. As the competitive process keeps the wages and work conditions of technicians at a low level, the job of field technician is now less commonly perceived as a step on the way to principal investigator status (McGuire and Walker 1999).

One major current development—the widespread use of digital recording—is having contradictory effects. On the one hand, digital recording can facilitate much of the interactivity, immediacy, and fluidity that characterizes a reflexive approach to excavation. But this is only so if the field excavator is fully trained to use these technologies. Digital recording, often associated with further systematization of work in large-scale projects and further codification may take the excavators further from the process of interpretation. The technologies may become dependent on specialists who intervene between the excavator and the interpretation. The analysis and interpretation become removed from the trowel's edge.

So once again, with these new technologies, there is the potential for the long history of a gap between the excavator and the interpretation to be continued. Once again the moment of discovery at the trowel's edge gets separated from the moment of study. Data are separated from analysis and interpretation. The excavator is forever pushed back into the realms of the "unskilled," a provider rather than a producer of data.

The purpose of the historical review has been to situate the development of field practices in archaeology within a social context. In particular, we have asked "who did the actual digging?" By asking this question we have been able to see that from very early on the excavation process was seen as unskilled and requiring little formal training. As a result, methods were developed so that directors of excavations, those that did not on the whole do the digging, could control and regulate the excavation process. These methods included the box method, baulks, sections or profiles, and codified formulaic recording systems. As field archaeology became more of a profession after the rise of contract archaeology in the 1970s, there was a shift in some countries to forms of excavating and recording which gave more responsibility and independence to the excavator. These methods included single-context recording, excavating in plan and the open method. But even in such cases the amount of authority that was delegated was limited, and there have been technological changes more recently, such as the use of digital recording, that can sometimes be used to again create a gap between excavator and interpreter.

This historical account has served to show that the old theoretical debate about the separation between data and interpretation in archaeology partly has a social basis. It is not an abstract philosophical discussion. It is about who is empowered to interpret. And on the whole the answer has been "not the excavator."

Many other related problems have emerged in this review. Even though we have seen an increasing cooperation between contract archaeology and the universities and most field archaeologists today hold a degree, there is still much evidence of a separation between contract archaeology and universities. Other problems include the backlog of unpublished material and the emergence of "gray literature" (Webster 1974:236), and the difficulty of incorporating indigenous voices alienated by noncollaborative archaeology (Downer 1997:32; Hester et al. 1997: 18; Swidler et al. 1997; Watkins 2000). They concern the separation of laboratory specialists from the excavation itself and the fragmentation of archaeological data (the "pots," the "bones," the "bots," etc.) into dispersed disconnected units of analysis (Hunter and Ralston 1993). People have recognized that problem orientation and codified procedures, necessary as they are, limit flexibility in relation to unexpected discoveries and multiple demands from the constituencies within which one works (Adams 2000:91; Rahtz 1974a). But above all, and most flagrantly, the review has pointed to the poor working conditions of many field archaeologists today. It is difficult to generalize as there are differences both between countries and sectors, but it seems that the role of the field archaeologist remains deeply problematic, even though the causes and nature of the problems may differ.

There are social, moral, and political reasons why this situation might be seen as unacceptable. But we want to argue here that there are also scientific reasons. In our view the low status of the excavator is associated with a less than optimal scientific approach. We will consider below how an alternative field approach that we term reflexive (Berggren 2001; Hodder 1999a) would have various characteristics that imply a changed role for the excavator. The practice of reflexivity can take many forms (Potter 1991:226, and for a more general definition see Lynch 2000). One definition of reflexive archaeology is that it is an approach that tries to provide systematic opportunities for field archaeologists to engage in narrative construction and to provide critique of those narratives in relation to data and social context. The approach also tries to make the process of interpretation visible to help archaeologists as well as nonarchaeologists reflect on how archaeological knowledge is produced. More specifically we will argue that a reflexive field method involves the following characteristics which all imply a changed role for the excavator: at the moment of excavation less of a separation of data and interpretation, throughout excavation and post-excavation more integration, and more involvement of other voices, and more documentation of the documentation. The scale of excavation is relevant here and much of what we have to say may be less relevant for small-scale excavations or individual surveys.

AT THE TROWEL'S EDGE

Is archaeological fieldwork a technical task or one that involves an intellectual process? Is it possible to define a set of practical skills that can be seen as "unskilled" in contrast to academic knowledge? Certainly many of the skills that are used in the field involve some component of classroom training, including planning, photography, Harris matrices, and sampling. These skills are used in relation to a wide range of practical knowledge about how to use a theodolite, how to sharpen a trowel, how to identify layers and describe their components, how to peel off layers, and so on. To be efficient and competent in such tasks involves much training, experience, and skill, even if such work is often described as "unskilled." But as well as these practical skills, we argue that the competent field archaeologist also needs to have a wide range of additional knowledge and skills. Such knowledge is of various forms and it could often be described as academic. There should be a knowledge of local cultural historical sequences so that pottery types can be recognized and relationships understood. There may be a need to know about ethnographic or historical parallels, so that features can be recognized. There will be a need to know about the range of scientific techniques that can be applied so that decisions can be taken about when and how to sample (for phytoliths, DNA, flotation, phosphate, radiocarbon, etc.). There will be a need to know about theoretical debates so that different possibilities for interpretation can be entertained.

Thus, archaeological fieldwork may be regarded as a technical task that involves an intellectual process. The divide between practical and academic skill may be bridged in archaeological fieldwork. Increased experience of the practical work leads to increased skill and knowledge of how to use previously acquired knowledge in the process of interpretation. This way our frame of reference is created and constantly added to. This process involves a silent component, an embodied knowledge that stems from practical experience (Edgeworth 1990; Shanks and McGuire 1996). From this point of view it is not possible to carry out archaeological fieldwork without involving the intellect.

We wish to argue that attempts to separate excavating from thinking lead to bad archaeology—that the separation of data collection from interpretation leads to bad science. This is primarily because archaeology is not strictly an experimental science. In other words, in most areas of archaeology one cannot repeat the experiment—of course you can excavate another trench but this is not like repeating an experiment in the lab because you cannot hold the variables absolutely constant. A closely related issue is that it is never possible to return to the same data because archaeology involves destruction (though see Lucas 2001a). This all means that the moment of excavation, at the trowel's edge, is the best chance the archaeologist will ever have to explore alternative interpretations (test competing hypotheses) about the data.

Therefore the moment of excavation should be a moment of great concentration of knowledge, voices, and interpretive narratives. It is at this moment that alternative interpretations can best be explored and a wide range of data taken into account. A British example of contract archaeology in which an attempt is made to foreground interpretation is Framework Archaeology and the excavations at Perry Oaks and Heathrow Terminal 5 (Andrews et al. 2000; Beck and Beck 2000). One of the goals is actively to involve the field archaeologist in the process of interpretation. The archaeological project is seen as research driven (even in a contract archaeology context) rather than as a recording procedure. Digging is seen as an intellectual as well as a technical process, and interpretive responsibility is given to excavators who are involved in the construction of an overall publishable site narrative. The aim is to empower all staff in the production of the site narratives, and during the excavation individual units or contexts are grouped into stratigraphic and interpretive entities to facilitate debate and narrative construction. The Citytunnel-project in Malmö is another example of contract archaeology in which the asking of questions and the setting aside of time for "why" discussions allowed a better integration of data and interpretation (Berggren 2003; Lindhé et al. 2001).

As the trowel moves over the ground it responds to changes in texture and color, but always in a way informed by a particular perspective. The knowledge of the archaeologist influences the way in which the site is excavated. There are many classic examples such as the inability of archaeologists trained in northern Europe to "see" mud brick walling in the Near East. But more generally, if excavators have limited experience and knowledge of what they are excavating (is this a human or animal bone, is this fourth- or third-century pottery?), they will be less able to excavate and interpret correctly. If they do not know that a yellow-green deposit they have come across is actually dung, they may misinterpret a stable as a house, or not see a slight foundation trench for a wall used to pen animals. (For other examples see Hodder 1999a.) If they do not look out beyond the individual context or unit they are excavating, they will not be able to deal with interpretative issues that involve other contexts and other sets of data.

So one aim of a reflexive approach is to get the archaeologists as they excavate to have as much information as they can so that they can make a good judgment about what it is they are investigating. From this viewpoint, excavating is not just a technique; it is a highly skilled and difficult balancing of lots of different types of information (Shanks and McGuire 1996). But how is it possible to empower the excavator with all the information that is needed? Nowadays, in many countries, excavators may be relatively inexperienced. And the specialization of archaeological skills and knowledge has led to a separation of field from laboratory and from university. Thus excavators often work in a relative vacuum, distant from the faunal specialists, soil scientists, and archaeobotanists who could provide information to be integrated in the ongoing process of excavation and interpretation. And equally the specialists often work in a relative vacuum without sufficient knowledge of contextual relationships. An artifact or feature excavated by an archaeologist has a meaning which depends on its relation to other objects and features.

The positive effects of an inclusion of different specialists at an early stage of planning research designs have been acknowledged and sought for some time. The British organization IFA states in its guidelines that all contributors to a project should be involved in its planning from early stages. Blinkhorn and Cumberpatch (1998) claim this has had little effect on the practical situation in British contract archaeology. But what we are seeing is an increasing number of explicit attempts where specialists are involved at the beginning of a project to participate in formulating research questions, and therefore have an impact on the research design as well as methods in the field (Adams 2000:96; Berggren 2003; Lindhé et al. 2001). In Framework Archaeology (Andrews et al. 2000), post-excavation, study, and analysis are brought into the excavation process.

Other trends counteracting the further separation of specialists from the excavation may be identified. The further development of in-house specialist skills may be a solution for excavating organizations. Employing specialists or field archaeologists with special interests demands a rather large-scale organization and a steady stream of excavations, ensuring a sound economic situation and use of the full potential of specialists. In large as well as small excavating organizations the further education of the already employed field archaeologists may be a solution, developing the situation where the archaeologist responsible for the excavation and writing the report is able to do more of the analyses by him or herself. Employing in-house specialists for specific projects sometimes in collaboration with the local museum is also practiced in Sweden (Berggren 2001 and see also Andrews et al. 2000). In these ways data specialists can be present to engage in interpretive dialogue with excavators.

At the research project at Çatalhöyük (Hodder 1999a, 2000) many different scientific specialists are brought to the site so that they can examine material as it comes out of the ground. The project has invested in on-site laboratories and in-the-field techniques (e.g., in-the-field phytolith or soil chemical analysis) so that a wide range of data specialists can work at the site. There is frequent movement between laboratory and trench as people seek each other's advice and try to enhance interpretation through increased information. This interaction is formalized at Çatalhöyük by "priority tours" which every day or two bring specialists in a wide range of different types of data to the trench itself so that a dialogue can take place between excavator and data specialist. The aim of these tours is twofold. Their first function is to decide collectively on which units (bounded soil units) should be prioritized for intensive study and sampling. The decision is made on a wide range of criteria (how many of a particular type of unit have been excavated so far, the importance of the unit for making sense of an area of the site, and so on), the criteria themselves being subject to negotiation. The material from priority units is fast-tracked through the system so that laboratory specialists can look at the material quickly and feed back that information to the excavators. So the second function of the priority tours is to inform the excavator what has been found in recently or currently excavated units. Specialists may pass on information about types of phytolith found, types of animal bone, fragmentation indices of bone and pottery, carbonized plant remains, densities of lithic debitage, and so on. In this way the excavator is empowered to make a more informed interpretation, and excavation strategy can be directed more efficiently. Digging in this way is all about listening, collaborating, discussing, and then making judgments as close to the trowel's edge as possible.

OTHER VOICES AT THE TROWEL'S EDGE

Many of the contributions in the book *Native Americans and Archaeologists. Stepping Stones to Common Ground* (Swidler et al. 1997) explicitly call for increased communication and mutual compromises between archaeologists and stakeholder communities. In the United States the general public and special-interest groups are guaranteed participation in the decision-making process of any project involving a historical remain on federal land that concerns them, in compliance with section 106 of the National Historic Preservation Act (www.achp.gov/publicpart.

html). Participatory guidelines have existed for some time in Australia (Australia ICOMOS 1981 and for an update of the Burra Charter see www.icomos.org/australia/burra.html) but this kind of participation is not required by law in many European countries. In Britain the Gardom's Edge is a project specifically aiming at raising public awareness about the remains in the area (Dymond 1998).

One example of an explicitly political attempt at public outreach to a specified interest group is the work of the Ludlow Collective directed to the working class in general and specifically the families of the workers of the coal mines in Ludlow, Colorado (Duke and Saitta 1998; The Ludlow Collective 2001). The collective states that archaeology typically serves the interests of the middle class. Instead, the project is directed towards working-class people. "It speaks to their experience, in a language they can understand, about events that interest them and about events that they feel directly connected to" (The Ludlow Collective 2001:104).

All this has an impact on the setting of research designs. Especially if the project occurs abroad, or in land claimed as ancestral by local groups, the setting of goals needs to be sensitive to interests beyond those of the "research design." The choice of questions is often in practice the result of a dialogue between multiple stakeholders. Sponsors, government agencies, contractors, local communities may all have their own purposes. The archaeologist has to embed the research design within the social world.

This implies that the experience of the excavator is not simply a matter of following codified procedures, but increasingly of adjusting those procedures to the interests of multiple stakeholder groups, including local communities. There has been much involvement of local communities in the construction of visitor centers and site interpretation, and there have been reflexive attempts to open the "site tour" to groups of different background (e.g., Handler and Gable 1997; Leone et al. 1987). But if, as we argue here, archaeological excavation itself is a highly skilled task, to what extent is it possible to involve varied stakeholder groups in the moment of interpretation at the trowel's edge?

The training of indigenous participants allows a fuller degree of participation (Watkins 2000). In many collaborative examples, close integration has occurred between archaeologists and Native Americans (Swidler et al. 1997; for Australia see Smith et al. 1995 and Smith and Ward 2000). This type of collaboration, when occurring at the archaeological site itself, may involve changes of method (Anyon et al. 1996). In excavations in the Andes, foreign archaeologists are often obliged to hold rituals to ensure the success of the project or to placate the spirits or gods on the recovery of a human or llama burial. In recent Caltrans archaeological projects in California, Native Americans and archaeologists have worked side by side in developing ways of interacting with Native American pasts (Dowdall and Parrish 2003). The non-Native American archaeologists have agreed to follow the rules specified by tribal rules and taboos. For example, women and partners of women who are menstruating do not participate in the excavations or laboratory analysis. There are other examples of how traditional native knowledge has been integrated in archaeological projects on tribal lands. One such example is the Leech Lake Reservation in Minnesota. Native Americans are hired and trained to carry out the work and their traditional beliefs are taken into consideration both during planning and fieldwork (Kluth and Munnell 1997. For other examples see Dean and Marler 2001; White Deer 1997).

But it is not possible for large numbers of unskilled people to be involved in excavation itself. One partial solution is to record and disseminate information in such a way that larger and more dispersed communities can be involved. At Çatalhöyük diary writing has been used (see below) to encourage a more open account of the interpretation process. The diary entries are placed on the project website. They allow a wider debate and dialogue about the interpretation of the site, especially when backed up with an on-line database (www.catalhoyuk.com). Experiments in using the internet to involve more communities in the process of interpretation have been at least partially successful. For example, McDavid (1997, 2000) has used a website about the Levi Jordan Plantation in Brazoria, Texas, to mediate relations between archaeologists, local community members, and descendants of both slaves and slave owners.

It is thus in our view wrong to expect archaeologists and students to go into the field with tight research designs that have been developed without consultation with stakeholders, and which are to be followed through to expected results. A reflexive approach involves a to-and-fro between initial hypotheses and the data. It also involves an interaction between initial hypotheses and the social world in which the data are embedded. This again implies greater openness and dialogue at the socially skilled trowel's edge. It means that the excavator may need to be trained in ethnographic or social science method, bridging between science and multiple interests, including spiritual interests (Dean and Marler 2001:35). It may involve the excavator being involved in diary writing and internet dialogue during the excavation process.

DOCUMENTING THE DOCUMENTATION

What do we mean by recording and what does the term *the archaeological record* mean (Patrik 1985)? Some say they imply a notion of a pre-existing record, to be discovered, preserved, deciphered, be it in a physical or written form, and that the archaeologist may be regarded as responsible for the management of this archaeological record. But if we instead agree that the only thing that exists are fragmented material traces of social practices in the past, it follows that the role of the archaeologist changes (Hamilakis 1999:69). We are not solely guardians of some record of the past, but also cultural producers today. Andrews et al. (2000:527) argue for the use of the term interpretation instead of record. For them the term "record" implies objective recording and an exclusion of humans both from the process of creating these records and from the production of the record in the past. Instead, Andrews and others would like to stress the act of interpretation. The term archive has also come increasingly to be used (e.g., Lucas 2001b) in order to denote the fact that the data that are retained are selected and placed within an institutional context. They are curated as part of a social process.

In positivist and empiricist approaches there is a clear separation between the recording of data and the following interpretation, with the former regarded as an objective process. This separation is maintained by some (e.g., Roskams 2001), while others acknowledge the subjectivity in the initial production of data. "The move towards a descriptive record is thus a move away from the historical realities with which archaeology should be primarily concerned" (Andrews et al. 2000:527). Even in reflexive approaches there remains a difference between what is recorded on the front page of the context sheet and the interpretation on the back side. In other words, there remains a difference between the information such as measurements, descriptions of soil color and texture, etc., and the free text that tells a narrative about the data.

As already noted, codified documentation in archaeology is central to the construction of archives that can be used and compared (Larsson 2000). Codification remains an essential part of a reflexive approach. But what is also needed is an enveloping of the codified records in a reflexive context so that people can later understand how interpretations were arrived at and reuse the archive by relating it to the agenda according to which it was constructed. The finds can best be reinterpreted through an understanding of that original agenda. Since archaeology involves destruction, the best way to allow later reevaluation and debate is to record the processes by which the data were produced. The method and the recording of data are components of the data to be recorded. Thus, the front side of the context sheet is viewed in a different way in a reflexive approach. It is recognized as historical and interpretive. It

thus has to be enveloped in documentation about its historical construction.

There are numerous ways in which the records can be embedded within an outer layer of documentation. For example, databases and archives can be tagged with a history that describes changes made through time. Diaries can be written which describe the thought processes of the excavators and laboratory analysts. Traditionally much archaeological recording was done in the form of diaries. Increased codification often led archaeological teams to dispense with such diaries and to use solely codified forms. But there remains a need for diary writing, and this can easily be achieved by typing straight into a computer. In the Citytunnel-project, mentioned above, the recording process is based on digital recording in plan, and context and feature sheets recorded in a database. Half-sectioned features are recorded by hand drawing. In addition to this the archaeologists' thoughts are documented in diaries, with possibilities for commenting on their colleagues' diary entries. Diary entries thus become part of the database and can be searched for keywords.

Another way of documenting the documentation is to use digital video. This allows visual information, sound and words to be used to provide a record of the excavation and post-excavation process. Such a range of information allows the excavation process to be embedded within a greater depth and richness of context than is possible in texts and pictures and drawings alone. The excavators can be shown explaining what they are finding and discussing their interpretations as they develop them. They can point out what they have found; and on-site editing allows insets and close-ups. The video clips can be added to the site database and can be recovered using keywords. In this way it is possible for later archaeologists to evaluate more clearly the claims that are made by the excavators. The later re-interpretation can make relationships between what was found and what the excavators were preoccupied with at the time. The video clips may show data that were not seen at the time or which can be reinterpreted with hindsight. They may show things that were missed, and they may explain why the site came to have the meaning it did for the excavators (Brill 2000; Emele 2000; Stevanovic 2000).

This fragmenting and multiplying of the archive allows authorship to be reconsidered. Even if an excavation is performed by a group of archaeologists, and the interpretations that make up the archive are the result of all the team members, the published report is often written by one or two, typically the site manager and perhaps an assistant. The many participants are mentioned by name in the report, but the personal contributions are not identifiable. But when the individual participants to an increasing degree write direct accounts of their interpretations, there is the potential for including a multiplicity of voices in publications and other output. For example, at Çatalhöyük the publications of the excavated features involve direct quotes from the diary entries of the excavators, and references to and quotes from videos. They also include direct quotes from the local community which is invited to participate in the post-excavation interpretation, as well as from the various specialists that had looked at data from a particular context. The end result is a patchwork of perspectives and points of view which can be identified as to authors.

CONCLUSION

We have left the question unanswered: does reflexive archaeology claim to be better archaeology or is it just different? In our view it is a better archaeology, for two sets of reasons. First, it is better science. It does not make false claims about finding what one expects to find or about imposing standardized methods. Rather it responds to what is found and tries to use a wide range of techniques to make sense of what is found. It tries to surround the excavator in greater knowledge. It is more rigorous because starting assumptions and taken-for-granteds are always being re-evaluated and open to critique, especially as different partners in the process bring their different perspectives. It records more data, including the phenomenological

(Edgeworth 1990). The emphasis on the integration of different types of data allows a site or region to be more fully explored and for more variables to be brought into consideration simultaneously.

Second, it is better because it is more socially responsible and thus more sustainable over the long run. It accepts the need for collaboration with diverse stakeholders and interest groups. It supports the need for site management plans (de la Torre 1997; Pearson and Sullivan 1999; Stanley Price et al. 1996) and long-term conservation and protection strategies (Matero 2000) as central components of the archaeological process. It seeks to provide archives that are usable and open to re-evaluation and critique. It is concerned with developing multiple ways of engaging with the site. As has been argued elsewhere (Hodder 1999a), this emphasis on social engagement with a diversity of groups is appropriate in a globalized world—by which we mean a world in which a major tension is between the local and the global. On the one hand, the archaeological site is increasingly embedded within local rights and identities. On the other hand, sites are increasingly of importance to diasporic groups, to international agencies, and corporate interests. They are increasingly available in globalized media such as the Worldwide Web. In such a context it becomes important for the archaeologist to look beyond the narrow confines of the discipline and accept a broader engagement.

In such a world of transparency, dialogue, multiple voices, and media, it is anachronistic that the moment of the production of archaeological data is seen as unskilled. In a nonexperimental science, the moment of production must be open to scrutiny. It must be seen as competently recorded, using the fullest information and scientific techniques available. In practice, archaeological excavation has become increasingly professional. But it needs fully to shake off its historical cloak of unskilled, unthinking labor if it is to participate in contemporary social contexts. The tensions discussed in this paper surrounding the excavator have a long history, and they impede not only the amelioration of the working conditions of "field technicians" today, but also the transformation of the technician into a social agent.

In describing various components of a reflexive archaeology it is clear that the role of the excavator is changed. At the trowel's edge, in the process of excavation, a wide range of often highly specialized data needs to be taken into account and a wide range of often conflicting voices need to be listened to and catered to. The excavator negotiates between these demands and the excavation findings. Creative solutions may need to be found to collaborative working contexts. A whole new layer of documentation is provided so that the excavation and interpretation processes are properly recorded.

The upgrading of field excavation may of-ten be difficult to resolve, as befits a problem with such deep historical roots. Institutional structures, training and education, work and employment practices, field methods, and social attitudes are all implicated. We have noted above many calls for such changes, including the reskilling and upgrading of field archaeology. In this paper we have suggested some specific solutions that individual projects have undertaken. But adequate solutions are of a larger and more intractable scale.

Acknowledgments
We would like to thank Danielle Steen for her help in conducting the research that led to this paper, and to the several reviewers for their constructive comments on an earlier draft.

III. The Impact on Theory

A third group of papers examines the effect of developing a reflexive, multivocal, and global archaeology on theory. In general terms new theoretical trends in social archaeology foreground a dialectical relationship between past and present, an indeterminacy and a focus on power/knowledge systems.

It has been argued so far that archaeologists today need to be responsive to a great diversity of social groups, and that the methods we use as archaeologists are embedded within a wider social matrix. We can thus talk of a "social archaeology," in which all our interpretations and activities as archaeologists are at least to some degree social. Chapter 8 reviews the history and growth of social archaeology and surveys the current trends. In particular it looks at post-structuralism, agency, and embodiment, and has a brief critique of behavioral and cognitive-processual archaeology. The chapter argues again for a dialogical relationship between past and present and between object and subject. There is never a socially neutral moment in the scientific process, but equally, socially biased accounts can be transformed by interaction with objects of study.

Many of the things we take for granted, like our conceptions of ourselves as individuals, or our notions about the biological body, can be shown to be socially and historically variable. Chapter 9 discusses this issue in relation to theories of agency. It critiques applications of structurationist and phenomenological approaches in archaeology for being insufficiently sensitive to cultural difference in the ways we look at bodies, landscapes, and agents. The chapter makes an attempt to summarize the individual lives of the Alpine Ice Man and the person buried at a late point in the use of Building 1 at Çatalhöyük. In fact, new evidence has meant that the lives of both these individuals were rather different from accounts provided here. More recent X-ray study of the Ice Man, now that he has been moved to Italy, has shown that in fact an arrow had been fired into his shoulder, after which he climbed into the mountains and died. As regards the Çatalhöyük individual, the identification of the small bone as a penis bone has now been rejected by the faunal team working on these data—no definite identification has been possible. At least these revisions show that it is possible to build up an ever-clearer picture of individual lives, and in them see the grain of larger-scale processes.

In achieving accounts of diverse individual moments within the movements of millennia, we reach perspectives that cannot be reduced to the "anthropological" or the "historical." At such moments, archaeology seems to stand in relation to other disciplines, but separate from them. Should archaeological theory ape theories of other disciplines, and should social archaeology aim to be an identikit of social anthropology? Or should it develop independently but in close dialogue with other disciplines? Chapter 10 argues that anthropology is an inadequate umbrella for archaeology because archaeology also has close links to history and the natural sciences, which are constrained by the links to anthropology. I argue that there should be flexible alliances within the social sciences and humanities generally and that archaeology should not be bound by anthropology—indeed in some respects archaeology can act as an umbrella for anthropology.

8

The "Social" in Archaeological Theory:
A Historical and Contemporary Perspective

The central importance of the social in archaeological theory has emerged over recent decades. Through the twentieth century as a whole one can identify an overall shift from the "cultural" to the "social" in theoretical discussions within archaeology. This is a grand claim and there are many exceptions and vicissitudes, but I hope in this paper to demonstrate the shift and to explain its importance.

A HISTORICAL PERSPECTIVE

It has long been recognized that the archaeology of the late nineteenth and early twentieth centuries in Europe and North America was primarily concerned with documenting culture historical sequences and influences. The culture concept, in so far as it was theorized by Childe and others, concerned shared traits. Stereotypically these shared traits were pot styles and fibulae types, but for many authors they included social features. Thus the social was seen as part of the cultural. For Walter Taylor (1948) the subject matter of archaeology was "cultural," and in his theorizing, the social aspects of culture are those involving shared traits (Taylor 1948:103). But there is little specific attention to the social itself; the focus is on culture.

A partitive notion of culture, in which the social is a subset of the cultural whole is perhaps most clearly indicated in Hawkes's (1954) response to Taylor. Hawkes, in presenting his famous "ladder of inference," argued that in achieving understanding of past cultures it was relatively easy to infer from archaeological phenomena to the techniques that produced them. On the next rung of the ladder it was possible to infer subsistence economies. Harder was inference about the social and political institutions of the group, and hardest of all, at the top of the ladder, was inference about religious institutions and spiritual life. For Hawkes, the social rung dealt with settlement patterns and it involved analyses in order to see if special, larger, chiefly huts could be identified. It dealt with burial data to see if ranking could be observed (Hawkes 1954:161–162).

For Grahame Clark, too, the social was a subset of culture as a whole. As a prehistorian he valued information from social anthropology in assisting the interpretation of early cultures. In his book *Archaeology and Society* (1957 [1939]) he saw culture as made up of component parts such as transport, technology, trade, religion, but also social organization (Clark 1957:175). Social units are "the main groups through and by which culture is shared and transmitted from one generation to another" (Clark 1957:169). Clark certainly gives social organization a central role in the cultural system because of its place in the transmission of culture. He also discusses demography, trade, specialization of production, and social differentiation as key parts of the archaeological account of the social. Language, writing, art, science, law are also seen as inextricably social. Although for Clark the social remains a component of the cultural, his links at Cambridge with social anthropologists possibly led him to a greater emphasis on the social than is found among American colleagues influenced by the opposing tradition of cultural anthropology.

Childe is often identified as one of the major theorists regarding the notion of culture in archaeology (e.g., 1925). But his Marxist interests also led him to describe (1960) the evolution of societies in stages defined by social theorists and ethnographers (as the savagery, barbarism, civilization scheme of Morgan). These same Marxist leanings also led Childe to discussions of the internal workings of societies that involved sophisticated accounts of social relations. In his 1939 book, *Man Makes Himself*, he looked at how cultural development in the Near East is very much concerned ultimately with adaptation to the environment. But he also recognized that it is social mechanisms that allow adaptation. He showed how information about survival is passed down through social traditions. He saw language as a social product, with its meanings created through the agreement of people. He saw discoveries and inventions in technologies as being social, linked to the emergence of specialized production and concentrations of wealth. Social and ideological mechanisms can also come to retard progress in his model, and in other work (e.g., 1952) he argued that cultural development became stagnated in the ancient Near East in comparison with Europe, because of social differences between despotic and superstitious elites in the East and more entrepreneurial, independent specialists and elites in Europe. But in the end, even for Childe, the social was just a subsystem within a wider cultural whole. It was thus dependent on other aspects of life, especially the economy and environment. Thus, for example, "on the large alluvial plains and riverside flatlands the need for extensive public works to drain and irrigate the land and to protect the settlement would tend to consolidate social organization and to centralize the economic system" (Childe 1939:159).

There was another sense, too, in which archaeology had a social dimension during these culture-historical, diffusionist, and evolutionary periods. For many, archaeology had a social role. Many archaeologists in the nineteenth and early twentieth centuries felt a social responsibility to provide museums for wider publics, even if the message advocated in those museums was paternalistic, nationalist, and imperialist. Some theorized at great length about social responsibility. At the end of his *Methods and Aims in Archaeology*, published in 1904, Flinders Petrie argued that the study of the past and archaeology led to social union and "the responsibility of man for man" (Petrie 1904:193). Grahame Clark discussed in 1934 the political links between archaeology and the state, and Childe (1949) discussed the social construction of archaeological knowledge.

The notion that the social is a part of the cultural remained in the New Archaeology, and in processual archaeology. The social was now often identified as a subsystem within an overall system. The frequent use of the term "sociocultural system" to describe the system as a whole perhaps identifies an increased emphasis on the social in processual archaeology. Indeed, much emphasis was expended using social terms such as band, tribe, chiefdom, or state to describe archaeological assemblages. Today a parallel practice is found among processual archaeologists who categorize societies in terms of social complexity (Johnson and Earle 1987). But in practice, in much processual archaeology, it remained the case that the social subsystem remained subordinate to the environment and to economic and technological subsystems. The intellectual debt owed by processual archaeology to ecological and materialist approaches assured that social relations were seen as deriving from or based upon other areas of life.

The continued partitive view of culture and the social is seen in Binford's (1962) distinction between technomic, sociotechnic, and ideotechnic artifacts. Some artifacts were part of the social subsystem but others were not. For David Clarke too, the social was a subset of the overall "sociocultural system." The "social subsystem" is "the hierarchical network of inferred personal relationships, including kinship and rank status" (Clarke 1968:102). His own work on the Iron Age Glastonbury site attempted to infer kinship organization from settlement data and material culture distributions (1972). In the United States, a parallel move sought post-marital residence behavior from ceramic distributions within sites (e.g., Longacre 1970). Although these early attempts to "play the ethnographer" in the past and infer prehistoric kinship were ultimately unsuccessful, they were part of a wider and successful effort by processual archaeologists to use settlement and burial data to make inferences about social group size and ranking.

A good example of a processual archaeologist with a strong commitment to the social is Colin Renfrew. He argued for the ability for archaeologists to reconstruct past social subsystems in his inaugural lecture at Southampton University (Renfrew 1973b). Later, in his book *Approaches to Social Archaeology*, he said that he was concerned to make "inferences of a social nature from the archaeological data" (Renfrew 1984:4). Like Clark before him, he wanted to make alliances with social anthropology, and he defined social archaeology as the reconstruction of past social systems and relations. Most of his work at this stage involved trying to identify the degree of social ranking in society and the systems of exchange between elites and social groups. He was also interested in issues of past identity and ethnicity. In a later inaugural lecture, at Cambridge University in 1983, he argued for a further shift from the social to the cognitive. In defining a cognitive-processual archaeology (see also Renfrew and Zubrow 1994), it can be argued that Renfrew saw the cognitive as somehow separable from the social—one can separate cognitive processes in the mind from their social contexts. This is a claim denied by much social theory and by post-processual archaeology as we shall see. The definition of a cognitive-processual archaeology again shows that for Renfrew the social is just a

subsystem that can be separated from other realms of life, including the cognitive.

THE CENTRALITY OF THE SOCIAL IN POST-PROCESSUAL ARCHAEOLOGY

In recent decades, not only the mind, but even the economy and the environment have come to be seen as social. The body and sex, too, have been pried from biology and placed firmly within the social realm. The overall goal of interpretation in archaeology has come to be to understand the past in social terms (e.g., Tilley 1993). This shift to the view that, crudely, "everything is social" has a number of causes. One is the shift within Marxist approaches inside and outside archaeology from the 1960s onwards toward the centrality of the social relations of production. Writers such as Friedman and Rowlands (1978) had much impact on European archaeology when they espoused a structural-Marxism in which the search for prestige goods could be a prime mover in the evolution of social complexity. This move perhaps opened the way for post-processual archaeologists to embrace social theorists from social anthropology (e.g., Bourdieu 1977) and sociology (Giddens 1979) who were interested in examining the micro-processes of daily life rather than the macro-economic constraints and interactions. These small-scale practices were seen as fundamentally linked to power. They were thus seen as social rather than as simply the product of "cultural" differences between societies. They were not just another cultural trait, but were the building blocks of society as a whole. Everything, from the body and its daily practices in the home, to the technology, economy, and to the landscape came to be seen as social. There was no separate social subsystem or social rung on the inferential ladder as all aspects of life were seen as integrated and dispersed along chains of social meaning (Tilley 1993:20).

Thomas (1993:76) looks back from a post-processual point of view and suggests that "generally, ever since we have had something which could be called a *social archaeology*, we have tended to set our sights on what might be seen as somewhat grandiose targets: social organization, ranking, stratification, empires." In a post-processual perspective, the aims are perhaps yet more grandiose, as everything becomes social. But on the other hand, Thomas is right that in practice the focus becomes less grand as every mundane aspect of daily life is explored for social meaning. The aims become more particular and specific, more holistic and less partitive.

Another important factor that encouraged an emphasis on the social in all aspects of life was the critique of positivism. Most processual archaeologists had espoused some version of the idea that theories could be tested in archaeology. From whatever source hypotheses derived, there could be an independence and an objectivity in the testing process. Theory could be confronted with data. In particular, much play was given to the idea of "middle range" theories that could mediate between high-level theory and data (Kosso 1991; Tschauner 1996). But the critiques of these positivist views had emerged early and continued through the last decades of the twentieth century. Wylie (1989) pointed out that it was ironic that processual archaeology should adopt a framework—positivism— just as it was undergoing radical critique within philosophy and in the social sciences. Gradually, this critique spilled over into archaeology and it is one of the main reasons behind the emergence of post-processual archaeology.

But there were also more down-to-earth reasons for the critique of positivism. It became clear that many of the communities served by archaeology saw the idea of neutral testing of theories as itself a socially biased claim. Many indigenous groups found themselves in conflict with archaeological scientists over the idea that science was socially neutral. On behalf of the Tasmanian Aboriginal Community, Langford (1983) argued that objective science does not have a natural right to study her culture. Mamani Condori (1989) talked on behalf of the Aymara in Bolivia and maintained the value of traditional knowledge in opposition to the positivist scientific attitude. In the United States, the con-

flict over the reburial of human remains of Native Americans has resulted in much disillusion over the sustainability of a neutral science perspective. "Scientific knowledge does not constitute a privileged view of the past that in and of itself makes it better than oral traditions. It is simply another way of knowing the past" (Anyon et al. 1996:15). A critique of neutral science also emerged from a feminist critique—a wide range of studies have shown both flagrant and subtle gender bias in supposedly neutral archaeological science (e.g., Gero 1996).

In more general terms, I have argued (Hodder 1999a) that the increased concern with alternative perspectives, multivocality, and identity issues in archaeology is linked to globalism, post-industrial societies, the information age, and so on. Writers such as Castells (1996) have looked at broad globalizing trends in economic systems, and Arjun Appadurai (1996), working from an anthropological perspective, has discussed the cultural components of this process, describing a new fluidity whereby the emphasis is on transnationalism and diaspora. Archaeology developed as a discipline in relation to nationalism and colonialism. Its embrace of the natural science model was a necessary part of its role as guardian of the nation's past. It can be argued today that the nation state is being undermined by international companies, by the dispersal of production, consumption and exchange, by large-scale environmental changes, by the internet, and so on. There has been much discussion of global and local processes that play off each other and together undermine the nation state. This is still a highly unequal process that favors the already developed centers of economic wealth, but it has new characteristics in which fluidity and diversity are important components, and in which a wide range of alternative voices have made themselves heard.

So what is the alternative to a positivist, hypothesis-testing archaeology? Many positivist archaeologists have stuck to some form of watered-down version of the hypothesis-testing idea because they fear that the only alternative is a form of relativism in which "anything goes." In other words, they fear that if there is no possibility of objective testing, then anyone's statement about the past, including fascist manipulations of the past, are equally as good as anyone else's. I know of no archaeologist who would take this line. There are various forms of relativism (Wylie 1994; Lampeter Archaeology Workshop 1997), and most archaeologists would accept that archaeological interpretation is and should be answerable to data. The question is really just a matter of "how."

Most post-processual archaeologists, and in my view most processual archaeologists in practice, use some form of hermeneutic relationship with their data. Even if processual archaeologists claim to be doing a positivist science, in my view (Hodder 1999a) this is often false consciousness, and a desire to ape the natural sciences. In practice, archaeology is not for the most part an experimental science. Rather, it is a historical science that works not by testing theories against data but by fitting lots of different types of data together as best it can in order to make a coherent story. This emphasis on fitting rather than testing is at the heart of the hermeneutic approach. Hermeneutics deals with the theory of interpretation as opposed to explanation (Ricoeur 1971; Thomas 2001; Tilley 1991). Within the positivist, processual approach it was claimed that events in the past could be explained by showing that they were examples of general covering statements. Theories of interpretation place more emphasis on making sense of the event in relation to what is going on around it, while recognizing that generalizations have to be used. In the hermeneutic approach it is recognized that the researcher comes to the data with much prior knowledge and prejudgments. The data are perceived within these prejudgments. The researcher then works by fitting all the data together so that the parts make up a coherent whole. The interpretation that works best both fits our general theories and prejudgments and it makes most sense of more data than other interpretations. The process is not circular, i.e., one does not just impose one's prejudgments on the data. The objects of

study can cause us to change our ideas about the whole. But never in a way divorced from society and from perspective. There is thus a dialectical (dialogical) relationship between past and present and between object and subject. There is never a socially neutral moment in the scientific process, but equally, socially biased accounts can be transformed by interaction with objects of study.

For all these reasons, then, post-processual archaeologists came to place more emphasis on the social than in earlier approaches in archaeology. In early post-processual archaeology, two good examples of this tendency are the ideas that material culture is meaningfully constituted and that it is active. One source of such ideas was ethnoarchaeological research carried out in the 1970s and 1980s by myself (Hodder 1982) and a group of students based at Cambridge (e.g., Braithwaite 1982; Donley 1982, 1987; Lane 1987; Mawson 1989; Moore 1982, 1987; Welbourn 1984). These studies, and the early development of post-processual archaeology were very much influenced by semiotic and structuralist approaches in anthropology (e.g., Barthes 1973; Leach 1976; Douglas 1970; Levi-Strauss 1968, 1970; Tambiah 1969; Turner 1969). But parallel developments were underway in the United States within historical archaeology (Deetz 1977; Glassie 1975) and in feminist-inspired prehistoric studies (Conkey 1989). These semiotic and structuralist ideas led to the notion that material culture has a meaning which goes beyond the physical properties of an object, and derives from the network of social entanglements and strategies within which the object is embroiled. This idea was explored in relation to historical archaeology in the United States (e.g., Leone 1982), in relation to ethnoarchaeological studies of modern material culture (e.g., Parker Pearson 1982), and in relation to feminist understandings of, for example, space and ceramic variation (e.g., Moore 1986).

The second, and overlapping, idea is that material culture is not just a tool that is passively used by humans as they follow strategies dictated by environment, adaptation, or societal rules. Rather, material culture is used actively to have an effect in the social world. It is used by agents intentionally pursuing strategies and monitoring outcomes—even if the intentions are often not consciously understood. Thus it is difficult to predict how material culture will be used—an interpretation of particular strategies is needed. This second idea partly derived from the ethnoarchaeological work already described. For example, in my work in the Lake Baringo area in Kenya, I found that despite frequent interaction between three regional groups ("tribes"), their material culture exhibited a number of distinct stylistic differences (Hodder 1982). Rather than attributing such patterning to "cultural" norms, I argued instead that material culture styles were used strategically to maintain notions of difference between the three groups, and that in this sense material culture could be said to play an active role in the creation and recreation of identities. The notion that material culture is actively involved in social processes rather than being merely a passive reflection of human behavior was subsequently elaborated upon by others (e.g., Shanks and Tilley 1987). The development of this perspective was heavily influenced by the "practice" or "action" theories of social forms as developed by Bourdieu (1977) and Giddens (1979). The emphasis on material culture being actively manipulated in order to legitimate or transform society was also found in Marxist-inspired archaeological studies in prehistoric Europe (e.g., especially Kristiansen 1984) and in historical archaeology in the United States (Leone 1982).

These two ideas reinforce the pervasiveness of the social and they lie behind many of the later developments in the various approaches termed post-processual archaeology. The underlying context for this shift towards a fuller recognition of radical cultural difference (differences in social meaning of material culture), and for the view that material culture is active, rather than passive, together with the shift from positivism, was the various economic, social, and cultural changes described by the term globalism (see above). The two ideas also led to two key areas of research in recent archaeology. The first concerns material culture as text, and the second theories of agency.

THE TEXT METAPHOR, READING THE PAST, AND POST-STRUCTURALISM

If material culture is always meaningfully constituted, then perhaps it can be seen as a text that is read (Hodder 1986). This idea has several attractive aspects. It puts the emphasis on the reader—on the notion that meaning does not reside in the object itself, but in the way that the reader makes sense of that object. The "reader" here is both the past social actor and the present archaeologist. The reading metaphor foregrounds the fact that different people will read the same data differently, a tendency for which there is much historical evidence. The reading metaphor refers to interpretation and thus links us to hermeneutics as discussed above. It recognizes that interpretations are fluid and will change through time. The material object has to be read in terms of prejudgments but also in terms of contextual clues. The text metaphor encourages us to focus on context— "with text." Rather than studying pottery and animal bones separate from each other and from their find context, the emphasis is placed on looking at pottery, animal bones, and find circumstance in relation to each other. In each context there may be distinct or subtle changes of meaning, but there may also be overall codes or rules used in the "language" of the material objects. The text metaphor thus invites us to make use of the world of semiotics—the study of signs and the systems in which they are embedded.

There has in fact been widespread use of semiotics and structuralism in archaeology over recent decades (Bekaert 1998; Helskog 1995; Parker Pearson 1999a; Yentsch 1991), and there has been a recent revival of interest as a result of a shift from Saussurean to Peircean perspectives (Preucel and Bauer 2001). There are clearly advantages to be gained from considering material objects as organized by codes and rules that give them meaning. Knowledge about symbols, signs, indices, icons, and so on can usefully be applied in archaeology. The layout of settlements or of decoration on pottery, the discard of animal bones and the arrangement of artifacts in graves have all been subject to semiotic and structuralist analysis. But there are also difficulties with the text metaphor when applied to material culture. In some important ways, material culture is not like a written text. Perhaps most significantly, the relationship between a word and its signified is normally arbitrary; but this is seldom the case with material culture. In most, if not all, material culture usage, there is some nonarbitrary link between material culture and its meaning—as when gold is used to indicate high status because it is rare and enduring. Also, material objects, such as those in a living room, are not arranged in a simple sequence as is the case with words in a sentence—there are often fewer clues about the sequence in which one is supposed to read objects on entering a room. In addition, many of the meanings of objects are sensual and nondiscursive—they are less open to conscious definition. The very fact that one cannot often be sure of the meanings of objects, their sensual nature and nonarbitrary relations, suggests that material objects are important mechanisms for manipulating social situations. Although the Peircean approach deals with many of these criticisms of the text model, it remains the case that semiotic approaches often deal inadequately with the social.

This same notion, that meaning cannot be adequately studied by reference to abstract "linguistic" codes, lies behind many of the post-structuralist approaches that have influenced archaeology (Bapty and Yates 1990; Derrida 1976; Tilley 1990). In Derridean post-structuralism, the critique focuses on the structuralist notion that signifiers have meaning through their difference from other signifiers. But these other signifiers themselves only have meaning by being opposed to yet other signifiers in an endless chain of signification. Also, the meaning of a signifier varies depending on the context in which it is found. It is thus always possible to deconstruct any analysis which claims a totality, a whole or an original meaning, a truth, because these "origins" of meaning must always depend on other signifiers. These forms of critique have been effective in undermining many of the a priori assumptions made by archaeologists. In other forms of post-structuralism influenced by Foucault (1979), the focus is on the forms of power that sustain particular forms of knowledge and regimes of truth. Foucault radically decenters the subject actor who is seen as caught within webs of power/knowledge. The meaning of texts or material culture is situated within discourse. By discourse I mean particular forms of knowledge that are historically generated within specific relations of power. Thus knowledge and meaning are always situated and always social. Meaning is not just meaning. It is always *of* something and *for* someone.

The post-structuralist critiques take us a long way from the interpretation of meaning divorced from society. They have led to large numbers of studies that explore the relationships between material culture, meaning and power (e.g., see the volumes of collected papers edited by Hodder et al. 1995; Thomas 2001; Tilley 1993). They have also led to attempts to explore new ways of writing that open up the meaning of the past to alternative readings by different groups, and which undermine the notion that there is only one valid interpretation. These experimental studies, often influenced by a parallel debate within feminist archaeology, involve the production of new textual strategies, ranging from self-reflexivity and dialogue, to hypertext and the inclusion of semi-fictional vignettes (Edmonds 1999; Joyce 1994; Moran and Hides 1990; Tringham 1991, 1994).

We thus see the importance of the social for any attempt to interpret meaning. But does all this critique of the text metaphor mean that we can no longer talk of "reading the past"? If material meanings are closely linked to power and to material context, if material culture is related to unconscious motivations and sensual experience, if its meanings are nonlinear and ambiguous, perhaps the very idea of reading the past is unhelpful. In my view, taking these various criticisms into account, it remains important to retain "reading" and interpretation as components of archaeological procedure. This is because we do not only read texts. As social actors we are involved in daily acts of making sense of, "reading," what is going on around us. This wider sense of reading refers to the larger process of interpretation—including making sense of textures, sounds, smells, power dynamics, and so on. Reading is a wider process than interpreting words on a page. It involves being thoroughly engaged in a social context and interpreting that context through a variety of senses.

AGENCY

One of the limitations of the structuralist and post-structuralist approaches is that, as we have seen, they often downplay the role of social agents. As already noted, the view that material culture is active, that it is wielded by agents to achieve social ends, was an important strut of early post-processual archaeology. But what is meant by agency theory and how can material objects be seen as active?

The emphasis on agency began as a reaction to the processual emphasis on behavioral responses to environmental and other forms of change. Is there really nothing to societies and their long-term development than the passive stimulus-response that seem implied by much processual and behavioral archaeology? In his recent description of a behavioral theory of material culture, Schiffer (1999:9) states that "readers may be nonplussed at the absence in the new theory of much vocabulary...such as meaning, sign, symbol, intention, motivation, purpose, goal, attitude, value, belief, norm, function, mind, and culture. Despite herculean efforts in the social sciences to define these often ethnocentric or metaphysical notions, they remain behaviorally problematic and so are superfluous in the present project." The discussion of

agency is a reaction against types of social theory in which intentionality is seen as irrelevant to the understanding of human behavior.

But beyond this starting point, how much can we say about past agency? Certainly, there has recently been increased archaeological interest in discussions of agency (e.g., Dobres and Robb 2000). In my view the first step in making sense of these discussions is to recognize that agency is itself a complex process that needs to be broken down into its component parts. Different authors in archaeology refer to different aspects of agency. For example, Barrett (1994) mainly discusses the context for action—the fact that the actor has to be situated in relation to power/knowledge in order to have knowledge and resources to act. He discusses the mobilization of space and resources in prehistoric monuments in Britain in these terms.

A rather different approach argues that there is an intentionality to agency and that this intentionality cannot be reduced to the context for action. Of course, some intentions may be nondiscursive in the sense that actors may not be fully consciously aware of their motivations. Intentions need, therefore, to be interpreted. Archaeologists routinely make these interpretations. When claiming that a ditch is defensive or that a large wall around a settlement was built to provide prestige, intentions are imputed. The defensive nature of the ditch may be determined from its shape and size and position, and from evidence of warfare and so on. The prestigious nature of the wall may derive from its nondefensive nature (in terms of construction material or location or effectiveness) and from a larger context of competitive symbolic behavior. Another form of intentional social action that has recently attracted the interest of archaeologists is resistance to dominant groups. The older Marxist view that subordinate groups are duped by dominant ideologies has suffered from theoretical and empirical inadequacies in the social sciences (Giddens 1979), and many archaeologists have sought to demonstrate that subordinate groups use material culture to counteract dominant forms of discourse. For example, Shackel (2000) detected hundreds of hidden beer bottles in his excavations of a nineteenth-century brewery in West Virginia. Shackel concluded that the workers were intentionally and covertly consuming the products of their labor, thus drinking the owner's profits (see also Beaudry et al. 1991). As another example, Joyce et al. (2002) argue that at the regional center of Rio Viejo, on the Pacific coast of Oaxaca, Mexico, non-elites inhabited the monumental platforms of the site's civic-ceremonial center after the collapse of centralized institutions at the end of the Classic period. According to Joyce et al. (2002), these commoners rejected the dominant ideology of the previous era by dismantling and denigrating the architecture and carved stones. Likewise, Brumfiel (1996) suggests that powerful Aztec ideologies of male dominance expressed in official carvings at the capital city are contested in the countryside by popular images that assert the high status of women in reproductive roles.

There are problems in these accounts of intentional resistance. As Joyce et al. (2002) note, is it not inadequate to reduce intentionality to a response to dominant groups—surely in most cases there are many more dimensions to agency? Also, resistance is often discussed as if groups acted as wholes, when in fact most societies have many cross-cutting divisions. This point has been made effectively by feminist archaeologists who have recently resisted the notion that "women" or "men" form one category. In fact, there may be many differences among women (or men) on the basis of age, class, sexual orientation, and so on. Meskell (2002c) in particular has attempted to break down social groups and study the varying actions of individuals within them. This raises the issue of whether groups can have intentions. In my view the existence of a group is part of the resources used for individual agency. To get at the intentionality of agency properly involves understanding the construction of self and private individual lives. While some examples are provided by Meskell (see also Hodder 1999a), for most archaeological contexts the

aim of accessing individual intentionality is an ideal. But it remains important to consider variability in intentionality within groups and to study the processes used within groups to negotiate and coordinate group behavior and consensus. It is also important to recognize that the atomized individual is itself a Western concept and that the very idea of "individual" agency is itself a social product. Conceptions of individuals and body boundaries vary through time and space. Indeed, these conceptions are part of the resources available to agency.

Any act can have intended and unintended consequences. Indeed another approach to agency takes the focus away from intentionality and focuses more closely on the impact of action on others and on the material world. These consequences can be short, medium, or long term. They can be local or "global." Perhaps the main way that this impact-view of agency has been used in archaeology is in terms of "power over" (Miller and Tilley 1984). Dominant groups are described constructing a monument, controlling exchange, or holding a ritual that persuades others or manipulates them ideologically. Or elites may control the labor of others through the use of force. In these cases, there is almost no attempt to infer the intention of the actors: it is assumed that the intention is irrelevant to the outcome—domination. Since the specific intention or meaning behind the action is of little concern, analysis focuses narrowly on the effects of actions (see Barrett 1994:1).

To say that material culture is active is thus to argue that material objects are given meaning within agency. Material objects are part of the stocks of knowledge that provide the context for action. They are manipulated as part of intentional strategies (to hide, mask, legitimate, disrupt, and so on). And they endure, often resulting in unintended consequences long after individual actions—they spread agency over time. But consideration of the agency of material objects also leads to another nuance. Gell (1998) has provided many anthropological examples of objects that are apotropaic—that is they protect people from illness or evil spirits. Boric (2003) provides archaeological examples from the prehistoric sites of the Danube Gorges. In some cases, apotropaic objects appear to act as people, to be agents themselves. In such cases the objects (appear to) have intentionality because they bring to mind associations that are meaningful to the person affected by the object. Indeed much intentional action only has effects because it is perceived to be agentful. Thus we "give" powers to others and to objects such that they can act on us. Much ideology works in this way. So in exploring agency as intentional action we need to recognize two phases—the intentionality of an actor before or within an act, and the ascription of intentionality to an act by participants or observers.

Agency is likely to remain a fruitful area of discussion in archaeology. On the one hand, archaeologists deal with huge expanses of time in which change often seems slow and incremental. There seems little room for intentional action outside the structures within which agency is embedded. On the other hand, archaeologists deal with intimate moments—the loss of a bone awl (Spector 1993) or the burial of a relative. To what extent are these small events determined by larger structures? To what extent is agency involved in transforming structures of power? To ask such questions is not to search for "free will." Such a notion implies that will and intention can somehow be external to society. The individual, will, and intentionality are themselves social. Rather, the aim is to understand the relationships between structure and agency when viewed over the long term.

BODILY PRACTICES

It can be argued that these discussions of agency deal too much with power and with rather abstract agents. We get little sense in many discussions of agency of embodied individuals. Theorizing the body has become a central theme in many areas of research, including philosophy, literature, cultural studies, queer theory, and anthropology. In archaeology, the route towards a problemati-

zation of the body derives from two main strands—practice theory and feminist theory.

From early in the development of postprocessual archaeology, the writing of Pierre Bourdieu had a special place. His outline of a theory of practice (1977) was attractive to archaeology because it foregrounded the mundane aspects of daily life which archaeologists spend most of their time excavating—the pots and pans view of the world. Bourdieu showed how the daily practices of movement around domestic space, the discard of refuse, the construction of an oven, all had social weight. Alarm bells went off for archaeologists when Bourdieu said that it was possible to instill "a whole cosmology, an ethic, a metaphysic, a political philosophy, through injunctions as insignificant as 'stand up straight' or 'don't hold your knife in your left hand'" (Bourdieu 1977:94). In his own ethnographic work, Bourdieu described how children learned social rules as they moved around the house, moving from "male" to "female" parts of the house, from "light" to "dark." Boys may be encouraged to stand up straight, like spears, and girls to look down and be deferential. In this practical way, people gain an understanding of the world that is both practical and socially meaningful. Often they cannot articulate the understandings in conscious speech very well—they remain a set of dispositions or orientations—a *habitus* that is practical rather than conscious and verbal.

In fact, similar arguments had been made by a long line of sociologists from Goffman to Giddens, and anthropologists, from Mauss to Leroi-Gourhan. But it was Bourdieu and Giddens that had most direct impact in archaeology. Bourdieu in particular dealt with material very close to archaeology, and it was easy to see the application of his work. Also, he attempted to bridge between structuralism and Marxism while at the same time to give an adequate account of agency. Bourdieu recognizes that the *habitus* is not the only way in which practice is produced. The regularity that we observe in behavior is also produced by norms, symbols, rituals, and objective material considerations, such as the location of actors in socio-economic hierarchies. But he was able to foreground the *habitus* in ways attractive to archaeologists. In doing so, he also pushed archaeologists towards a discussion of the body. He was concerned with bodily stance and with bodily movements about houses and other spaces. These were the prime mechanisms of social enculturation.

A similar move toward a consideration of the body derived from debates within various strands of feminist archaeology. One of the main aims of much feminist archaeology has been to put people back into the past, and to put faces on the "faceless blobs" that stalked the multihyphenated systems of processual archaeology (e.g., Tringham 1994). Beyond this general aim, in much early feminist archaeology a distinction was made between sex and gender, the first referring to the biological sex of the body, and the second to the cultural and social way in which that body was adorned or given meaning. This distinction was seen as being important methodologically, since skeletons in graves could first be identified by biological anthropologists, and then, on this reliable basis, patterns of artifact associations could be studied. More recently, archaeologies of sexuality have responded to a wide range of historical, literary, and anthropological work (e.g., Laqueur, Foucault, Haraway, Butler) which argues that simple dichotomies between sex and gender are difficult to maintain (Joyce 1998; Meskell 1999; Schmidt and Voss 2000; Yates 1993). Sex is not in fact a "given." Rather, descriptions of bodies and sexes change through time. There is no natural, stable, sex, but rather a set of discursive practices that help define what is natural and biological.

Some examples of archaeological studies that use the idea that bodies are socially constructed include Treherne's (1995) account of the appearance of toilet articles at a particular horizon in the European Bronze Age. He argues for a changing aesthetic of the body and of personhood as a part of wider social changes. Joyce (1998) discusses human images from Prehispanic Central America and

shows how they actively constituted theories of the body. Only certain postures were selected from the range of daily bodily movements to be represented in durable material such as fired clay and stone. This discourse, which materialized some representations of the body but not others, reinforced and naturalized a particular social philosophy.

At least in relation to practice theories, it can be argued that insufficient account is given to ways in which agents can transform structures. We are still left with rather faceless agents determined by larger forces. How can we get closer to what it feels like to "be," or to be inside someone's body? In attempt to achieve a fuller account of embodiment, many archaeologists have been influenced by the phenomenology of Heidegger (e.g., Thomas 1996). Some of the most important aspects of the discussion of Heidegger in archaeology have been the critiques of binary oppositions between culture and nature, and between mind and body. What this means in archaeological applications is that attention is again focused on the ways in which bodies move around sites and landscapes. Rather than looking at the plan of a monument, attention is paid to the ways in which people moved around and experienced the monument.

In many of these archaeological accounts, the emphasis is placed on the way that relations of power are served in the layout of monuments and landscapes (Barrett 1994; Thomas 1996; Tilley 1994). In these accounts it is suggested that social actors are forced to perceive the world and to interact with each other in certain ways because their movements are constrained by the built environment. This focus on power again threatens to take the discussion away from lived experience and toward the structures of power that are seen as binding bodies and their movements. Often the accounts seem to assume a universal body. But two bodies moving around the same landscape or monuments may not see it in the same way. Much depends on the social meanings and values that are given to sites in the landscape, and much depends on the specific social positioning of actors.

It is inadequate to describe the movements of bodies and sensual experience without embedding bodily experience within social meaning. The studies discussed in this section have made great strides in that they have moved away from the body as a natural substance onto which the social is mapped, and they have rejected the idea that space is an abstract entity, a container for human existence. Rather they see space as part of the structuring of social existence, part of the process by which social actors experience and respond to the social world (Tilley 1993:10). But phenomenological approaches have their own problems. In particular, they need to be sensitive to radical cultural and social difference in basic ways of seeing the world, and they need to be reflexively critical about the different ways that different bodies can experience the same monuments and landscapes.

CONCLUSION

I hope it has become clear in this account how in contemporary social theory in archaeology "everything is social." We have seen how concepts that might seem neutral, natural, or biological, like space, bodies, sex, the environment, have all come to be seen as social. The same could also be said for other terms not discussed here such as time (Lucas 2001a). Certainly good arguments have been made that technology cannot be separated from the social (Dobres 2000; Lemonnier 1993). Even materiality itself is now seen as social, and Latour (1988a) argues that objects are like people, in that both have agency or can act in the world. The notion that the meaning of a thing is not stable but depends on context and social entanglement has been made by Nick Thomas (1991). But we can go a step further and argue that our very selves develop in relationship with the object world, and that the boundaries between self and object vary historically and socially (Merleau-Ponty 1945).

The reasons for this shift from the dominance of culture to the centrality of the social have been discussed above, but they are part of a wider move against universalist and essentialist assumptions. Even truth is now seen as an effect of the social (Foucault 1979). In critiquing "culture" and "society" as essentialist or Western, the aim is to focus on the particular and the variable. No attempt is made to argue for a universal definition of the "social" and its workings. Rather, the term refers to the diversity of human experience. Of course, in other quarters of the social sciences there are counter moves toward the real, the universal, and the evolutionary. Certainly one of the main challenges in social archaeology over coming decades will be reconciling the tensions between new advances in biological and biomolecular archaeology (Jones 2001) and social theoretical approaches.

I have not discussed at any length other "social" approaches in archaeology. This is because they do not attempt to engage with social theory in the social sciences and humanities as a whole. For example, Schiffer (2000) has edited a book entitled *Social Theory in Archaeology* and in this and other work he has developed a behavioral theory of material culture. But I noted above that in developing his theory he rejects everything that most anthropologists, sociologists, and historians would regard as central components of the social. He focuses on material interactions and performance as if they could be isolated outside the social. Even in his edited volume, the tensions involved in trying to build a social theory without the social become clear. In that volume, Feinman describes an interesting categorization of societies into network and corporate. But he accepts (Feinman 2000:49) that the important *why* questions remain. Unless one is allowed to explore the daily manipulation and reproduction of social micropractices, knowledge and power, it is difficult to see how a fuller account can be achieved. As another example, Nelson criticizes behavioral approaches to the choices involved in artifact deposition saying (Nelson 2000:61) "the social context of the choices could be more fully explored." She recognizes the need to introduce agency-based approaches to abandonment studies, but her account does not benefit from the full range of available social theory.

A similar indication of the need to embrace a fuller social theory is seen in Darwinian evolutionary archaeology. For example, O'Brien and Lyman (2000) try to build bridges to social theory by discussing the role of history in their theoretical perspective. Their own account of history focuses on the selective environment that led to the appearance of cultural traits and then on pursuing the historical lineages of the traits that ensue. A full account of the selective environments and performance characteristics that lead to some cultural variants being selected would need to consider social power, agency, meaning, and so on, i.e., all the rich social world (environment) in which cultural traits are embedded, are selected, and transmitted. Once all that has been done one is back with the full world of social theory, and with history as social, cultural, constructed, and created as well as being materially based. In order to provide an adequate account of an evolutionary process, a full social theory would need to be incorporated.

Much the same point can be made about cognitive processual archaeology (e.g., Renfrew and Zubrow 1994). Here an attempt is made to argue that one can talk in universal, nonsocial ways, about the mind and its cognitive processes. The focus is on the early evolution of the mind, the strategies used in knapping flint, the systems of weights and measures used complex societies, and so on. The difficulty is again that this approach is underlain by the assumption that mind can be separated from society. For Bourdieu and Merleau-Ponty, the mind is born of the social world of objects. But Renfrew and his colleagues wish to maintain an objectivist position untrammeled by the meanings, desires, and intentions of the social world. Lakoff and Johnson in their book *Philosophy in the Flesh* (1999), however, argue that even color has no independent reality. "The qualities of things as we can experience and comprehend them depend crucially on our neural makeup, our bodily interactions with them and our

purposes and interests " (Lakoff and Johnson 1999:26). Cognition is not outside the social, and cognitive processual archaeology needs to become fully post-processual if it is to be successful in understanding past minds.

On the other hand, to argue that everything is social is not to argue that it is only social. Clearly there are aesthetic, emotional, and material aspects of life which, while being thoroughly social, cannot be reduced to the social. Rather, the more important aim in foregrounding the social is to recognize the indivisability of human experience— its nonpartitive character. Most of the approaches discussed here try to be nondichotomous—in terms of culture/nature, mind/body, agent/structure, self/society. The central point is that everything is infused with the social, so that attempts to ignore the social are bound to be limited and partial. Future developments in the discipline, however biological and natural science they might be in initial motivation, will need to engage with the full range of social theory.

It might be argued that recognition of the social nature of material culture and of the way the past is constructed derives its influence from anthropology, history, and related disciplines. But there is also a sense in which recognition of the centrality of the social acts as a springboard for archaeologists to contribute to other disciplines. Certainly, there has been a widespread increase in the use of the archaeology metaphor in the social and humanistic disciplines. This metaphorical use of archaeology goes back to Freud, Husserl, Benjamin, and more recently to Foucault and Derrida. But there are more specific recent links that suggest a social archaeology can contribute more widely. Certainly, there is a widespread interest in many disciplines in materiality, in the ways that the social is constructed in the material, and in the ways in which materiality is active and constitutive. The success of the *Journal of Material Culture* is one indication of the extent of these interests and the archaeological contribution here is clear. Archaeology and heritage come together in accounts of monuments, identity, and memory (Meskell 2002a; Rowlands

1993) that are part of wider discussions in the social sciences (e.g., Connerton 1989). The archaeological and the material also allow windows into the nondiscursive aspects of social life, especially when viewed over the long and very long term. The social present can be seen as the long-term product of slow moves in daily, nondiscursive practices (e.g., Hamann 2002). In these various ways, the focus on the social in archaeology allows a port of entry for archaeology, heritage, materiality, and the long term to contribute to debates in a wide range of related disciplines.

Acknowledgments
I would like to thank Danielle Steen for her help in the literature search used for this paper, and Scott Hutson for discussions regarding theoretical points raised here.

9

Agency and Individuals in Long-Term Processes

INTRODUCTION

Archaeological data raise the issue of scale in a most extreme form. On the one hand, the processes observed by archaeologists stretch out over spans of time which are difficult or impossible for individual actors to comprehend or perceive. These are the processes of the long term, the rise and fall of complex political systems, the slow transformation of subsistence technologies, the *longue durée* of *mentalités,* the battleship curves of styles, and so on. Archaeological emphasis on the long term is reinforced by patterns of survival and recovery. From many periods and areas, few sites survive or few have been excavated with modern scientific techniques. Thus, there is little choice but to talk of the large scale, the generalized, the gross patterning. There are also sociopolitical reasons for the archaeological focus on the long term. For example, archaeology grew in Europe as an inherent part of nationalism, to provide a long-term basis for the nation state, and reference to the long-term archaeological past is an integral part of many indigenous claims to territory today. Within the Western academy, archaeology identified itself as a separate field of inquiry by opposing its concern with the long term to the shorter spans dealt with in sociocultural anthropology (in the United States) and in history (in Europe).

On the other hand, archaeological understanding of the long term is built up from traces of the smallest and least significant of acts. Our data are produced by the dropping and breaking of a pot and the kicking or tossing of its sherds. They are produced by the discard from meals, the knapping of flint, or the scratching on clay. True, there are also the walls of houses and temples protected in tells and the monuments built to last in open landscapes. But even these we increasingly understand as constructed at particular moments in time for specific historical purposes; the social meanings of these temples and monuments do not stay the same. Again, there are sociopolitical factors involved. Archaeologists in Europe defined themselves as different from historians by their concentration, not on elite texts, but on the mundane practices and residues of daily life.

These radical differences in scale inherent within archaeological data and within the archaeological discipline, might be supposed to have encouraged theories which deal fully with the relationships between individual events and large-scale process. On the whole, however, and especially over recent decades, in both processual and post-processual archaeology, archaeologists have eschewed the small scale in favor of long-term trends. It was particularly in traditional culture-historical archaeology that attempts were made to conceive of the "Indian behind the artifact," for example in identifying the individual "hand" of the painter of a Greek vase

(Hill and Gunn 1977), or in discussions of the intentionality of Caesar crossing the Rubicon (Collingwood 1946). But since the 1960s, the emphasis has shifted to the "system behind the Indian behind the artifact." Despite the rhetoric of many recent theoretical perspectives in archaeology, in what follows I argue that insufficient attention has been given to the role of small-scale events and processes within the long term. I argue that archaeologists have come to focus on agency and on the *construction* of individuals, selves, and subjects. I argue, following Meskell (1996; Knapp and Meskell 1997) that this constructivist position is inadequate, and particularly inappropriate for dealing with the particularity of archaeological data: the radical differences of scale. I argue that there is a need to shift from agency and the construction of social beings, to individual narratives of lived lives and events.

AGENCY

In my view, the early uses of the term "agency" in post-processual archaeology have to be understood in terms of an opposition that was being made with the term "behavior." The use of the latter term, even if not associated specifically with behaviorism, was seen by critics as implying a passive stimulus–response view of human action, and as implying the description of events from an external, distanced point of view: "her arm was raised" as opposed to the agency-centered view that "she raised her arm."

The notion that material culture was active derived from a critique of the view of social systems as peopled by actors who respond predictably to events and produce material culture as byproducts of those responses. It could be shown that individual actors actively used material culture (Hodder 1982) in their competing, contradictory, and changing strategies. An emphasis was thus placed on intentionality, and it was this that became central to discussions of agency (Hodder 1986; Shanks and Tilley 1987). While in my own early texts on this subject there was much discussion of individuals, no attempt was made to identify them specifi-

cally. Rather, the reason for foregrounding individuals was to make a theoretical point: that we needed to consider how people were actively pursuing specific actions and intentions. "The individual" was at that point a theoretical prop to the emphasis on intentionality.

Another reason for the early emphasis on the individual was to foreground indeterminacy. Rather than large-scale systems and processes in which individuals were caught and determined, the theoretical focus on the individual underlined the idea that human beings were able to monitor the effects of their actions and act in novel, creative ways. So again, it was not a matter of identifying individual agents but of emphasizing at a theoretical level the move away from behavioral and deterministic perspectives.

If early work on agency was couched in terms of intentionality and indeterminacy, the concept soon came to be overtaken by a different view: that agency amounted to "the power to act." In my view, this shift reflects the long-standing inability of the discipline to cope in theoretical terms with the individualized and with the small-scale. And indeed, the effect of this shift was that the emphasis on individuals was lost, a trend noted by Johnson (1989).

Agency thus came to be seen in terms of the resources needed in order to act (Miller and Tilley 1984; Shanks and Tilley 1987). These resources were both material and symbolic (informational). The control of prestige goods or esoteric knowledge was seen as the basis of power, both power *to* and power *over* (Miller and Tilley 1984; Shanks and Tilley 1987). An example of a study in which power is related to resources without explicit consideration of individuals is provided by Walker and Lucero (2000). Many such perspectives on agency derived from Foucault and Giddens (Miller and Tilley 1984), and they have increasingly been subject to criticism in the social sciences (e.g., Turner 1994), mainly because they do not in the end provide an adequate theory of the subject and of agency. Despite an apparent emphasis on the duality of structure and agency, Giddens is criticized for leaving little room for transformative action.

We can see the limits of the structurationist view in many of its applications in archaeology. Agency appears in these applications to be routinized, and materially and objectively structured. A good example in archaeology is provided by the "big men aggrandizers" discussed by Hayden (1990). There is perhaps an androcentric aspect to the focus on power (Meskell 1996). There is little emphasis on intentionality as individualized, small-scale, and transformative.

For example, Barrett (1994) provides one of the clearest and most successful sustained applications of structuration theory in archaeology. It is clear, however, that he wishes to get away from specific moments of intentionality and from accounts of meaningful and transformative action (but see also Barrett 2000). He argues that "we have not uncovered what those monuments meant" (Barrett 1994:1). In discussing Neolithic and Bronze Age monuments in Britain, practices sometimes appear to become separated from mind. "Monumentality originated in neither the idea nor the plan but rather in the practice and in the project" (1994:23). This seems to be denying discursive intentionality, idea and plan too completely. Perhaps as a result, Barrett's agents seem caught in long-term structures with a materialist bent. For example, Barrett argues that in the British early Neolithic the use of monuments and landscapes is generalized. Thus, a wide range of activities occur at "ancestral sites." This pattern is linked to long fallow agricultural systems and generalized rights to community land. In the later Neolithic and early Bronze Age a shorter fallow system implies closer links to the land, the closer definition of inheritance and tenure, and the clearer marking of burial locations on the landscape. Barrett's emphasis is on the practical mastery of material and symbolic resources within routines and locales. He foregrounds practices and their material structuring. There is discussion of how "people" control and respond to the choreography of place, but no account of individual lived lives. Agency is seen in terms of

resources: what is available to allow action to take place, rather than in terms of individual forward-looking intentionality and creativity.

SUBJECTS AND SELVES

Notions of individuality and individual creativity have become highly suspect within many of the social sciences. It is clear that many of our contemporary Western notions derive from historically specific concepts of individuality and intimacy (Giddens 1992). In particular, Foucault (1977) has demonstrated the way in which discourses emerged in the late eighteenth and nineteenth centuries associated with the identification, surveillance, and disciplining of persons as individuals. In more recent times, new information technologies and new global production, distribution, and consumption processes have emphasized the fragmentation and individualization of time, space, and product (e.g., Castells 1996). The individual is increasingly seen as a particular historical product of capitalism and, in particular, of late capitalism.

However, the concept of the individual self has been rescued by anthropological and historical perspectives which chart changing concepts of self and the body across time and space. For example, Moore (1994) provides a discussion of how in different ethnographic concepts different conceptions of the body boundary can be found. In Western societies we tend to see the outer skin as the boundary of body and self. In other societies, the boundary of self may extend to include objects in the world around. The way is open to explore cultural variation in the factors which lead to different constructions of the self and of subjectivity. In archaeology a relevant study is that by Treherne (1995). Treherne discusses changing concepts and practices of the self and the body during the European Bronze Age. Why do toilet articles such as tweezers and razors appear at a particular moment in European prehistory? Treherne shows that such articles are related to evidence for increasing individualism: warfare, bodily ornament, horses and wheeled vehicles, the hunt, and the ritual consumption of alcohol. While all these activities are related to the rise and transformation of a male warrior status group, Treherne argues that the key is a changing aesthetics of the body. He describes the "warrior's beauty" and his "beautiful death." This aesthetics is a framework of meaning linked to a set of practices which is quite specific historically and which is part of a distinctive form of self-identity. This life-style crystallized across Europe in the mid-second millennium B.C. out of roots in the previous few millennia. The institution of the warrior elite was to survive into, and in part give rise to an aspect of, the later feudal order in Europe.

Elegant as such accounts are, the aim is not to examine agency in terms of the forward-looking intentionality of individual lives. Rather, the focus is on the social construction of subjectivities as part of the unfurling of long-term processes. This constructivist view of bodies, selves, and subjects is also seen in recent applications of phenomenological approaches in archaeology. For example, Thomas (1996), Gosden (1994), and Tilley (1994) have all looked to Heidegger and his idea of "being in the world" (also Barrett 2000). These authors use phenomenology to focus on how the subject experiences the world through the body. In particular, they explore how subjects experience monuments and landscapes as they move through them and carry out practices in them.

These phenomenological approaches are important in that they attempt to break away from approaches which foreground structures and systems binding people into particular modes of behavior over time. They seek to undermine the notion of universal oppositions between culture and nature, mind and body, meaning and practice, structure and agent. Rather they place emphasis on the local and the personal: the lived experiences of individuals inhabiting monuments and landscapes. They also show that the sites and monuments never had one single meaning. Rather the meanings were continually changed through time (Bradley 1993). The site or monument is not a static structure but the product of a long cycle of reordering and renegotiating.

For example, Thomas (1996) describes the ways in which Neolithic Linearbandkeramik houses were centers of experience of the self and of the environment. The daily practices of cutting down trees, moving earth, respecting older houses, living in and using the building created a sense of place. People came to "know" a place as part of "being-in-the-world." The similarities of form of Linearbandkeramik houses and megalithic long tombs over vast areas are not seen in terms of a common meaning. Indeed, Thomas argues that the houses or tombs did not have a common meaning. All that was shared in northwest Europe was a "material vocabulary" (Thomas 1996:135). The similarities are presumably produced by the routinization of practices. But why did people keep doing the same thing with their house plans and tomb plans? And why these specific plans?

The answers to these questions are again often given in terms of the organization of material resources and in terms of the social construction of subjectivities within power strategies. For example, Tilley (1994) argues that the placing of prehistoric monuments in the landscape is related to material factors. The need to control and fix meanings in the landscape is linked to herding and the control of animals, migratory routes, and pastures. Treherne makes a related point in relation to Thomas's (1996) work:

> Thomas' attention is given to the manipulation of individual bodies, and concomitant notions of subjectivity, through the dominant interpretations of built or acculturated space fixed by hegemonic groups.... What he is really concerned with is an external process of subjectification. (Treherne 1995:125)

So once again, the lived experiences of individual bodies located in a particular time and place are not explored, despite claims to the contrary. There is too little emphasis on subjectivity and self as constructed by individual agents.

INDIVIDUAL LIVES

I have argued so far that a notion of agency as involving intentionality and indeterminacy has become overshadowed in recent debates by a perception of agency in terms of the availability of resources and of the structuring of lives within long-term and large-scale processes. There is little room in such accounts for the individual construction of events and processes. An adequate account of agency needs to supplement structurationist and phenomenological accounts with dimensions of experience which can be gained from an examination of individual lives.

There is, however, a different tradition in archaeology which points towards a less constructivist position. This is work influenced by Feminist and Queer theory. Feminist archaeologists have for some time been concerned with the general ideas of "peopling" the past and of putting faces on the "faceless blobs" which seem, according to most archaeological accounts, to have inhabited much of prehistory (e.g., Gero and Conkey 1991; Tringham 1991). But it is particularly radical notions of difference and the performativity of sexual identities (Butler 1990) which have led to detailed attempts to reconstruct the individuality of past lives (e.g., Knapp and Meskell 1997; Meskell 1998).

Within these more radical notions, emphasis is often placed on the ways in which the same subject can take on different identities. Indeed, an "individual" is itself a larger whole constructed from individual events. We cannot assume that the acts of a subject will always amount to "an individual," that is a distinctive pattern of behavior associated with a single body. The potential exists to build up evidence of individual characteristics in archaeology. For example, the artist's "hand" is identified by repeated peculiarities of style or technique. Individual variation in the knapping of flint has been recognized from the refitting of cores. Repeated physical movement can be identified from the examination of skeletons (Molleson 1994). For example, certain bodies are found to have repeatedly sat in certain positions while grind-ing, or to have repeatedly used their teeth to clean fibers and so on.

So rather than starting with "individuals" we need to see how "individuals" and other wholes such as sites, cultures, and exchange networks are constructed, not solely by large-scale processes and hegemonic groups, but through the intentionality within particular and individual events.

Any construction of individual lived lives involves starting off with the traces of individual events. The evidence excavated by archaeologists is usually the result of a palimpsest of individual events. Certainly the individual events can sometimes be extracted from the palimpsest (the breaking of a pot identified from refitting within a general spread of pottery, the digging of a particular posthole within a pattern of postholes, etc.). It is often possible to work out the intentionality and decision-making involved in individual event sequences, as in work on *chaînes opératoires*, without relating those sequences to a particular embodied individual. In other cases, as discussed below, it may be possible to link individual events and individual sequences of events together as the products of a particular person. It is necessary to attempt to build up from the former (events and event sequences) to the latter (embodied individuals) so that the construction of the individual in a particular society can be approached. It is rare that archaeologists can identify named individuals; it is rare that they can piece together anything approaching a full account of an individual life. Yet we routinely have evidence of fragments of lives. The challenge is to build up these fragments into the fullest possible accounts of individual lived lives, by grouped together events and sequences of events wherever possible.

The focus on the individual event is important for a number of reasons. First because of the indeterminacy of levels, that is, that events are not determined by the structures within which they are embedded. Structure and system can never be fully instantiated in the moments of daily action except provisionally and partially. In the practice of the lived moment it is impossible for all the abstractions and constraints of systems and structures to be present except in the simplest of terms and most provisional of ways. This is because of the complexity and size of the system, unacknowledged conditions and incomplete knowledge held by actors, different perspectives and interpretations of appropriate action, and an inability to predict all its consequences.

There must, then, always be a disjunction between event and structure. One can never adequately explain one level by another; the systems, structures, and events are simply not equivalent. If there is not a determinate relationship between large-scale and small-scale, macro- and micro-scales, then it cannot be sufficient to focus all archaeological endeavor on the large-scale. To do so is to treat all variability as "noise," as indeed it has been treated through recent decades in archaeology. Despite the New and processual archaeological emphasis on variability, the aim was always to reduce variability to "trend + noise." As already noted, the emphasis on general trends has continued in most post-processual archaeology. Rather than treating variability in these terms it can be approached as the situated construction of difference.

Another reason for the need to describe individual actions and lives at the micro-scale, is that it is at the human scale that contradictions and conflicts are worked out, lived through, and resolved. A full explanatory account cannot remain at the level of the interaction of variables. In fact these variables interact through the lives of individuals, in the compromises they made and the solutions they found. The structures are worked out and reproduced in the bodies of historical lives.

This is why it is not enough merely to identify individual events and persons. The inadequacy of such an approach is evident in the studies of prehistoric "bog bodies" in northern Europe (Coles and Coles 1989; Glob 1977). The detail which can be gained of the last moments in the lives of these individuals is remarkable. Their last meals can be described, and the processes of their death inferred. Their hair style and clothing can be clearly seen, and the state of their fingernails gives an indication of the mode of life they had lived. Yet, the very isolation of these bodies in wetland areas means that we understand very little of the social contexts in which the individuals lived and died. We still do not understand why the deaths occurred, whether they had a ritual or penal or other character. We can say little about how these individuals fitted into or reacted against the structures that surrounded them.

INDIVIDUAL LIVES:
THE EXAMPLE OF THE "ICE MAN"

In some such cases there is more potential for placing well-preserved bodies and the specific instances of the deaths into a wider and transforming social structure. For example, I have suggested that the evidence regarding the "Ice Man" found in the Austrian Alps (Spindler 1993), both allows a window into an individual life, and provides an opportunity to explore how that life dealt with and contributed to the contradictions generated by large-scale processes (Hodder 1999a).

The body was dated to 3300–3200 B.C., and the man, who was between thirty-five and forty years old, was associated with a wide range of equipment and clothes. These artifacts and the body itself allow Spindler to argue that the Ice Man had, in his life, been both connected to and disconnected from wider lowland society. The man was clearly integrated into exchange networks and had recently been traveling through lowland agricultural areas. Lowland communities may have depended on him as a metal trader, hunter, or shepherd. On the other hand, the man was obviously highly self-sufficient. He carried an extraordinary amount of equipment with him which allowed him to travel and survive in upland and cold conditions. There is evidence of independence and self-sufficiency, and a concern with the care and healing of his own body.

The clothes and the food of the Ice Man thus suggest an independence and an experience of surviving in a harsh and dangerous environment. Yet he had close contact with other groups and his existence depended on lowland communities. Lowland groups in turn depended on him and his like for the exploitation of upland environments. We see an individual threading a life together, one involving contradictions between dependency and self-sufficiency. We sense the duality in his commitment to and need for long-term social relationships with lowland groups, and his need to break away from such dependencies to live on his own.

Looked at on another scale, we can see the Ice Man and the contradictions which ran through his life as part of larger-scale processes. Large parts of Europe at this time were undergoing a shift from societies based on a corporate sense of lineage towards societies in which individuals and small groups competed for access to exchange goods (Thomas 1987). An important part of this change was the spread of the use of secondary animal products and the greater exploitation of upland areas (Sherratt 1981). In terms of symbolic change, I have argued there was a shift from the corporate group symbolized by the domestic hearth to individualized groups associated with hunting, warring, and exchange (the *agrios*; see Hodder 1990).

These large-scale transformations in economy, society, and ideology could only be achieved through the actions of individuals as they worked through the dichotomies between older systems and the practical world in which they lived their daily lives. In the Ice Man's life we see him struggling, even to his death, with contradictions which translated in his context into an opposition between upland and lowland. The lowland groups to which he had access may still have practiced collective burial and thus were part of the older system in Europe (Barfield 1994). His own life-style became necessary as people increasingly went into the mountains to obtain stone and ores, to herd sheep, or to hunt. These new developments ushered in a life of independence, harshness, and individual opportunity. The Ice Man found individual solutions. He found a way of carrying embers in a birch bark container. He had his own "med-

icine kit" in the form of two pieces of birch fungus attached to his left wrist. He got someone to make tattoos on him to protect him or to heal a strain or wound. We see in all this the intentional creation of a new world, breaking away from but dependent on the corporate. We see the small-scale drama within the large-scale movement of millennia.

AN EXAMPLE FROM ÇATALHÖYÜK
Another example I wish to provide deals not with long-term change but with long-term stability. One of the most remarkable characteristics of the early Neolithic mound sites in central Anatolia such as Aşıklı Höyük and Çatalhöyük is that the buildings, streets, and internal settlement organization stay very stable over millennia. How were the structures behind these continuities reproduced? How did individual action make sense of the structures and regenerate them? I want to attempt to answer these questions by considering a case from the recent excavations at Çatalhöyük (Hodder 1996).

In Building 1 on the north part of the East mound (Fig. 9.1), over sixty burials were found beneath the floor. The floor and wall plaster resurfacings suggest that the building was used for about forty years. It is therefore assumed that those buried in the building had lived in this and adjacent or other buildings. Examination of the skeletal evidence suggests some family resemblances among the bones (Theya Molleson and Peter Andrews; see http://catal.arch.cam.ac.uk/catal/catal.html). The last burial in the building was distinctive in a number of respects. This was of an older male but with the head missing (Fig. 9.2). The specific removal of the head was not observed in the other burials, but head removal is known from depictions in the Çatalhöyük art. "Vultures" are shown picking the flesh from headless corpses. Since excarnation does not seem to be indicated by the human bones from the site so far examined in the new excavations, it seems likely that the practices associated with death in the art refer to mythology. Alternatively or additionally, head removal was restricted to individuals of special and/or ritual status.

BUILDING 1
PHASE 2 - OCCUPATION I

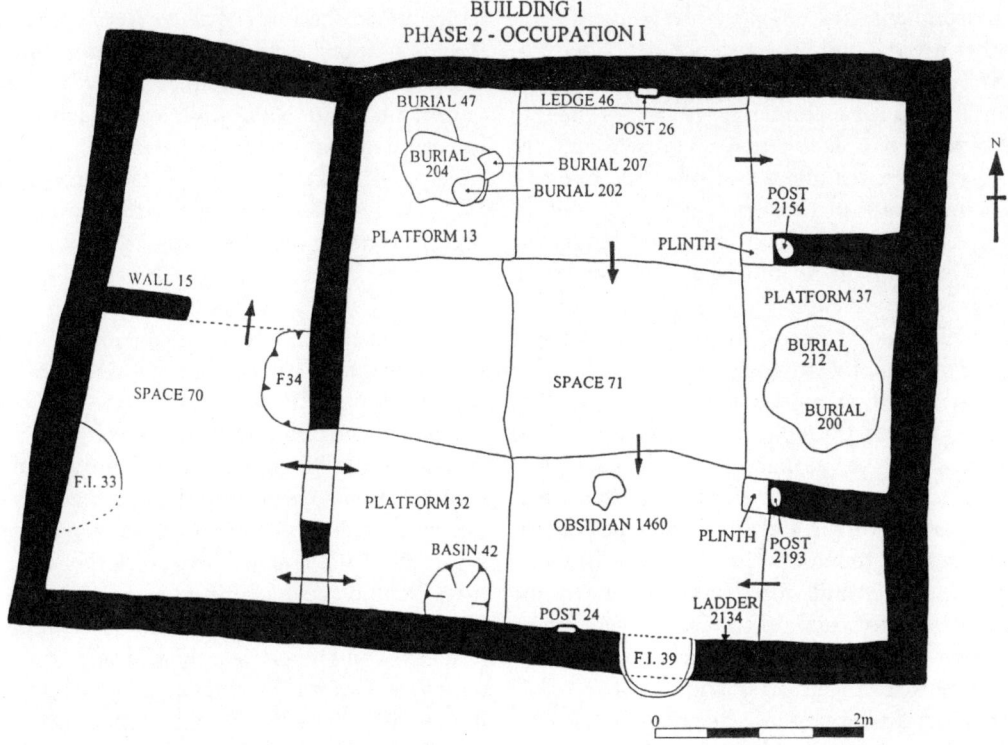

Figure 9.1. Plan of Building 1 at Çatalhöyük.

The special character of the headless burial was confirmed by his association with an unusual object, a small bone worn as a pendant. This bone proved to be the deformed penis bone of a small weasel-like creature.

The special status of this individual was thus implied by the removal of his head, by the penis bone, and by the fact that his burial was the last to occur in the building before abandonment. In addition he was buried under what seems to have been the main platform, centrally placed, within Building 1.

What else can we say about this individual and the way that he lived his life? Examination of the human bones from beneath Building 1 has suggested the possibility that the forty-year life-cycle of this house follows the life-cycle of the extended family buried beneath its floors. The early burials include high proportions of young individuals; indeed, as the building grows older, so only old individuals are buried within it. This suggests that the building was first founded by a young family head. His and/or her children then ei-

ther died or moved away, until only older individuals were left and finally the building was abandoned. When the building was abandoned it was purified by burning and intentionally filled in. Soon afterwards, however, someone dug down into Building 1 to remove a bull sculpture from the main internal wall.

It is reasonable to argue from the special treatment of the last burial, the headless man, that it was his death which finally led to the abandonment of the building. He may well have been the individual who founded the building and became the family head. If so, we can say something about this particular man's death and life. His death led to the removal of the great ancestral sculpture from inside the house. In his life, he would have witnessed the deaths of many of his siblings, cousins, and children. The infant and child mortality rate for those buried in the house is very high. It is not too difficult to argue that the penis bone worn by this elder had something to do with fertility. Perhaps this man

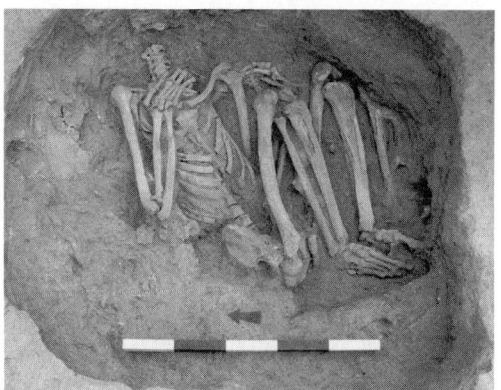

Figure 9.2. Headless male burial from beneath eastern platform in Building 1.

came to use such symbols and other special powers to protect the family and help it to deal with the death of so many of its children.

Indeed, we have increasingly come to argue at Çatalhöyük that much of the "art" may have been involved in protection, mediation with ancestors, and reproduction. The personal and individual solution found by the elder in Building 1 was perhaps part of a pattern which assured the continuity of an art devoted to dealing with loss and instability. In terms of the interaction of variables over the long term, we can see that the symbolism and "art" created links to the ancestors, that it mediated with the spirit world. And we can see that behavior of this type was necessary in the context of early agriculture and large settled communities. It is through the individual life that these interactions take place. We can get a surprisingly full picture of the elder of Building 1. We can look at the hearth he must have known so well, crawl through the same entryways he must have used. But we can also see how he dealt with tragedy and loss, and how his particular solution carried his family through forty years and many deaths. The use of symbolic representation to deal with ancestors and spirits was part of a long-term structure, but we glimpse its working in individual circumstances.

NARRATIVE WINDOWS
It is clear in the examples given above that the details even of prehistoric individual lives can to some extent be put together. But accounts

of such lives seem to demand a rhetoric rather different from that associated with log-normal curves and input–output diagrams. An intriguing link has begun to emerge in recent literature between the discussion of individual lives and the writing of narratives. In terms of the history of archaeology a fine example is provided by Joyce (1994). In historical archaeology, Spector (1993) has created an evocative narrative of the lives of individuals at the moment of early contact between colonial and Native American groups.

In my view, the switch to a different narrative mode may often be an integral component of a commitment to the small scale. Because of the indeterminate relations between the long term and the individual act, it is inadequate to describe and reconstruct individual lives and events in terms of macro-processes using the rhetoric of the distanced observer. It is not enough to describe the interaction of variables. Rather, the aim is to capture the way these variables are understood and dealt with (including the contradictions) in the practices and concepts of individual experiences. How do people struggle with the forces which appear to enclose them? A narrative account is needed because the macro-processes do not fully account for what is being observed at the small scale. There is a difference between causal and interpretive statements. Causal explanation deals with the interrelationship of variables at a distance, in the abstract, removed from the specificity of events. Interpretation in the form of thick description (Geertz 1973; see also Sinclair 2000) attempts to include accounts of the contingent and historical specificity of events.

This emphasis on narrative is also important because of the public interest in the human scale of the past. The popularity of Spindler's book on the Alpine Ice Man is remarkable. It demonstrates the public fascination with the detailed and the individualized. It demonstrates the public need to sense a human scale in the vast expanses of archaeological time. The narrative windows which we construct around individual events and lives create a point of entry into the long term for the nonspecialist.

CONCLUSION

For much of its data, archaeology can only give a general systemic view; it can describe the flow of cultures or systems, the rise of complexity, the collapse of states and interregional networks of exchange. The data are often too scanty to allow anything else, and the ability of archaeologists to paint grand syntheses with a broad brush is impressive (for a recent argument in favor of "grand narrative," see Sherratt 1995). But there are moments in archaeology which capture the public imagination when very rich and detailed information is found: an Ice Man, a Pompeii, a Shang tomb, or a Tutankhamun. We should not scoff at this: the popularization derives from a fascination we all share. It invites narrative. It provides a window into the workings of the grand systems which we so painstakingly monitor for so much of our archaeological lives.

It is not only the sensational finds which allow windows into the fine grain of temporal sequences, however. Indeed, it could be argued that archaeologists are better equipped at studying specific moments and daily rhythms than larger scale processes. Archaeologists can reconstruct in great detail the sequences of actions behind the knapping of a flint nodule. Knowledge of the sequences involved in making and firing a pot may be understood down to a few minutes. Seasonal activities may be constructed from tooth growth or shell middens. Medieval archaeologists may be able to reconstruct the daily routes from house to field, and the weekly passages from house to church and back again. In many ways, it is the human scale which is the stuff of archaeology; it is the larger scale which is more distanced from archaeological material.

I would argue, however, that few approaches in archaeology adequately recognize that different types of account are needed at different scales. Archaeologists have developed effective techniques for dealing with the large scale and the long term. When it comes to individuals and events, there have been few successful studies. Rather than abstract mathematical modeling of diversity and contingency, attention must be paid to lived experience. Rather than focusing on agency in terms of the resources (symbolic and material) needed to act and on the hegemonic control of action, attention can be directed to the intentionality and uncertainty of daily life. Rather than accounts of "being" which remain materialist, dichotomous, and disembodied, narrative interpretations are needed of the specificity of meaningful action (Gero 1991; Kus 1992). Grand syntheses of the long term may not be commensurable with small narratives of lived moments (Marquardt 1992), but both are needed in an archaeology which accepts roles for intentionality, uncertainty, and individual creativity in human behavior.

10

An Archaeology of the Four-Field Approach in Anthropology in the United States

My dominant reaction to the question of the four-field approach in anthropology in the United States is "why only four fields?" A related reaction is "why should I as an archaeologist accept anthropology as an umbrella discipline or as a meta-discourse?"

Of course, my response to this issue is as an archaeologist trained in Britain and Europe, where archaeology is more closely tied to history. By this I mean that most archaeology departments in Europe are not in anthropology or ethnography departments. Rather, they are within departments or schools of history, or classics, or Oriental studies. The training of students and their background are commonly in the arts and humanities rather than in the social sciences. In many cases, independent archaeology departments teach their own degrees without a larger umbrella (such as anthropology), but the institutional ties of departments and museums are often with history in some form.

The location of archaeology within anthropology within the United States is itself a quirk of history, as much as is the location of archaeology close to history and classics in Europe. The historical conditions which led to the varied alignments of disciplines in different parts of the world include both the internal developments of the disciplines and their alliances, as well as the wider political context. Within Europe, archaeology is tied historically and politically with the project of the nation-state. In the United States it is tied to colonialism and empire (Trigger 1984). As a result, in Europe, archaeology has a self-sufficient status linked to history and the invention of tradition. In the United States, the relationship with the precolonial past is more complex and is made relevant through anthropology.

In the second half of the twentieth century, archaeology in the United States came further to embrace the mantle of anthropology, and make a virtue of it. That was in the context of universalizing science and cross-cultural generalization. There are those in archaeology in the United States who still hold to such schemes—particularly selectionist and behavioral archaeologists. Indeed it is probably still the case that most archaeologists in the United States retain some version of this vision. My own comments are thus highly idiosyncratic in this United States context, since I do not take for granted such universalizing aims and I have not been part of a tradition in which anthropology has some form of natural right to define archaeology.

But I would argue that there is an emergent and different historical context in which both anthropology and archaeology find themselves—which is that of globalism, and the new forces of plurality and reflexivity (Hodder 1999a). In my view, the link between archaeology and anthropology in the United States is being undermined by changes in wider historical and specific disciplinary contexts. As for the wider context, the archaeological past has come to play a variety of social roles, from the commercialism of the heritage industry to identity formation among a diversity of social groups. Universalizing accounts, which might link archaeology to a generalizing (and outdated view of) anthropology, seem less relevant. As for the specific disciplinary contexts of archaeology and anthropology, there is again diversity. Archaeology as a discipline is both more mature and more fragmented than it was. It has too many kaleidoscopes of variation to be encompassed within one "anthropological" scheme.

Again I must stress the idiosyncracy of my view. While I think that many archaeologists, including many in the United States, would agree that archaeology is more internally divided than it has ever been, many would decrie this situation and would argue for a need to restore order and unity. For example, Schiffer (2000:vii–viii) fears that archaeology might become like sociocultural anthropology with no "common ground, no core set of concepts and principles…I hoped that we could, at all costs, avoid that unpleasant outcome." My own view is that this diversity is beneficial for the discipline; it creates dynamism and pushes research forward. I feel fortified in my view on this by work on other disciplines, such as the studies by Galison in physics. Galison (1997) sees physics as divided into multiple cultures which engage in a trading zone of competing ideas and approaches. The "whole" of physics is actually an unstable but productive compromise between groups with different assumptions, methods, and aims.

The variation in archaeology today extends across a wide spectrum, and many volumes have appeared recently trying to capture this diversity in theory and method (e.g., Ucko 1995). At one end are those archaeologists who hold to the natural science image of the discipline, to positivism, and the anthropological label. These approaches claim a "scientific archaeology." They include processual, cognitive processual, behavioral,

and selectionist views. At the other end there is a bewildering variety of post-processual views including feminist, phenomenological, dialectical, and hermeneutic approaches. Post-processual archaeology is a term that emerged in Britain in the 1980s as a reaction against processual archaeology. Although it can be seen to encompass a wide diversity of positions, many were and are held together by a critique of the positivism of processual archaeology, by an embrace of history and agency, and by an engagement with meaning and practice. As post-processual archaeology has moved on from its early phase of critique, the degree of diversity has increased, and other terms, such as interpretive or reflexive archaeology are now often used (Thomas 2001; Tilley 1993).

The variation of approach in archaeology is important in the context of the debate about the four-field approach. The behavioralists for example reject much of sociocultural anthropology, especially those parts that might be tinged with post-modernism or which concern themselves with meaning, agency, or discourse. It seems to me that similar tensions between archaeologists and sociocultural anthropology abound in the U.S.—there seems to be a real faultline that is thinly held together by tradition, training, placement issues, etc. It seems to me much healthier if in such contexts the arbitrariness of the historical connection between archaeology and anthropology is admitted, and the disciplines, or parts of them, go their own ways and forge new alliances.

There are many ways in which one might argue for major harm done by the location of archaeology within anthropology within the United States. Some of the problems concern the restraint in such a context on the development of debates with other disciplines, such as debates between archaeology and history (achieved more effectively in historical archaeology—Morris 2000). But also the development of archaeological science has been impeded. I refer here to the numerous techniques and skills described as archaeometry. There appear to be few graduate programs in archaeological science in the United States in anthropology departments. It is common, if not usual, for these to exist as Masters programs in the UK and Europe, and in my view this is a very important development. The use of scientific techniques in archaeology (such as XRF, SEM, micromorphology, ancient DNA, etc.) depends in my view on the training of researchers competent in both the techniques and the problems to which they can be applied. I am sure that the reasons for the paucity of such training in anthropology programs in the United States are complex, but the location of archaeology within sociocultural departments and within social and behavioral funding agencies may be relevant. Also in the United States there seems to have been an unhelpful confusion between scientific archaeology and archaeological science.

So it seems that some parts of archaeology would be better served either by separating from anthropology or by aligning themselves to human geneticists, the natural sciences, biology, behavioral sciences, and so on.

The distance between some archaeology and sociocultural anthropology often seems great. For example, recently Schiffer (1999: 9), a behavioralist, noted in his new book that "readers may be nonplussed at the absence in the new theory of much vocabulary...such as meaning, sign, symbol, intention, motivation, purpose, goal, attitude, value, belief, norm, function, mind, and culture. Despite herculean efforts in the social sciences to define these often ethnocentric or metaphysical notions, they remain behaviorally problematic and so are superfluous in the present project." The gap here between behavioral archaeology and anthropology appears cavernous. Most of sociocultural anthropology seems devoid of interest for Schiffer. Given such views and divergences of opinion it seems unhelpful to continue to pretend that archaeology is anthropology, or indeed that it has anything to do with anthropology at all.

However, other approaches in archaeology focus exactly on the themes which are discarded by Schiffer and which are of such interest to sociocultural anthropologists. In particular, most post-processual archae-

ologists have forged close links to many in the social sciences. This trend is seen, for example, in the new *Journal of Social Archaeology*, which aims to cover themes with broad interest in the social sciences. For example, its first issue included an interview with Arjun Appadurai, and its editorial board has archaeologists but includes many others such as Judith Butler, Sherry Ortner, Bryan Turner, and Sylvia Yanagisako. There are perhaps many reasons why such authors from a range of human sciences should be interested in archaeology. At least one such reason might be the widespread fascination in the human and social sciences with the metaphor of archaeology. The idea of carrying out "an archaeology" of contemporary discourses, institutions, cultural traits, and so on has different resonances in different contexts. But the widespread use of the metaphor suggests that an archaeology of anthropology might be feasible—and thus that archaeology could provide a meta-discourse for anthropology rather than the other way round.

As an example of the cross-cutting alliances between post-processual archaeology and mainstrean social-cultural anthropology in the United States, I would like if I may to refer to my own personal experience. I have never taken an anthropological course (by which I mean a course taught in an anthropology department) in my life (though I have taught many), and I do not see myself as an "anthropologist" as that term is defined by many archaeologists in the United States. And yet I feel very much at home in the Department of Social and Cultural Anthropology at Stanford, where I now teach. In fact I feel much more at home there than I would in most archaeology departments. Why is this? Sun, sail, and cocktails certainly help, but the main reason is undoubtedly that we read the same books and have the same theoretical and methodological interests even though we supposedly are in different disciplines. On the whole, I feel that we can talk to each other better and that we have more in common than I do with an archaeologist who is a selectionist or behaviorist or hardline processualist. The starting assumptions are the same, whereas everything is alien when I talk to my non-post-processual colleagues in archaeology. I have a similar experience when in a psychology seminar on agency or in a geography seminar on landscape—there is a commonality of major texts and orientation.

I believe that this personal experience of mine is part of a larger pattern, which is that post-processual archaeology is much closer to mainstream sociocultural anthropology in the United States than it is to some other forms of archaeology, and that it has common interests with groups in other disciplines. Another example of the forging of new alliances that cut across archaeology, anthropology, and adjacent disciplines occurs with material culture studies. For some years now there has been a convergence of interests and a unifying of literature around the theme of material culture. At University College, London, there is even a subdepartment of material culture that includes both archaeologists and anthropologists. One can then develop a new vision of anthropology and the social sciences in which groups of co-workers come together around themes and perspectives such as social agency and meaning (Stanford), material culture (London), or selectionism. In each group the alliances are in different directions and they extend out to include researchers outside the traditional four fields, such as those in history, psychology, cultural studies, or biology. In such a context there is no need for a meta-discourse provided by anthropology or by any other one discipline. Rather, strategic alliances can be made with biology, psychology, art history, or classics. But in each case the alliance is founded on area studies (such as Near Eastern studies) or themes and topics such as selectionism, behaviorism, phenomenology, feminism, and so on. This would allow people of like mind and like interest to engage with each other in fruitful ways, and

without the constraints of "big brother" anthropology.

Of course, the danger of creating alliances of this type is that students trained within one of these areas, themes, or topics would end up narrow and unaware of the full range of argument across the human sciences. It is for this reason that I would prefer an organizational structure in universities which retained disciplines much as they stand for teaching, but which rewarded still further realignment across disciplines in terms of advanced teaching and research.

In conclusion, there are clearly many strains in the current relationship between archaeology and anthropology in the United States. I have not mentioned a further important factor—the professionalization of archaeology in cultural resource management. This development often creates tensions between field practitioners and "anthropological archaeologists." In the current state of diversity of archaeology and anthropology in the United States, there are many signs that indicate that it is in archaeology's best interests to forge disciplinary relationships that are unfettered by the four-field scheme. While the individual disciplines of the four fields may continue to provide a useful framework for teaching, advanced teaching and research have already moved in directions characterized by fragmentation and the formation of new interdisciplinary alliances beyond the boundaries of the four fields. In this more complex, open, and fluid world of ever-changing intellectual alliances, the major challenges are organizational and infrastructural. How is it possible to preserve some semblance of disciplinarity while at the same time allowing for changing allegiances and changing interest groups? Apart from its nostalgic value, the four-field scheme offers only restrictions in such a context.

IV. Dialogue and Engagement with Prehistory

A final set of papers deals with new interpretations of prehistoric sites and monuments. The interpretations focus on agency, power/knowledge, and the development of societies through the negotiation of, or dialogue between, subject positions. They lead toward a recognition that archaeological interpretation and debate need to involve engagement with stakeholder groups.

Chapter 11 responds to debate and criticism regarding my earlier (1990) volume *The Domestication of Europe* in which I argued that the concept of the *domus* was central to the adoption of farming and a settled way of life in the Near East and Europe. The aim had been to argue that the onset of farming could not just be studied in terms of economies and climates, but that it involved equally important social and conceptual shifts. In this paper I emphasize the *domus* as a "seamless web" between economy, society, and culture. Thus the *domus* is dialectical—a unity with internal tensions. It is a set of practices, but also an idea or an orientation embedded within "objective conditions." Its duration is the result of its generality, narrativity, and practical nondiscursiveness.

The *domus* also plays a part in Chapter 12, which looks at the Haddenham sites in eastern England where I worked on a long-term project with Chris Evans. As in Chapter 9, the focus is on how a small window into long-term change can identify some of the tensions through which people lived their lives. The dialectical tensions are grouped around the gradual emergence over millennia of a separation of "wet" from "dry" at the fen edge. These long-term cycles take us from the Neolithic, through later prehistory, and into the Roman period. The separation between "wet" and "dry" takes on renewed significance in more recent historical periods as the fens came to be drained and transformed by wealthy dryland farmers from the south, causing much social conflict. So the meaning of things (this time "wetness") changes through time in different social conditions.

If our interpretation of wet and dry at the fen edge in eastern England is influenced by our knowledge of recent historical events, it can also be shown that many of our interpretations of the landscape in British prehistory are embedded within historical and contemporary notions of landscape. Chapter 13 was written as a review of Mark Edmonds's (1999) *Ancestral Geographies of the Neolithic: Landscapes, Monuments and Memory*, but it includes a wider discussion of recent British prehistoric research dealing with landscapes. The chapter argues that some British prehistory has an unwitting nationalist and elitist nostalgia. These comfortable and familiar interpretations are not subject to critique because of the lack of diversity and multivocality in British prehistoric archaeology (but see Parker Pearson and Ramilisonina 1998). When looked at from the point of view of the cultural diversity with which one is familiar in, say, California, some of the pre-histories reviewed seem like comfortable English accounts bolstering the national imaginary.

The "origins" of farming are often discussed as if they had an event-like character that could be linked causally to other variables. Centralization, sedentism, agglomeration, and domestication are often looked at in similar ways. But what of the small negotiations in the practices of daily life that lie behind these major, highly visible changes? Chapter 14 looks at the formation of large settled villages or towns in the Near East and Europe in terms of practice theory and memory. It provides detailed accounts of floor deposition practices, and thick descriptions of the continuities in individual houses. The chapter argues that socialization through daily practice in the house, plus memory construction, were important aspects of social regulation during these periods. The daily negotiation of space and memory within the house can be see as creating the possibilities for larger-scale settlement agglomeration, and for the more event-like changes we associate with the "origins" of farming and settled life. Causality is here distributed or dispersed into the daily practices of the mass.

As one picks apart the changes associated with early farming and the formation of large settlements, it is fascinating to note that different parts of society were not in step with each other. At Çatalhöyük, the art and symbolism show little or no evidence of any inter-est in or importance of domesticated plants and animals (Chapter 15). Ritual, the social process, and "art" and symbolism seem largely concerned with wild resources. We seem to be seeing a dialectical process whereby social prestige remains tied up with wild resources, even though domesticated plants and animals are increasingly important. Ultimately, of course, domesticated resources come to be so important that social prestige becomes very centered on their control. But initially the new forms of accumulation are used to bolster an older system of prestige. This dialectical relationship between economy and social power develops very slowly, over millennia.

Chapter 15 asks questions that have been formulated by archaeologists, even though many of the issues it raises, such as the role of women in early agriculture, are of interest to other groups such as the Goddess followers. In the final chapter in this volume, Chapter 16, we return full circle to the globalization issues raised at the start. To what extent is it socially and ethically acceptable to ask and answer questions from within the academy, without reference to diverse stakeholder groups? This final chapter brings together the different parts of the volume in that it links questions of multivocality to specific interpretations of prehistory. It argues that it is not only archaeologists who should "set the agenda" (Yoffee and Sherratt 1993), and it reinforces the view that archaeologists are active members of society.

11

The *Domus*
Some Problems Reconsidered

As we came to the top of the mound in the heat of midday, we blinked at the dark trench cut down perhaps 15 meters. The ladder leaning against the section seemed dangerously vertical. Gradually our eyes became accustomed to a remarkable sight—on the section wall facing us, the house walls which had been cut through seemed to rise the full height of the mound. Closer inspection identified floors and infill deposits at different levels within the gigantically tall houses, and the walls themselves had clearly been built by building later walls on earlier walls. And yet the continuity in the use of space was quite remarkable. At another point on the mound, a street had been sectioned which again seemed to have continued in use, endlessly resurfaced, from the bottom to the top of the mound. We had come to visit the aceramic Neolithic tell at Aşıklı Höyük on the eastern edge of the Konya Plain in central Turkey. What we had seen stretched credulity beyond its limits. What type of social system could produce such rigid continuities over such long periods? Surely in any society of which we are aware today households expand and contract in size, they create new alliances and have changing needs, and all this variation is expressed in the changing size and form of buildings? There seemed to be no building "phases" on the site, at least if the one sounding was anything to go by. The mound was built from single houses, continuously reused and relived in through long periods of time.

I will return to the issue of continuity throughout this paper, but the initial point I wish to make about the Aşıklı Höyük experience concerns our implicit assumptions about the relationship between architecture and society. The reason I found the tall houses difficult to cope with was because I saw houses as reflections or expressions, however active, of social form or social process. Thus the house should ebb and flow with the changing fortunes of social units defined, at the house level, primarily in terms of kinship. I came to see later that this privileging of the social against the material was an underlying problem, both in my writing about the *domus* (Hodder 1990) and in much archaeological discussion of the social meanings of built forms. Perhaps the Aşıklı houses did not "represent" or "express" social units, but formed those units. Perhaps it was residence in the house which defined the social group. Perhaps the houses stayed the same, built on top of earlier houses, because social groups defined themselves in relation to a fixed form—if the house did not remain the same there would be no basis for the social group.

Recent preliminary work at Çatalhöyük has confirmed the general impression of houses built on top of each other, using the same walls, over long periods of time during the ceramic Neolithic. Here there is more variation, with midden or courtyard areas later built upon and earlier houses being transformed in form and function. And yet surviving sections at the site in places show continuous walls rising many meters. In southeastern Europe, Tringham (1991) has suggested an overall trend during the Neolithic and Chalcolithic. Houses are initially placed directly over earlier houses, but gradually through time they are placed to the side and other strategies concerned with continuity are used. For example, Tringham suggests that the burning of houses is often intentional and can be seen as a cleansing or ritual closure. Bailey (1990) has noted that the replacement of houses in the fourth millennium tells in Bulgaria is inversely proportional to the frequencies of house models. It is as if continuities created by the physical reuse of houses can also be dealt with by the handing on of heirlooms and by rituals of closure and renewal.

No one living on the upper levels of Aşıklı or Çatal would have been able to see the tall houses with their continuous walls reaching to the bottom of the mounds. The continuity of walls is visible only after the event to the surgical archaeologist. The tall walls are presumably an unintended consequence of a set of practices which concern the rebuilding of later walls on earlier walls and the retention of house forms. The functions of rooms may well have changed through time, and initial work at Çatalhöyük has provided some evidence of this. The main aim was thus not functional but architectural continuity. The practices which reused walls and inserted new floors on rubble and infill materials within those walls were creating a continuity with the past. In reconstructing the building, the practices constructed a history. Within the continual walls things changed, events occurred, artifacts were passed on, rituals took place. But all these events were markers physically channeled into one sequence, written into a history.

The research question underlying the use of the term *domus* is why do houses (or in northwestern Europe their tomb equivalents) play such a central role in the archaeology of the earlier Neolithic in Europe and the Near East? Why are houses often large or elaborate and why are the domestic ceramics often dec-

orated? The first part of an adequate answer to such questions is to understand the house as a "seamless web" (Latour 1988b) linking the material and the cultural. The practices that produced the continuous walls of Aşıklı and Çatal were part of the economic production and social reproduction of a group which also passed on artifacts, held rituals, and buried ancestors beneath floors. The term *domus* attempts to capture the dual nature of the house as material and economic on the one hand and social and ideational on the other. The *domus* was both metaphor and mechanism.

The second part of an adequate answer concerns the specific ways in which histories were created in the rebuilding of houses and in the practices and rituals of continuity with which they were surrounded. In the earlier Neolithic, burials occur under floors in the Near East and at sites such as Lepenski Vir in southeastern Europe. This, and the examples given above, indicate the importance of creating a specific history based on individual houses. All this creates a long-term group with its own memory and practices. The art and sculpture at Çatalhöyük are inward looking. There is little evidence of decoration on the outside of houses, which are closely crammed into the settlement with "courtyard" areas used as large refuse pits. The art in the houses would have been difficult to see from the outside since entry is through the roof at the farthest end of the house. There are also many differences between the art and sculpture found in the different houses at Çatalhöyük. It remains to be seen whether the same differences between practices in individual houses are retained through time. But it seems possible that the consequence was the identity of a small house-using group, with its own culture and its own history.

Given this, what are the "objective conditions" within which the *domus* was reproduced? The term *objective conditions* is here taken from Bourdieu (1977) and refers to the "world out there" to which individual actors have to accommodate. It includes both material and economic factors and the social relations in which such factors are embedded. Certainly intensive hunting and gathering and early agriculture involve increased inputs of labor and greater dependence between individuals as they jointly invest in clearings, fields, artifacts from which a return is delayed. It becomes necessary to hold the group together over longer periods of time. But there is not, in this description, any a priori reason why the house should become the focus of joint labor and its continuities the focus of longer-term dependencies between people. Certainly, early agriculture involved the need to create histories, but why through the medium of the house?

Part of the answer to such questions might involve a consideration of one aspect of the objective conditions—that is the particular technologies involved in early agriculture in the Near East. The early cereals required intensive joint labor in harvesting, threshing, winnowing, sieving. Grinding stones and ovens occur on early sites and while it is not certain that the earliest sites saw bread being made, cereal grinding and baking may have been involved. Land cannot have been a major limiting factor at this time, and so the main problem would have been the relations between people and their labor—could adequate labor be brought together at the right moments and over considerable spans of time so that individuals could depend on obtaining a return from labor? At least parts of the production process which transformed cereals into food, such as grinding and cooking, would have been well suited to be undertaken in the house, and since the size of group involved in joint labor in early agriculture could have been small, the domestic unit was appropriate.

It would be of interest to compare the role of the house in other areas of indigenous agricultural development to see if the type of technologies involved had an impact on the role of the house. In the central Americas, maize does not require threshing and it was often not ground into flour. The domestic context may have been able to play different roles in different areas. Similarly, domestication in the Near East comes to involve animals which have to be separated from wild herds. In this practice of separation and tending away from the wild, an opposition is set up between domestic and wild which may reinforce the importance of the domestic unit and of the house as metaphor.

The practices of early agriculture also involve storage—at least of seed grain and grain or flour for consumption. Storage pits occur in early Holocene sites, often in or near houses. Certainly the house provides a convenient and well-guarded location for the separation and identification of goods "owned" by productive units. Reproduction, too, becomes of major concern where limits to growth are provided by labor rather than land, and certainly the household is well suited as a location for the rearing and nurturing of children.

I have argued that early agriculture, at least of the type found in the Near East, involved a suite of practices which were appropriately centered in the house. I am not arguing for necessary or materialist relations, since none of the practices has to be located in the house. I will mention below other factors which made the house the center of group production and reproduction. But agriculture, which largely functions at the domestic scale, is likely to encourage an emphasis on the house, and as agriculture intensifies the organization of production may become less house centered—and indeed in Europe later in the Neolithic, the importance of the house appears to decline with the introduction of the exploitation of the plough and secondary animal products (Hodder 1990). Thus it was in small-scale agriculture in the earlier Neolithic, involving intensive food preparation and separation of domestic from wild animals, involving storage and where labor rather than land was the main limiting constraint, that the house became an appropriate location for economic as well as social and cultural processes.

The main problem was how to form and hold together small groups over the long term, without coercion and without modern technologies of power. How was it possible to "bind" people together? In part the answer to this is just that people were bound together by their joint investment in agricultural labor. But even in small communities there are those at times fully involved in reproduction while others grow old or are too young to work in the fields and so on. How can this group as a whole come to see itself as a "bound" group? And if Bender (1978) is right in arguing for social differentiation at early phases, the problem for individual units of production and reproduction was to enhance their own unit at the expense of others, through exchange, increased production, ritual superiority, and the like. In a competitive process the aim was to bind people in a small local group into a common strategy.

The house was an appropriate practical location for the binding of people and for the creation of a common history. The joint project of house building and rebuilding, the activities framed within its historical walls, the rituals specific to each house, the heirlooms passed down from the ancestors buried beneath the walls: all these practices created a frame within which people were bound, literally and by ritual ties and historical associations—a common past. People came to be bound between the walls, metaphorically domesticated as they also had to become practically domesticated. The walls at Aşıklı and Çatal had to remain the same because it was the historical associations of those bound within them that created a group continuous through time.

Perhaps more can be said about the particular social forms which clung so rigidly to the *domus* as a primary generating principle. In a somewhat evolutionary vein, Lévi-Strauss (1983, 1987, 1991) has defined house societies which have a specific form of social organization. They have a type of social structure which is a hybrid or transition between kin-based and class-based societies. As well as kinship, other factors such as wealth, power, and status begin to be important in the formation of social groups. Lévi-Strauss's distinction between elementary and complex structures is here being blurred. Elementary structures of kinship have positive marriage rules which specify the category of kin from which a spouse must be taken, and so choice of spouse is based on kinship alone. There are thus networks of marriage exchange which give coherence and solidarity to society. In complex systems, on the other hand, non-kinship factors such as wealth, power, and class determine choice of spouse. Social integration is now provided by political and economic institutions. House societies still see the world in kinship terms but economic and political considerations come to play an increasingly important role.

It is not necessary to embrace the evolutionary implications of Lévi-Strauss's model to see the potential importance of the idea that "the house" can provide the basis for non-kinship relations and even for the construction of kinship groupings. In a recent volume devoted to a consideration of Lévi-Strauss's hypothesis (Carsten and Hugh-Jones 1995), examples are provided of house societies without marked stratification. The main criteria of house societies are rather continuity and the passing on of wealth. Lévi-Strauss argues that the house is a grouping which endures through time. Continuity is produced by the succession and replacement of humans but also by passing on fixed or movable property and by handing down special names and titles. In many of the cases discussed in Carsten and Hugh-Jones (1995) ritualistic property and heirlooms are important in creating continuity, as is the right to make and use ceremonial ornaments. These sacred regalia or ritual roles which are passed down are likely to vary from house to house as part of the attempt to maintain separate rights and identities (cf. Barth 1987).

One of the most distinctive aspects of the elaborately painted and sculpted houses at Çatalhöyük is their variability. The layout of each house shows some uniformity but the scenes and sculptures vary considerably. Little work has yet been completed on whether houses retain styles of ornamentation over time, but certainly some plaster reliefs, such as the facing leopards, were frequently resurfaced. In some cases there is evidence of replastering walls up to 50 times. Together with the evidence for the reuse of walls, the overall emphasis on continuity of distinct houses is apparent. I have already noted that Tringham makes the same emphasis for southeastern Europe. As yet we do not know the kinship relations between those who used the same house over many generations, although analysis of the bones from beneath the floors at Aşıklı and Çatal may provide some information in this regard. But it certainly seems possible that social relations in these sites were not based solely or primarily on kinship. The importance of the continuity of the physical building and the centrality of ritual at Çatalhöyük imply that practical and ritual processes may have formed the basis of the house group. It is also possible that the increasingly intensive use of domesticated resources was associated with shifts in size of the smaller-scale units of production and changes in the division of labor within those units. Even if such realigned groupings were based on kinship, the formation of new kinship relations as the basis of the house group may have been underpinned by other factors, practical and ritual.

I have noted that, at least in Europe, the importance of the house declines in the later periods of the Neolithic (Hodder 1990) and so it is tempting to agree with Lévi-Strauss's evolutionary stage of house societies between elementary and complex forms of social structure. Certainly in the late Neolithic, new forms of power based on exchange rather than descent and gradually leading to greater centralization of political focus imply a breakdown of the continuity model. However, house societies occur in a variety of different social contexts (Carsten and Hugh-Jones 1995), and they lead to very different social forms after the earlier Neolithic in Europe and the Near East. Perhaps all we can say with some security is that initially in the Near East and southeastern Europe, houses are inward looking and continuities through time are rigidly adhered to. But through time, burial increasingly occurs outside the house, ceramics which are passed between houses

are decorated, and more and more emphasis is placed on the facades or entrances of houses—the going in and the coming out (Hodder 1990). The importance of the house ultimately declines as relationships between groups and their political coordination increase. The house societies of the Near East and Europe thus play a particular role in the development from kinship-based societies to those for which kinship may still have been central but in which other dimensions of power came to be significant.

So far I have argued that the *domus* involved an economic, social, and cultural emphasis on the house and its continuity through time. I have further suggested that it was reproduced because it was an appropriate practical and symbolic model in a certain set of "objective conditions" which included the practices of a particular form of early agriculture and social relations based on kinship in the domestic unit but increasingly expanding to include other forms of power. Thus from the Near East and southeastern Europe to the Bandkeramik of Central Europe, and even to Orkney where houses and tombs of a local style look so like each other, the house occurs as central because it is appropriate to the particular set of conditions set up by early European agriculture. Wherever early European agriculture develops in the context of small-scale social units, so the house is a central social and symbolic focus as well the basis for the organization of production. Everywhere, people are domesticated through the practices and meanings of the house.

As already mentioned, the house model may be appropriate to a given set of conditions but those conditions do not determine the use of that model. Thus as well as considering the objective conditions it is also necessary to evaluate the loose historical ties between groups in Neolithic Europe and the Near East to see the spread of a specific idea. I have argued (Hodder 1990) for historical connections between different parts of Europe and for the spread of particular aspects of the *domus* over large areas. For example, many of the ceramic traits and symbolism of houses (e.g., use of bucrania) occur in Anatolia and southeastern Europe. In Central Europe a particular emphasis on long linear houses with elaborate entrances develops and shows historical continuities with the linear tombs of northwestern Europe.

The objective conditions within which house societies developed in the Neolithic are sufficient to explain neither the durability and reproduction of the general emphasis on houses nor the specific forms that the houses took. It is also necessary, therefore, to consider the historical development of a set of structuring principles embedded within houses, their uses and symbolic meanings. In the most general terms these principles concern the house as creating continuities between past and present, in all realms—economic, social, and ritual. A linked idea is that by being embedded within a social group with long-term memory within a house, individuals became "domesticated." In more specific terms the principles concern, for example, the importance of cleansing the house with fire at the ends of periods of use. Such deliberate burning is as common in the Neolithic of southeastern Europe as it is in the burial mounds of northwestern Europe. It should be clear from what I have already argued in this paper that these structuring principles are not just "ideas" in peoples' heads. They may not have been always consciously expressed, and they are as much ingrained in practices as they are symbolically meaningful.

I wish to suggest three reasons for the durability and reproduction of these structuring principles beyond their appropriateness in a given set of conditions. The first is that the principles lasted for millennia and survived translation into numerous contexts because they were very general and simply defined. The very generality and simplicity of the principles meant that they could be applied in a variety of different contexts. We would thus expect to see the same principles reappearing wherever loose historical ties existed between groups and provided the

medium for the transmission of change. Thus the emphasis on the continuity of the house could be translated into any small-scale society which was attempting to intensify domestic production and create its own history, whether it was hunter-fisher-gatherer (Lepenski Vir) or full farming (Çatalhöyük). It could be applied to dense villages in southeastern Europe and Anatolia and in the scattered homesteads of the Bandkeramik. It could be translated into houses for the dead in societies with more dispersed and less permanent settlement in northwestern Europe, where houses themselves were not long term enough to provide a focus for the handing on of rights and duties. But if the *domus* endured for millennia partly because it was general and simple, how can we explain the disconnected reappearance of the same principles without apparent historical connection? For example, I have already mentioned the Orkney evidence. Here houses and tombs and henges were built with common forms and with common principles (such as the importance of square stone-lined hearths). The emphasis on the house is certainly there, but its particular manifestation seems independent and distinctive. Another example of the presumably disconnected appearance of similar traits in similar conditions is provided by the evidence for female breasts on house walls in Turkey and southern Central Europe. The examples from Çatalhöyük claimed by Mellaart (1967) are supported by clay figurines with naked breasts in domestic contexts. The examples from Lake Constance are more clearly breasts and are associated with a wooden building with other painted clay reliefs (Arnold 1993). The latter are dated to the Pfyn culture. The enormous spans of time and space with which we are here dealing suggest that something other than the diffusion of traits is involved.

It is often the case that general principles are transformed locally and cannot be explained by direct borrowing. Unless it is argued that some psychological predisposition is triggered by the same objective conditions some other mechanism must be found. It may be appropriate to consider general principles reproduced in myth and folklore. Thus the general principle gets passed on in a nonmaterial form and "resurfaces" in the material record in often different guises, each a local translation of the general into the particular. The loose historical associations which reproduce the *domus* thus occur at the level of general myth rather than solely in terms of the borrowing of specific practices.

The second reason for the long-term durability of the house model of and for society in Neolithic Europe and the Near East is that it has an internal logic. By this I do not mean that the *domus* principles determined the direction of cultural change for millennia. Rather, I mean that social change had to be made sense of in terms of existing principles or their transformation. Another way to say the same thing is that we live in narratives (Hodder 1993; Ricoeur 1984). The story of our lives has to unfold, it has to have a certain coherence, the different parts fitting together into a whole which is continually being rewritten. The building of house walls on earlier walls, the burning or closing off in order to end a period of use, the blocking of megalithic burial monuments are all acts which create narrative relations, beginning and ending, constructing histories within a particular frame of walls, contesting stories. Thus the *domus* endured not simply because it could be widely applied in different contexts but because as it was applied in different situations the new had to relate to the old within a narrative. For example, at the site of Haçilar in Turkey in the sixth millennium the earlier importance of symbolism within the house appears to decline as relations between houses and wider community relations increase in importance. The elaborate symbolism is now transferred from houses to domestic ceramics, still related to the house but more visible and mobile and able to be used in the relations between houses. In Central Europe, the same process is dealt with in a different but equally logical way. Here, houses become trapezoidal, and façades, entrances, and outer walls become more elaborate, as relations between houses become more important. In each case, after the event, and with long-term hindsight, the principles seem to unfold with an inexorable logic. But the sense of "logic" is only experienced as the coherence of a narrative linking past and present. It is a narrative character of human lived experience that creates the apparent temporal structures of the archaeologist's long-term gaze.

The third reason for the durability of the *domus* principles concerns the integration of idea and practice outlined earlier. As I have described it, the emphasis on the continuity of the house was embedded within a series of practices. These practices were partly economic, involving the long-term investment of labor, the grinding and cooking of foods. But they were also social, involving relations with ancestors, the passing down of artifacts, rights and privileges, and the control of esoteric knowledge. And they were also ritual, involving rites of closure and renewal. In all these practical activities the group was reproduced. But all that reproduction was framed or bound within the physical walls of the house. In a very practical way the events which took place in the house were "caught" within a sequence—at Aşıklı a hermetically closed sequence, constructing a time-space continuum lasting centuries or even millennia. The materiality of the house was used to construct a series of practices which, even if only because they were "framed," told a narrative of continuity.

Now, it has been widely recognized, from Pitt-Rivers to Bourdieu and Giddens that most practices are not discursively available. In other words, we may know what to do and be aware of the effectiveness of our actions but be less able to describe and explain them verbally. As Bourdieu demonstrates, the implicit nature of practices does not mean that they are any the less organized or socially meaningful. The principles are there, within the practices, even if we cannot describe them. It is this taken-for-granted character of practices which contributes to their durability. The principles of most practices are not brought out for conscious discussion except when contradictions or conflict emerge. For the most part, the principles remain undiscussed, the background to our daily lives, the residues of past consciousness.

The emphasis on principles embodied and practically embedded might be seen as contradicting the inference made above that the *domus* principles were handed down in myth. Certainly I would argue that the disconnected appearance throughout the European Neolithic of different versions of the same idea about the centrality and continuity of the house suggests that the idea may have been passed on in nonmaterial form, at least in some instances. But the conscious use of the principles in mythical narratives does not contradict their practical embeddedness. Ricoeur (1984) argues for a dialectical interaction between stories we tell about ourselves and our practical experience of time. In local contexts in the European Neolithic these spoken and lived narratives could take on a particular form, embedded within local myths and local traditions of practice. Another way to make the same point is to note that mythtelling is itself a practice in which general principles are used implicitly and explicitly. The principles might at different times be reproduced in different domains of practice (myth, burial, the house itself, etc.), appearing and reappearing in the archaeological record depending on the survivability of domains. Thus the durability of the *domus* principle was aided both by the general nature of the told stories about the continuity of the house and by the implicit nature of the practices which embodied those principles.

I have suggested how house societies in Europe might have been reproduced. On the one hand, the longevity of a set of objective material and social conditions provided the context for the long-term use and dissemination of house-centered practices and metaphors. But in answering the question "why did these particular material and social conditions last so long?" we have to consider the dialectical relations between the "conditions" and the actions which produced them. Thus, on the other hand, a set of generative principles for action, based on the house, had enormous longevity because of their appropriateness to the "conditions" which they produced, but also because they were general and simple, made narrative sense, and were embedded in implicit practices.

MEGALITHS AS THE CREATION OF HISTORY

I wish now to look at the linear tombs of northern Europe and the British Isles in order to explore the way in which the general house principles, and especially the continuity of the house, were translated into a particular form of practices suited to a particular set of economic and social conditions within the general frame set by small-scale mixed farming of European domesticates. As with the houses of southeastern Europe and the Near East I will argue that a "house" of people was created through the construction and experience of a common history.

As Kinnes (1992) as demonstrated for the long barrows of the British Neolithic, the tombs were often used for a series of activities spread over a long time. In some cases the burial use of megaliths was relatively brief (as at West Kennet and Hazleton North, Saville 1990). For the wood-chambered tombs such as Haddenham the numbers of burials are relatively small and the sequence of activities long (Hodder and Shand 1988). A brief summary of the sequence of activities at Haddenham will indicate the extent to which people participated in the project in different ways at different times, creating an overall narrative and building a common historical experience and memory.

A site was chosen, on a late Mesolithic settlement, and an orientation. Premortuary structure activities took place. A large tree, an oak, was chosen, cut, and specialist expertise used to split it longitudinally into planks up to 8 meters long. The wood was carried to the site, some of it several tons in weight, requiring joint labor. Turf was stripped from the burial area and mounded as the big uprights were set in the ground. The wooden chamber was built and the earth heaped up around it in an organized way, different soil being placed in different parts of the mound and the turf being carefully stacked. Over the years, as people died, the roof of the chamber was lifted off and the bodies placed inside. Sometimes their flesh and the sinews holding the bones together were cut. People stopped using the tomb and closed off the façade with a bank of earth which was added to as pots were deposited as offerings at the front. The last time the roof of the chamber was taken off, the big uprights were cut down and the front of the chamber filled with turf and small wood. The roof was replaced and the turf set alight. The whole thing burned very slowly and was then covered by an extension to the mound. Even then the use of the site was not finished. Burials were added over the years into the top of the mound.

I have outlined the sequence of activities at Haddenham because over many years many people would have been involved in different aspects of a common project. Although the uses of the tomb changed through time, persons with different skills (how to orient a tomb, how to split wood, how to deflesh a corpse) were involved and at times larger mobilization of labor was needed. People came together to carry out activities at the tomb and were thus caught in a joint project. They had a common history. The tomb itself framed a set of activities through which people were channeled. How they were channeled changed through time as the narrative changed. Indeed the use of the tomb can be seen as involving a continual tension. On the one hand there is the communal nature of the mound building and the open area in front of the façade. On the other hand, and apparently contradicted by the funnel entrance leading up to the tomb, there is no entry into the chamber from the front; access is blocked and few people are buried in the tomb. The communal group seems to be in dialectical tension with limited access to the tomb itself. The narrative history was thus a contested one, but even in the dialectic a common history was created. A continuity through time had been constructed.

Perhaps another way in which continuity

was emphasized can be seen in the mounding of earth and turf which is such a distinctive aspect of the Haddenham sequence, associated with its more communal phases. In particular, as part of the ending of the use of the chamber, turf was stacked in the entrance area and on top of the dismantled posts. This act, associated with the controlled burning of the chamber at the end of its use, and associated with the mounding of earth and pot deposition in front of the façade, can be interpreted as linked to the idea of burial and renewal. The link with burning reinforces the emphasis on ending, cleansing, and thus renewal. Even if renewal is not part of the interpretation of these rituals, the formal and elaborated acts of closure certainly suggest a concern with continuity.

An overall emphasis on continuity in the use of tombs in northern Europe has been suggested by Gramsch (1993, 1995). In particular he has documented the widespread occurrence of the placing of tombs on houses or in relation to domestic debris. Such evidence strengthens the link to the *domus,* but it also emphasizes the creation of history—the construction of links to the past. The association of burial with domestic discard may also have helped to create liminality through inversion—the sacred linked with the dangers and impurities of dirt. Life would thus be constructed out of death and decay. But it is my main concern here to emphasize the social construction of a common if contested history.

Gramsch notes the recurrent phenomenon of barrows erected upon layers of cultural material consisting of charcoal, sherds, flint and bone tools, animal bones, etc., but often also incorporating features such as pits, ditches, hearths, and postholes, and in some cases clear buildings. It is possible that such material is connected with ritual or construction use of the site prior to or during the building of the tomb. It has at times been suggested that the domestic material under barrows was intentionally dumped as part of ritual. Gramsch argues for a domestic interpretation of the pre-mound activity for a number of reasons. First, some of the cultural layers are very extensive, spreading well beyond the grave area (e.g., at Lindebjerg, Wollschow, and Wartin). Second, the composition of materials in the cultural layers is very similar to that from settlements not associated with barrows. The material includes hearths, and types of flint and pottery found frequently on settlements. Wall daub, clay discs, and bowls are found in the cultural layers but rarely with purely ritual features. In Denmark, beakers involved in façade rituals or placed in the graves are decorated more elaborately than sherds from both settlements and cultural layers beneath barrows. Third, in several cases (e.g., Bjornshølm and Mosegarden) the structures below the mounds indicate an occupation more substantial than short-lived ritual activities, including several huts, fireplaces, activity areas, and dump areas.

It would be possible to argue that the tombs were placed over houses and settlements not because of an emphasis on continuity but simply because the abandoned settlements offered cleared and unwanted land for tomb building. That some greater intentionality is involved is suggested by the high frequency of such placements and by their sometimes deliberate nature. For example, in several tombs in Kujavia, rubbish is heaped over the graves, and in some cases in Denmark, the graves are sited very precisely in relation to earlier buildings.

Large stone and wood tombs are associated in northern and western Europe with different types of economy. But in general terms the associated settlement patterns do not include large bounded, permanent sites with dense concentrations of large houses. Farming communities which lived away from the rich loess lands of Central Europe may have been rather more mobile or dispersed and small scale. The overall objective conditions that sustained the use of megalithic tombs over the long term included dispersed settlement in which houses themselves could not function to provide a focus for continuity. But a "house" of people could be constructed in the joint practices repeated over time at large, stable tombs.

But given the variety of economies within which megaliths functioned it is necessary to consider other factors too that sustained the longevity of their use. Bell (1992) has noted the ways in which ritual practices embody social relations and meanings. Certainly the practical construction of the tombs involved bodily participation between people who thus became tied to each other through their joint labor. Richards (1990) has described for Orkney the parallels between houses, tombs, and henges, and shown the way in which bodily movement and orientation in each referred to the other monument types. The repetition of similar practices in different domains would have underlined the emphasis on continuity. Certainly too, the practices at many tombs must have involved a distinction between communal events at the entrances and the experience of exclusion and separation in relation to the activities inside the burial chamber. Thus long-term relations are constructed, but so are the social divisions contained within them.

The durability of the tomb practices may have in part derived from their implicit, taken-for-granted nature. However, death rituals are likely to have occurred less frequently than many practices associated with houses. Even if annual or more frequent offerings were made at the tombs, the activities there are likely to have involved more conscious effort to reconstruct sequences of events and performance. There may have been debate about what was the "right" thing to do. The implications of this are that the tombs offered more opportunities than the houses for the manipulation and conscious framing of the structures of bodily experience.

That manipulation worked within a narrative constructed around the sequence of events at the tombs, which would have had both specific and general components—specific to the history of that particular tomb and general in relation to other widely found narratives and myths on which the particular made comment. Andrén (1993) has shown in a very different context the way in which burial practices can "tell a story" or be embedded in myth. Some of the components of these narratives may have concerned continuity and renewal. Whatever their content, they may have provided the bridge between infrequent practices at the tombs. But the embedding of ritual practices in myth or narrative produced another realm of practice in which general ideas could be retold and transformed over the long term.

CONCLUSION

In discussing Neolithic houses in Europe and the Near East it is unhelpful to separate too rigidly economic, social, and ritual factors. Rather, the houses are a context, a locale (Giddens 1984), in which economic, social, and ideological resources are mobilized in strategies focused on creating a long-term small-scale "house" of people. These different resources are thoroughly interwoven within practices. They form a seamless web (Latour 1988b).

I have argued that the *domus* or house was an appropriate context for practices concerned with creating long-term continuities within small-scale units depending largely on domestic production. Where houses themselves were not stable enough themselves to provide the fixity for the group, as they had been at Aşıklı Höyük, other strategies were followed such as the building of new houses near earlier ones in small clusters (as in the Bandkeramik cultures of the Rhineland) and such as the construction of tombs, sometimes over houses and settlements. The objective conditions in which house societies could develop in Europe and the Near East lasted a long time and this partly explains the longevity of the importance of the house in the archaeological record.

But lest our seamless web be broken and a materialism introduced, we should also ask why the objective conditions were themselves reproduced over such a long period. The answer to this question concerns the structuring principles through which the objective conditions were reproduced. These structuring principles concerned practices dealing with the continuity of the house, its boundedness, the burning and other rituals associated with closure, the importance of entrances, and so on. The reproduction of such general principles across enormous expanses of space and time has been understood in this paper in relation to three factors beyond the continuity of objective conditions.

First, the structuring principles were general and simple and could thus be applied in a variety of different specific contexts. As part of their generality they could occur in more than one domain. As a result they might exist in myth even if not present in any archaeologically recognizable material. Second, the general and simple principles were understood within a narrative structure. New developments had to be made coherent within an existing framework, or the framework had to be rewritten in order to accommodate change. As a result, sequences of cultural change involving the house appear to "unfold" with a certain internal "logic." Third, the principles were embedded in practices which were generally implicit and thus were continued as part of the unacknowledged conditions of action. Where the practices were largely ritual in nature, the greater opportunity for manipulation by dominant groups may have led to a further reason for the conservative retention of tradition over the long term.

12

The Wet and the Dry
Interpretive Archaeology in the Wetlands

The Fenlands of eastern England have long been studied by archaeologists and palaeoenvironmentalists. Their work has shown the gradual encroachment of the sea, the formation of lakes and backswamps and, ultimately, the formation of large-scale peatlands. The relationship between human settlement and the water's edge has always been studied in terms of economies, the use of resources, and environmental adaptation. But our knowledge of European legend and mythology suggests that the water's edge may have had deep symbolic significance in myth and ritual. It would be wrong, however, to assume that such water-related myths were unchanging and unchallenged. In this paper I describe archaeological research in the Haddenham area on the southern fen edge. The locations of domestic and ritual sites in relation to the changing fen edge are shown. It is clear that the significance of water in social and ritual strategies changed through time, from the Neolithic, through the Bronze and Iron Ages, and even up to recent centuries.

INTRODUCTION

The Haddenham project in Cambridgeshire, England (Hodder and Evans n.d.) provides us with a very small window through which to look at large-scale and long-term processes in human-environment interactions. The aim of this paper is to explore whether some of the patterns observed in this small area might be seen as examples of general processes in Britain and adjacent areas of Europe. The location of the project area in relation to the changing fen (i.e., swamp) edge invites a consideration of links between settlement and ritual and wetland environments. In large parts of British and northwest European prehistory and history there is an association between wetness and ritual, especially burial ritual. From the placing of Palaeolithic painted cave sites near springs, to the placing of hoards and bodies in rivers and bogs in northwest European prehistory, to the King Arthur legend, there is an apparent continuity. Does the Haddenham window allow us to gain glimpses of a long-term structure through which beliefs and actions give certain cultural values to wet areas? Or are the continuities produced by us as onlookers? Is wetness placed in fact in different ways in different narratives at different times in different social conditions?

THE ENVIRONMENTAL SEQUENCE

In order to examine how wetland areas and wet margins in the Haddenham region were used in prehistory, it is necessary to understand where "the edge" was at different times. However, the edge itself is not easy to define even today (Figure 12.1 shows the edge at one point in time). The boundary between wet and dry moves back and forth in the different seasons, and in different years. In any

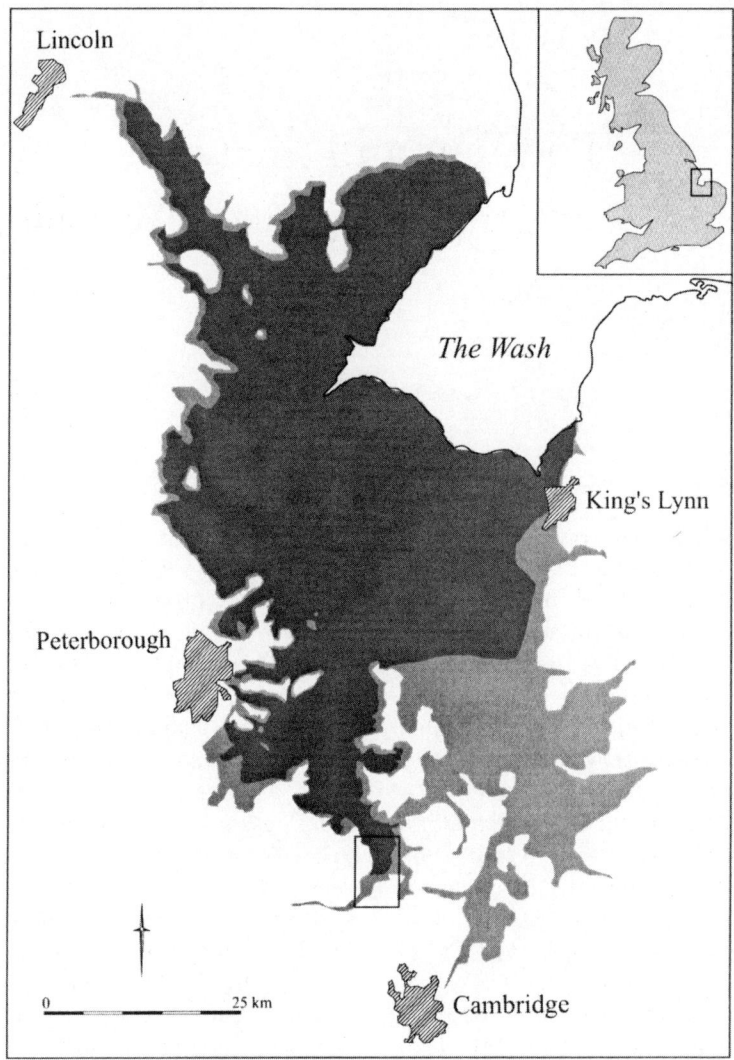

Figure 12.1. The Fenland ca. 2300–2200 B.C., with inset showing its location in Great Britain. Silt is shown in dark gray and peat in light gray. Modern-day cities are diagonally hatched. The Haddenham site is shown by the box at the southern tip of the dark gray area.

case, there is a gradation of zones from dry land to swamp or, during marine incursions, to sea. These zones include dry land, transitional woodland, fen carr (i.e., reedy wetland), sedge fen, reed swamp, salt marsh, mud flats, sea. As a particular place on the landscape changes through phases of encroaching wetness it may go through these and other phases. There will be an overall process of change rather than a well-defined edge. The process will be highly variable locally, with different embayments responding

differently, with alluvium and peat blocking water flow in certain directions, and with the changing courses of the rivers.

Our most reliable evidence for increasing wetness in the Haddenham area is from the borehole sunk into the Great Ouse roddon (ancient raised riverbed) 1 km to the north of the long barrow (Fig. 12.2). Here waterlogging and peat formation, resulting from a rising water table, occurred at −2 m OD (ordnance datum) around 4500 B.P. In the pollen sequence, zone HA1 indicates a well forested

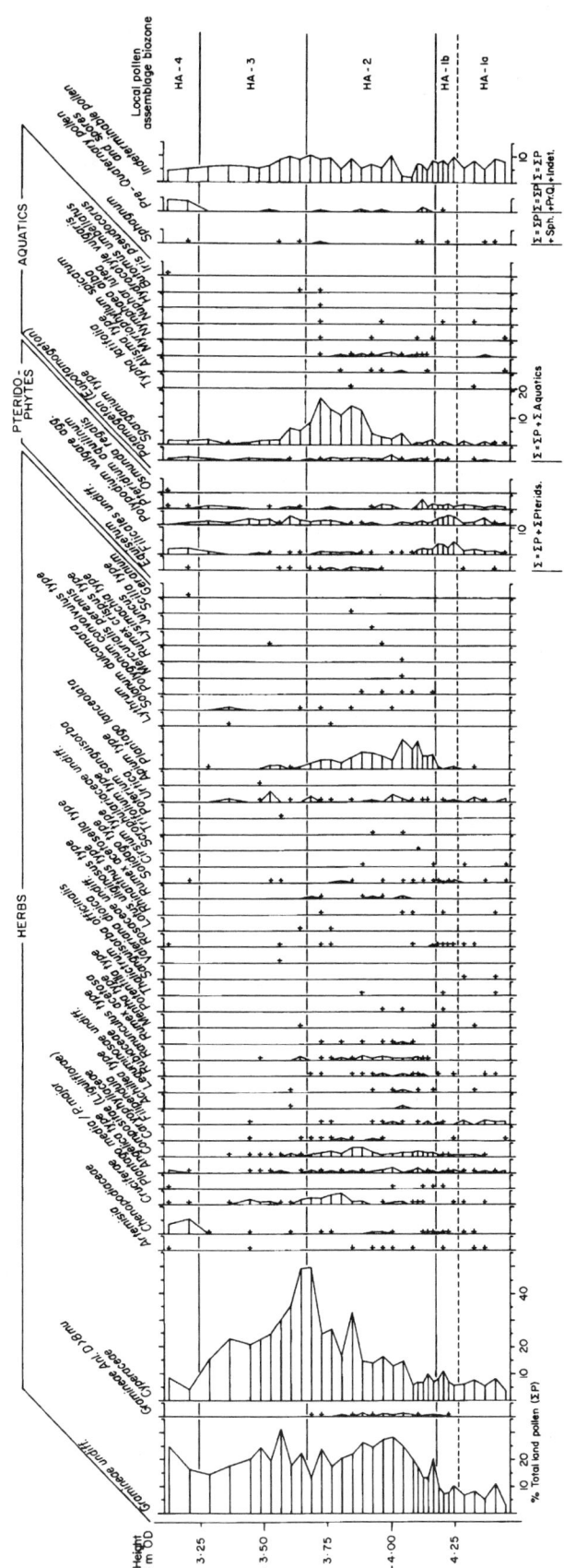

Figure 12.2. Pollen sequence from the Ouse channel to the north of Haddenham, analyzed by S. M. Pelgar in 1988–1989.

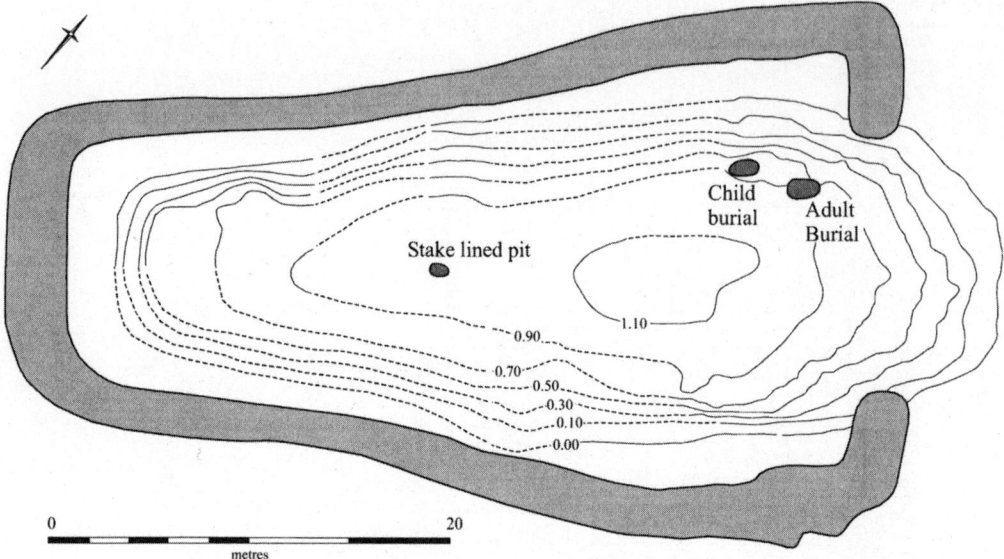

Figure 12.3. The long barrow at Haddenham.

environment with an elm decline (the 1A/1B boundary) at 5420 B.P. There is some indication of some clearance at this time. Generally in this zone the following may be reconstructed: closest to the river channel there was probably wet alder fen carr. As one moved away from the river channel the woodland would have changed as the ground became drier with oak and ash increasing until on the gravel terraces and higher ground the woodland was dominated by linden. The HA2 zone sees an overall drop in arboreal pollen, especially linden, with much evidence of clearance and cereal growth. Toward the top of the zone the pollen suggests the replacement in the channel environs of fen carr woodland by sedge fen and reedswamp, indicative of a rise in groundwater level.

Unfortunately, this sequence is the only evidence we have locally for the period of the causewayed enclosure and long barrow. The long barrow (Fig. 12.3) is dated to 4700 B.P. and the enclosure (Fig. 12.4) to 4500 B.P. and on into the Late Neolithic. Thus the monuments are contemporary with increasing wetness in the environs of the pollen core, but this is 1 km from the long barrow, while the causewayed enclosure is 4 km upstream on a gravel terrace with heights above 0 OD. It is extremely unlikely that either monument was

immediately adjacent to very wet conditions in the Neolithic. Both were built on dry land although the long barrow, built on land at just below 0 OD and probably only 1 km from a meander of the Ouse, was certainly not far from sedge fen and reedswamp.

Reeds found within the marl in the base of the long barrow ditch indicate wetness in the ditches soon after construction. A pollen core taken from adjacent to the long barrow shows reedswamp prior to the arrival of the marine Fen Clay at 3590 B.P. The base of the Fen Clay here is at −0.30 m OD, and the relatively late date for the marine incursion is corroborated by the finding of Fengate wares and Rusticated Beaker pottery (early second millennium B.C.) sealed beneath Fen Clay near the long barrow. The maximum extent of the Fen Clay in the area is 3600–3200 B.P.

On the Upper Delphs, a raised dry area to the south (Figs. 12.4, 12.5), the Neolithic and Bronze Age land surface is at approximately 0 OD to 2 m OD, with local channels reaching to −50 m OD. The Fen Clay does not reach into this area, and the local effects of increasing wetness are late. A pollen core taken from the Upper Delphs itself indicates dry land usage dated 3500–3100 B.P., with a rising water table dated to 2830 B.P. This fits well with the late Bronze Age date for the ap-

Figure 12.4. Aerial photograph of the Haddenham site. The causewayed enclosure is seen as a crop mark (double arrowheads). The island (light-colored) in the peat (dark-colored) on which the enclosure is built is called the Upper Delphs.

pearance of wet conditions in the adjacent Willingham Mere, a wetland to the south. There is archaeological evidence for flooding on the top of the Delphs by the later middle Iron Age and on into the Roman period.

Thus, much of the Upper Delphs was dry during the marine incursion and on into the late Bronze Age. But even here generalization is difficult. The lower terraces by the ancient Ouse are close to 0 OD and transects show they are only a few meters from the Fen Clay and lower peats of the channel environs. There is evidence of wet deposits at least in the upper fills of the barrow ditches in this area. The north and west fringes of the Upper Delphs may have been at least seasonally wet during the second millennium B.C.

Overall, within the Haddenham region, areas downstream near the river channel showed increasing wetness perhaps around 4500 B.P., with the Fen Clay arriving at 3950 B.P. Then Fen Clay reached its maximum in the second half of the second millennium B.C., and there may have been some marginal effects of this on the lower terraces of the Upper Delphs near the Ouse where round barrows (i.e., burial mounds) occur. But the Upper Delphs as a whole remained relatively dry until the first half of the first millennium B.C., with flooding occurring on the Delphs from the mid Iron Age onwards.

The Haddenham region occurs at the point at which the Ouse flows out into the Fens. But in more specific terms this was a

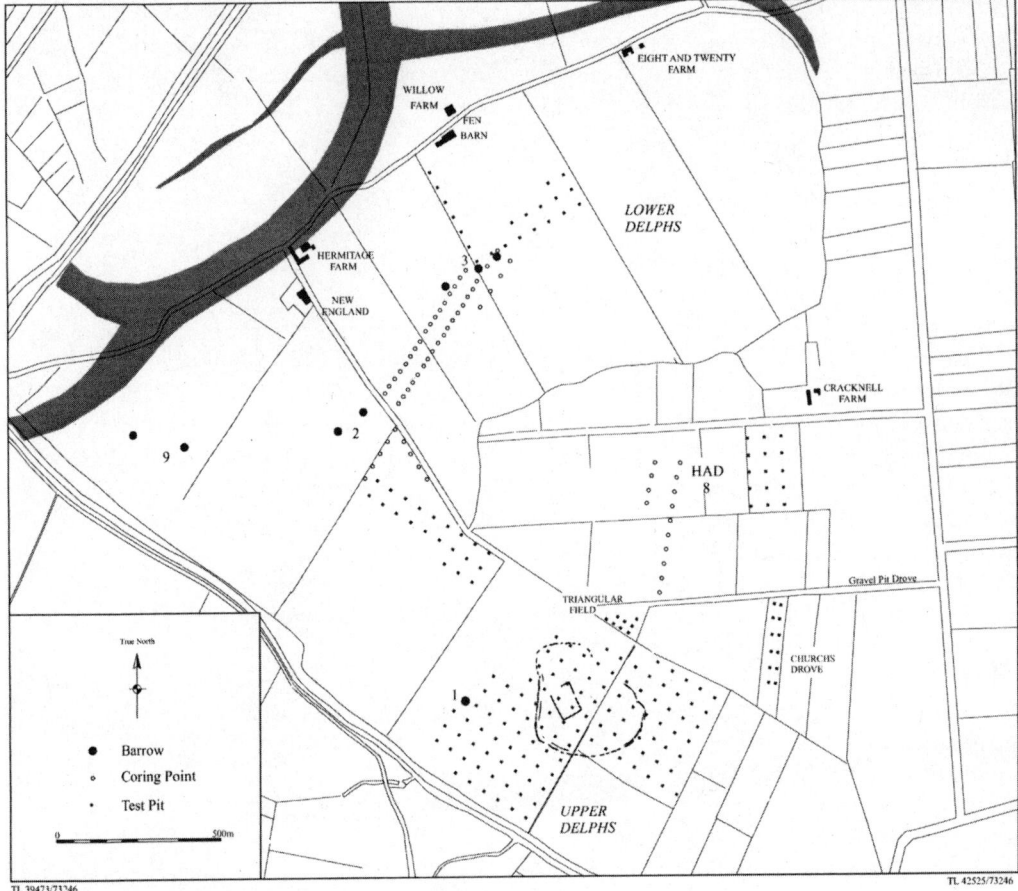

Figure 12.5. The sampling regime on the Upper Delphs. The causewayed enclosure is shown (on the left), as are Bronze Age arrows (upper center and right) and Romano-Celtic temple (Had 83). The outlined trapezoid represents the area shown in Figure 12.4.

changing environment which became increasingly wet through time in a complex sequence—probably with local backwater swamps, changes in river course, and local embayments and meanders which we cannot monitor in detail. But certainly in the Neolithic this was largely a dry land environment and parallels should be sought up the Ouse. Only later was it a proper fen edge and then fenland environment.

SETTLEMENT AND CULTURAL HISTORY
Attempts to sample this changing landscape have to deal with the fact that the prehistoric surface was submerged in peat and alluvium. Ploughsoil surface finds were few and far between in the whole area apart from a flint

scatter. Yet flint scatters observed on the present surface had to be evaluated in terms of submerged scatters and sites.

In evaluating the submerged landscape, aerial photographs and dyke surveys were used. The aerial photographs (e.g., Fig. 12.4) showed a causewayed enclosure and later sites and monuments on the higher Upper Delphs. Field walking and dyke surveying discovered emerging round and long barrows. But our main effort was to situate the visible sites into a wider understanding of the more deeply submerged landscape where air photography was of little value and where the buried prehistoric soil had not been disturbed by recent ploughing.

In order to provide systematic coverage

and to allow sampling for artifact and other densities, a "shovel pit sampling" method was used (Fig. 12.5); soil samples were dug up in a grid-like pattern, and the soil was sieved in order to count artifacts. This method used on the Upper Delphs picked up highly localized activities around individual Bronze Age, Iron Age, and Romano-British enclosures. These concentrations could not be explained in terms of altitude, depth of soil, depth of peat cover, etc., and so are taken here as indicating prehistoric and Romano-British activity. In the wider area there is an overall pattern of low densities near the ancient Ouse, but there are localized concentrations of struck flint.

How are the varying densities of flint across the ancient landscape to be interpreted? There is a general correlation between higher densities of struck flint (above 4–5 per m²) and evidence of occupation features on excavation. Whether these are really "sites" or "settlements" rather than foci of generalized activity within a wider low density of use partly depends on period, as we shall see. More recent work by the Cambridge Archaeological Unit in the south Cambridgeshire area has demonstrated the very complex relationships that may exist between flint scatter densities and underlying features and types of site. Any attempt to construct a universal cut-off point between sites and non-sites is thus of limited value. More useful is to understand the overall landscape use through time.

A number of Mesolithic scatters have been identified in the Willingham-Over area, and at Earith. One scatter near the long barrow at Foulmire Fen was sampled by the project. The flint assemblage can be dated typologically to sometime in the period after 9000 B.P. (Middleton pers. comm.). The site consisted of a small concentration of artifacts within a broader low density spread on a low sand rise. No features could be definitely linked to the Mesolithic occupation, which had at least partly been scooped up to form the long barrow mound. Given the gap of time involved, there is no evidence that the long barrow was intentionally located on or by the Mesolithic site.

In the earlier Neolithic the pollen shows clearance from 5400 B.P., gradually becoming more extensive. The dating of the flint scatters in the landscape was based on the sequence provided by the causewayed enclosure and other comparisons (Middleton pers. comm.). Settlement from this period appears to be relatively dispersed across the landscape but with a variety of localized "sites." There is a dense scatter of Mildenhall ceramics and settlement pits at Barleycroft Farm, to the southwest on the other side of the ancient Ouse (Hodder and Evans n.d.). Overall, there is little to suggest anything more than relatively impermanent settlement. The Haddenham areas as a whole, including the Upper Delphs, has lower densities of activity than the Barleycroft Farm area.

How is the long barrow positioned in relation to this settlement pattern? It is one of a group of two or possibly three in the area to the north of the Upper Delphs. There are several strands of evidence that converge to suggest that the long barrow was placed in a marginal environment:

1. Sampling of the prehistoric soil in the field around the long barrow produced very low densities of artifacts.

2. Middleton (pers. comm.) concludes from the condition of the struck flint on the Mesolithic site that it had not undergone a substantial degree of post-depositional trampling. This evidence does not suggest a high degree of post-Mesolithic activity near the long barrow.

3. The Neolithic worked flint from the long barrow itself leads to a similar conclusion. The low densities of Neolithic flint at the long barrow and in particular the low densities in the flanking ditches support the idea that the barrow was located away from dense settlement.

4. The soil from beneath the barrow shows evidence of forest development and clearance (French pers. comm.). Limited tillage is indicated but the soil fabrics were not considered sufficiently heterogeneous to suggest prolonged tillage.

5. Another point perhaps not directly

related to the argument is that the use of the tomb appears fairly short term and slight. There are low phosphate readings from in front of the tomb, little pottery deposition, and a low number of bodies placed in the tomb.

Overall, then, the long barrow was placed away from settlement, near the river, in an area which had been cleared but which had not seen intense agricultural use. However, it would be wrong to assume that such peripheral or marginal locations automatically imply that the dead were just being shifted aside, to an unwanted edge. Rather, the activities at the tomb point to an important series of ideas about clearance, continuity, and durability.

For example, Morgan and Darrah (pers. comm.) have shown that most of the wood used in the chamber probably came from one large, long-lived oak cleared from the wildwood. The wood had been cut using a particular technique, tangential splitting, which enabled very large timbers to be produced. The resulting "megaxylic" construction consisted of large, solid slabs of a type of wood that is very long-lasting. The impression is that technological choices were made that foregrounded duration and continuity.

A concern with continuity through time is also seen in the treatment of bones. Cut marks on the human bones indicate a concern with defleshing, and there is some rearrangement of defleshed bones at the back of the chamber. The theme of clearance is suggested by the large-scale removal of turf beneath and around the barrow. The themes of continuity and clearance are again suggested by an elaborate process of building up the mound, careful stacking of turves, and at least brief breaks in the construction of the mound. There is careful dismantling of the chamber, involving lifting off the roof, cutting down the main uprights, filling the front chamber with layers of turf, replacing the roof, and submitting the dismantled chamber to a slow controlled burn. There is a sequence of burnings, depositions, and pot placements across the façade—this front area sees a complex process of mounding and closing associated with pottery deposition.

Overall, the initial activities at the tomb seem to be concerned with clearance, duration, and continuity, with proper rituals at closure. They are not themselves marginal or unwanted activities, despite their peripheral location. Indeed, the marginal location could have been intended to create links to ideas about clearance. Continuities through time were created in the context of clearing new soil and the uptake of new land.

Turning to the causewayed enclosure, we have less precise dating without dendrochronology, but there is a series of the five ^{14}C dates from 4600 to 3600 B.P. The lower fills of the ditches contain Mildenhall ware and show much complex recutting, mounding, and incorporation and perhaps "placement" of axes and human bones. Looking at the evidence from the struck flint, overall levels of deposition are quite low in the lower ditch fills and in the enclosure itself at this time. The primary ditch and palisade have little evidence for flint implement production. The enclosure shows a lower intensity of use than at the Barleycroft Farm settlement(s).

This initial phase at the enclosure is brought to an end by activities involving burning (as in the long barrow) and higher intensities of use. The upper ditch fills include a range of late Neolithic and early Bronze Age wares. This later use of the enclosure includes higher densities of flint within the ditch circuit. The struck flint in the upper levels of the ditches has much evidence of core reduction and implement production. Such a change in the nature of the use of the enclosure is supported by the appearance of small pits, postholes, and a grain pit, all suggesting a shift from more "ritual" to more "domestic" activity, although densities remain lower than in the settlement areas near Barleycroft Farm. This later use is also associated with a closing of some of the gaps in the palisade and ditch circuit in order to produce a more closed or "defended" site.

It is argued here that the use of the enclosure was associated with competitive control over labor, as expressed in earth movement. The larger and longer ditch segments are most closely associated with possible "placed" deposits, higher densities of lithic and ceramic finds, and more recuts (Hodder 1992). There are also more animal bones in the more elaborate ditches and some association between areas of complex activity in the ditches and higher frequencies of cattle. One interpretation of this evidence is that small social groups vied with each other in terms of the ability to mobilize labor in the digging and maintenance of ditches. The more successful groups were also able to gain better access to prestige goods used in rituals and were more able to resource feasting behavior.

It should be pointed out that we can no longer argue for a unique Neolithic ritual focus at Haddenham. Further up the Ouse at Meadowlane, St. Ives, the recent find of a segmented monument needs further excavation. At Godmanchester the trapezoidal ritual monument and cursus (long parallel prehistoric banks) are of comparable date to the Haddenham monuments. The latter are probably part of a wider, perhaps riverine, series. We cannot, as we have already seen, argue that the Haddenham area was an edge between dryland and wetland at this time. Nevertheless, at the local level, we can argue that burial and ritual were initially associated with locations away from settlement and, in the case of the long barrows, by the river.

THE LONG-TERM SEQUENCE

The Neolithic use of the Haddenham landscape as described above can be clarified through comparison and contrast with its later use (for details of the latter see Hodder and Evans n.d.). Through time a different relationship with the environment emerges which is more influenced, both practically and conceptually, by the edge between wet and dry. But so as not to imply that the social and cultural changes are just environmentally produced, I wish to start with a transformation already visible in the long barrow and causewayed enclosure and in a sense "introducing" later round barrow activities in the area.

As we have seen, both the long barrow and the causewayed enclosure are, with great deliberation, "closed." These acts of closure involve a wide range of activities from dismantling and burning to soil dumping and infilling and artifact deposition. In these ways, monuments constructed to allow multiple access are made less accessible or inaccessible. This restriction and ending presages the use of later round barrows in which soil is mounted over burials so that further access is denied. This shift is normally seen in terms of changing from a communal to an individual focus. We wish to twist this conventional interpretation round by focusing on the idea of closure itself.

The human bones in the long barrow and in the enclosure ditches could initially be accessed and involved in continuing rituals. Their materiality and circulation would allow them to be used as devices in continuing social strategies. Since specific bones of ancestors were involved, links to particular individuals could have been maintained and reproduced. The productive and destructive aspects of individual ancestral spirits could have played a direct role in social life. Here we have all the emphasis on continuity described above. But the act of closure distances the present from the past. Links to the ancestors become generalized and remote, perhaps as new forms of generalized exchange begin to emerge (Barrett 1994). But more specifically, the closing of access to the dead in the long barrow limits the ability of individuals to manipulate past ancestors for contemporary gain. This "leveling" process is continued and developed in the round barrows.

It is of great interest that as the dead become more remote from the living through the process of closure and mounding, so too the dead in the Haddenham area are increasingly moved to spatial margins. At the end of the Neolithic and into the Bronze Age, settlement is concentrated on the higher land and there is a continued focus of activity in and over the causewayed enclosure, including the construction of a rectangular enclosure. A series of round barrows was built, in particular along the terraces adjacent to the Ouse. Two of these have been excavated, containing material dating to the fourth millennium B.P. as well as Collared Urn and later secondary cremations.

The landscape sampling in the Haddenham area indicates very low densities of all indicators near the round barrows on the terraces. The upper fills of the barrow ditches contained waterlogged material and we have seen that the lower terraces by the Upper Delphs are close to the Fen Clay by the mid-fourth millennium B.P. The marginal and river edge location of these barrows is repeated in the Barleycroft area to the south. Here recent work has shown a separation between "lived areas" on the higher ground away from the river, and "areas of the dead" lower down nearer the river.

It is possible that an earlier association between burial and peripheral locations came to be transformed into an association between burial and marginal river-edge locations. Certainly the long barrow was situated in a marginal area. The low intensity of activity in the early phases of use of the causewayed enclosure may again suggest a relatively marginal location. We have argued that this association of burial and burial-related activities with the margins may have made sense in the context of the importance of ancestors in the organization of labor for the uptake of new land. But an "accidental" conjuncture then occurred: the wetlands began to encroach up the Ouse and those margins near the river became not just marginal but also wet. The practices involved in the meaningful use of the Neolithic landscape resulted in margins and the whole suite of ideas concerning mounding and renewal began to become associated with the wet. This conjuncture was to have a long-term impact locally, however much it was informed by and added to more widely found schemes. The riverine distribution of barrows and ring ditches in the middle and upper Ouse is well established, but in each case we would need to evaluate the relationship to contemporary

settlement before claiming any special link between burial and the river.

More generally in Bronze Age contexts in eastern England, there are good reasons for arguing for a special relationship between burial and water. For example, in the eastern fens in Norfolk, early Bronze Age bodies are found placed in wet environs—in one case on a wooden platform. Deliberate disposal of the dead seems the most likely explanation of these wetland placings. Late Bronze Age skulls dredged from the Thames may provide a wider example (Bradley 1990), although interpretation of these is complex. Deposition at the Flag Fen alignment indicates the more general disposal of "wealth" in wet areas. Since both bodies and "wealth" are deposited in wet areas, a component of this "burial" activity may have involved social display.

As already noted, peat development encroaches on to the Upper Delphs around 800 B.C., and in Willingham Mere at about the same time. From the middle Iron Age onwards there is seasonal flooding on to the highest points of the Upper Delphs island. But prior to this flooding, in the middle Iron Age, a field system was laid out which linked together a series of enclosures. A number of sites on the island have produced evidence of ploughing dated to this phase. It is likely that it is this ploughing which led to the flattening of and soil development over the causewayed enclosure—the Neolithic meanings of the landscape were by then, perhaps deliberately, "forgotten."

Of the three middle Iron Age enclosures examined by the project, the main excavations took place at Haddenham V. Unlike the faunal assemblages from the other enclosures, and indeed of any other site of any period in the Haddenham area, the Haddenham V faunal assemblage is clearly indicative of a wetland economy. There is much beaver, together with swan, pelican, crane, heron, mallard, coot, and curlew. There is evidence of butchery marks on these bones. But what is of special interest here is that the ritual deposits of animals at the house entrances in Haddenham V are of sheep and do not include wetland species. This certainly suggests that the opposition between "wet" and "dry" had a symbolic or ritual significance. But this opposition had little impact on the arrangement of practices in the landscape. We have little knowledge of burial practices at this time. The tops of the Bronze Age barrows do have limited and casual Iron Age utilization. This may have been as dry "stations" for foraging wetland resources. Despite the continuation of "wet/dry" symbolism, there appears to be a gap or rupture here. The fen edge is exploited as a specialized economic resource rather than as a predominantly ritual focus.

The link between the fen edge and ritual returns in the Roman period after settlement had retreated from the Upper Delphs. In the second to fourth centuries A.D. a Romano-Celtic shrine was located on a Bronze Age barrow (Fig. 12.5). This shrine has some association with death, as indicated by the sub-floor deposits of sheep head and feet burials with coins placed in the sheeps' mouths. The placing of such a shrine on an ancient burial mound can hardly have been accidental. This link between ritual (associated with death and burial) and the wet edge is superficially similar to the Bronze Age uses of the edge. But there are important differences. The placing of sheep burials beneath floors recalls the sheep deposits in the earlier Haddenham V houses (see above). But the placing of coins in the mouths of sheep suggests a local manifestation of a state cult or religion. The shrine is part of a more concerted and large-scale exploitation of the fens and fen edge as documented by the construction of canals. The concern of the shrine is less with the reproduction of local productive units, and more with the larger scale processes of Romanization, transformation, and exploitation. Local wetlands were incorporated into a larger sphere both materially and ideologically.

It would be possible to continue through time and argue that the building of medieval monasteries on fenland islands was part of the continuing link between ritual and wetlands. But again, behind this superficial similarity, there is more of a rupture than a continuity, since the ascetic ideals of remote locations derive from a very particular medieval religious, social, and economic system. However, the interpretation of these ideals in terms of wetland margins could have been influenced by longer term understanding and practices in the Fens.

LOOKING BACKWARDS

There are many seventeenth-century descriptions of the Fens and Fenlanders as putrid, loathsome, lazy, wild, vagrant, lawless, and poor. The Protestant work ethic and the Christian virtue of "honest" labor were seen as contradicted by the predatory Fenland existence. But this negative valuation of the wet as opposed to the dry cannot be seen as timeless. What was the particular social context in which the negative seventeenth-century evaluation of the wet fens was produced?

From the seventeenth century, drainage proceeded at a fast rate. The wealth generated by drainage did not often go into the hands of the Fenlanders themselves. Outside interests transformed an economy based on pastoralism and fishing and fowling to one based on arable farming. The justification for this transformation and exploitation was often in terms of the narrative of progress and improvement. Higher profits and rents were a major motivation behind land reform, but this was justified in terms of the negative valuations given to the Fens, which were seen as being in need of "civilizing" and "improving." The recent opposition between "dry" and "wet," drained and undrained, came about historically in terms of the clash between two sets of social interests, the "dry" dominant over the "wet."

In concluding, we can take a lesson from this historical example and look back and try to evaluate the differing social contexts under which "wet" and "dry" were regarded differently at different times in the Haddenham sequence. In the earlier Neolithic, the link to wetness itself is less demonstrable even though the long barrow and the one adjacent to it are by the ancient Ouse. But peripheral locations do seem important, in relation to the issues dealing with clearance, durability, and continuity. The social context here is small-scale, relatively mobile groups trying to establish long-term dependencies in the organization of society and labor. Groups compete with each other in their ability to organize labor, but specifically in relation to the clearing and working of new land. The emphasis on deturfing, digging, and mounding in the long barrow and causewayed enclosure expresses this competition, and the peripheral locations of burial and ritual can be understood in terms of the setting of such competition in the uptake of new land.

Through the later Neolithic and Bronze Age in the Haddenham area, the link between burial and marginal wet areas becomes clearer. Onians (1951) argues that in Indo-European thought, "wet" was seen as life, and "dry" as death. Water and rivers are the source of fertility in seeds and in humans. Wetness is life-begetting. Water is the source of life and of the earth. The dead can be revived by being near water, since water germinates new life out of old. This is a description which could be used to make sense of the location of burial mounds near water, and of the offerings of wealth deposits in water. The social context that we have come to understand for this period is one of status rivalry and display (Barrett 1994; Bradley 1990). In the Haddenham area it is perhaps not unreasonable to argue that the productive and reproductive power of water was being used to create social prestige for local competitive groups who buried their dead by the water. While such an interpretation might be widely relevant to the Fens and to the riverine distribution of barrows in the Ouse, we cannot presume that similar notions underlay the location of barrows elsewhere in Britain. Each case would have to be argued on local grounds, and the increasing wetness of the fens does offer a very particular environment. However, both Bradley (1990) and Thomas (1991) have suggested links between material, rivers, and water extending back from the Bronze Age into the Neolithic.

Even if a link between round barrows and the regenerative power of water is discounted, the barrows represent a social process

that extends one already developed in the later use of the long barrow (and causewayed enclosure). By restricting access to the bones of the ancestors, individuals and groups were limited in their ability to manipulate ancestral claims. There is little evidence for increasing social differentiation. Rather, the closure of the long and round barrows suggests an increasing fear of the dead, who had to be set away from settlement. The elaborate mounding of the round barrows indicates a continued concern with regeneration and renewal. But the increased separation of the dead from the living is part of a long-term process found throughout Europe, which I have described as the rise of the "agrios" (Hodder 1990). The "agrios" involves a new code of social relations based less on lineal ties between domestic producers and more on exchange, and a social code of relations between men based on warring, hunting, drinking, and feasting. In this emerging world, which was to have such long-term significance in the Bronze Age, the dead still had regenerative power, but it was a dangerous power, one that had to be controlled and set apart lest it harm the new forms of relations among the living.

CONCLUSION

We have tried to argue that the wet edge was not always the same thing, either materially or conceptually. The opposition between wet and dry was not always given the same meanings. Behind the apparent continuities in the ritual use of this particular environment are social and economic ruptures that go hand in hand with transformed ways in which the wet landscape is used symbolically. In the earlier Neolithic, wetness itself does not seem to have been so important. More important was the creation of long-term labor relationships to deal with the uptake and maintenance of cleared land. In this context, margins had a particular significance. But then the water began to encroach, first up the channel of the Ouse, and then seeping out into the surrounding landscape. In this conjuncture between environment and culture, by the later Neolithic and Bronze Age in the

Haddenham area, the significance of margins came to be linked to wetness. In the middle Iron Age the wetlands were used primarily economically, exploited by highly specialized small communities involved in the trade of, for example, beaver skins, and involved in either wetland or dryland economies. In the Roman period settlement retreated from the encroaching water's edge, but a wet location was chosen to link larger-scale processes of Romanization with local cults—perhaps as an ideological justification for increasing exploitation of the Fens.

As the appearance of the Fens changed through time, so did their social meanings. Their interpretation ebbed and flowed with as much cultural force as did the natural processes of change.

13

British Prehistory
Some Thoughts Looking In

This (Edwards, 1999) is a wonderful book, beautifully written, an elegant summary of Edmonds's own views and of the conclusions of an exciting new generation of British prehistorians. The book has also set me thinking about a wider set of issues. Especially when read in California, the book offers a reflective moment. It invites a consideration of the way in which British prehistorians have come to see the monuments and sites which fill up (and here is the issue) "their" landscapes.

The book provides a general interpretation of the earlier Neolithic in Britain, covering aspects such as landscape, subsistence, burial, and exchange. The largest part of the text concentrates on the evidence from causewayed enclosures. The chapters in the book alternate between general interpretive accounts of the archaeological evidence, and (in bold type) more fictional and imaginative essays. At the back of the book a dialogue with Barbara Bender about its content is presented.

From the point of view of the perspective I take in this review, the book is both an ending and a beginning. Appropriately published in 1999, it represents a moment of change in the way the past is construed. On the one hand, looking backwards perhaps to the nineteenth century, we see nationalism and nostalgia. On the other hand, looking forwards to a globalized relationship with the past, we glimpse a new openness and multivocality.

NATIONALISM AND NOSTALGIA

It is now widely argued that archaeology emerged as a scientific discipline in the context of nationalism (e.g., Daniel and Renfrew 1988; Diaz-Andreu and Campion 1996). Colonialism and imperialism also played an important role, especially in the United States (Trigger 1984), but an initial impetus in Europe in the eighteenth and nineteenth centuries was the construction of unity and history within the emerging nation states. Earlier periods and groups such as the Celts, Slavs, Greeks, Turks, or Germans were looked to, to provide a unity and sense of national pride. The success of this strategy is evident in contemporary Europe where, in contrast to many other parts of the world, members of nation states have an unproblematic relationship with the monuments and artifacts found on their territories. Monuments and sites are seen as belonging to and owned by the nation state, and especially middle and upper class groups take their relationship with monuments and sites for granted. The monuments help to create a sense of belonging, a being part of. The relationship between people and their past is seen as self-evident.

Within the British, or at least the English sense of nation, nationalism and nostalgia are intimately tied to a rural fantasy, and in this archaeology has long played a role. Whether we consider Turner's paintings of

Stonehenge, or Hardy's romantic dramas centered on the same site, or Victorian picnics on barrows and monuments, or whether we fast-forward to English Heritage and the National Trust protection of rural landscapes, we see a mixture of nation, romance, and nostalgia ingrained within a rural idyll. Throughout, there is a comfortable sense of knowing, of belonging, of familiarity within a rural landscape.

This background helps me to make sense of what seems to be a contradiction within much recent work on British prehistory which takes an experiential or phenomenological perspective. It is of interest that this recent work arrives at the same end point—the bodily experience of moving around monuments and landscapes—whether the starting point is the phenomenology of Heidegger (as in the case of Thomas 1996 or Gosden 1994) or the very different structuration theories of Giddens (as in the case of Barrett 1994). What seems contradictory in this work is that on the one hand a critical, reflexive stance is taken, but on the other hand the moment of experiencing past monuments is not opened to critique (Hodder 1999a; Meskell 1996). Rather, the bodies that are described moving down a cursus, or into a causewayed enclosure or henge, are not placed within a different frame of meaning and are not adequately situated within an alien discourse. The bodies become universal bodies, and their relationship with "their" landscape becomes taken for granted and unproblematic. For example, when Tilley (1994) takes a walk down the Dorset cursus, he seems to be "taking a walk" in a very contemporary sense. When Barrett (1994) and Thomas (1996) describe individuals moving around henges, or when Bradley (1993) discusses how Neolithic houses were centers of experience, there is little account of alternative views, radically different understandings of our relationship with place (despite the theoretical emphasis on just such issues). It is almost as if one sees in such writing not the self-critical, reflective social scientist, but the lord of the manor "taking a walk" around his estate, surveying "his" landscape, entirely

comfortable within a familiar land and nation to which he "belongs."

In some ways, Edmonds seems aware of these issues and tries to move beyond them. His experiential accounts are more careful and more nuanced than many others. He does try to place human action within a situated frame of meaning. For example, in chapter 5 he suggests that we need to see stone tool production as not just practical but situated within a landscape of social memories (p. 49). I will refer to more such examples below. But in other ways, Edmonds repeats what has become the dominant interpretation of the earlier Neolithic in Britain without critical appraisal. He seems to take his interpretations for granted, to be comfortable with them. The monuments in the landscape have become familiar to him.

In the postscript dialogue to the book, Bender (p. 157) refers to the repetition of this taken-for-granted set of ideas as a mantra, and this does seem an appropriate word. All the new terms of the dominant discourse regarding British prehistory are repeated without critique. This is true both of the use of general social theory and of specific interpretations of the earlier Neolithic. As regards examples of the social theory mantra, on page 58 we learn of "routines that people followed," and of "knowledge of how to go on," and on page 134 that "monuments are often fundamental to...social memory." As regards the mantra that describes the interpretation of the earlier Neolithic, on page 63 we read that treatment of human bones in Neolithic burial monuments "could conceal differences of authority," and on page 64 that "a forecourt emphasized the place in which only a few could stand and speak." "Enclosures were concerned with the making and remaking of the social order" (p. 123). Treatment of bodies and objects in burial was "a narrative" (p. 124).

The mantra-like nature of these claims is indicated by the fact that for many there remains little evidence. On page 90 Edmonds argues that the recutting of ditches in causewayed enclosures "was not simply the result of some routine process of ditch cleaning and maintenance: it was a product of more purposeful acts." This claim has never in my view been demonstrated—it has become an unquestioned taken-for-granted. On page 99 "enclosures were arenas in which identity and authority were brought into being"; monuments were projects in which people had a limited sense of what they were doing. There is no evidence for such claims. As Edmonds states (p. 100) "there is much scope here for speculation."

On page 162, Edmonds says that he wants to avoid writing a "past-u-like," but the mantra has become uncriticized. The discourse has effectively silenced conflicting claims and allowed grand arguments to be based on minimal data. The shift to the Neolithic is described as piecemeal, small-scale, uncoordinated, dispersed, gradual, with the people at the time not being aware of the transition (p. 68) when the actual evidence for transition is very slight. In chapter 8 there is an account of rotten flesh being picked off human bones by hand. There is no evidence that defleshing occurred in this way. The movement of individuals across causeways into enclosures "meant an acknowledgement of seniority and difference" (p. 113). Other unsubstantiated claims are that "the dead pass through Wayland's Smithy rather than ending up there" (p. 58), and that "there were many ways of dying. There were good deaths and bad deaths" (p. 58).

The mantra occurs because of the effectiveness of a new dominant discourse. According to this new canon it seems to have been accepted that we know how earlier Neolithic communities interpreted the world in which they lived. There is a comfort from the discourse. But I would also argue, and I shall pursue this further below, that the lack of internal critique stems from a familiarity with landscape which comes from believing it is yours and that you are part of it. In order to make my case further, I wish to turn to the way in which Edmonds's text is written.

Each of the main chapters starts with a poetic account of the English landscape. These accounts are of the familiar and nostalgic. Few except educated English readers would recognize the sonority and power of writing such as this. "Upon the edge of the Vale of Pewsey a chalk ridge hangs above the arable, an area of grazing and hawthorn scrub. We know it now as Knap Hill. Coming to this vantage in the low light of morning or as the sun starts to set, the shadows reveal a chain of ephemeral features..." (beginning of chapter 9, p. 80). Or at the beginning of chapter 7 (p. 56) we find the following: "Walk along the Ridgeway south-west from Uffington. Keep the White Horse behind you, Dragon Hill and the Vale over your right shoulder. Half an hour or so will bring you to Wayland's Smithy." We are drawn into the Neolithic by familiar paths and by-ways, recounted in terms redolent of centuries of prose and verse. The Englishness and the rural nostalgia stand out. It is this, I argue, which at least partly lies behind the unsubstantiated claims of the new prehistory. The past is familiar and the rhetoric supports the familiarity. We "know" what the past means.

A different but related point can be made concerning the bold fictional accounts in the alternate chapters. While I welcome these, for reasons to be given below, I sense a use of words and phrases that hints of the rural exotic. On page 106 we read that "her uncle had shown her the way in this making." Other phrases include "when she had seen ten summers." The writing is often beautiful, but in the unusual phrasing and in the short stunted and repeated words such as "The signs were good" (pp. 51–52) there is a sense of a static and stereotypical other—"That was the way at these times" (p. 131). Perhaps I am reading too much into the rhetoric used in these accounts, but they seem to me to make the Neolithic past exotic yet desirable. It seems that this past is constructed as traditional and other-worldly, but familiar because stereotypical tropes are employed.

One of the distinctive aspects of the whole book is the complete lack of references in the text, although a bibliography is provided at the end. The lack of references could be seen as positive in that it makes the text more accessible. The lack of evidence for claims, and the lack of substantiation for interpretations could be seen as the necessary product of writing a popular book. This may be true and some of the positive aspects of Edmonds's popular account will be discussed below. In my view, the book remains specialized and I doubt that it will work as a truly popular text. It rather summarizes the dominant view in British prehistory. In which case, should not the general reader be allowed some indication of the evidence on which the story is based? Edmonds is better placed to offer informed critique than any of his readers. The lack of evidence, reflection, references seem to make the text more elitist and less penetrable. For example, on page 121, when talking of causewayed enclosure ditch placements of skulls, he suggests that "perhaps the heads that were sometimes buried retained their eyes." The way this is stated makes it difficult for a non-specialized reader to know whether there is any evidence for this. At Godmanchester in Cambridgeshire "assembled companies may have sought spiritual help in renewing the fertility of the land" (p. 105), but how, might the general reader reasonably ask, can archaeologists make such claims?

TOWARD GLOBAL DIVERSITY

So far I have suggested that aspects of Edmonds's text and of recent British prehistory, in particular the contradiction between a reflexive approach and a non-reflexive account, can be made sense of in terms of a long cultural tradition in which landscape is central to claims of national belonging, and in which rural monuments are owned and made familiar. In such a context, the past is self-evident and there is little potential for critique and debate. It is possible to "speak for" people in the Neolithic because in some sense (a sense defined by the politics and rhetoric of nationalism) "we" and "they" are one.

It is distinctive that the phenomenological approaches in British prehistory have had little impact in the United States, and I think in other strongly multi-ethnic societies. The idiom of "speaking for" experiences of people in the past seems to make less sense in these countries. In a recent discussion in California it was suggested to me that one cannot imagine most U.S. archaeologists describing Native American experiences of monuments (Preucel pers. comm.). Such a "speaking for" would be seen by many non-Native and Native Americans alike as insensitive. Some non-Native Americans argue that their use of categories of complexity to describe early societies in the Americas has to do with the feeling that it would be inappropriate to go beyond such external descriptions to define internal experience. These may be some of the factors that inhibit the use of phenomenological approaches in the United States, at least in the way they have been used in the UK. Native American rights, reburial, and African-American identities mean that the context of the archaeological past in the United States is colonialism and imperialism (Trigger 1984). The comfortable space provided by the "oneness" of nationalism in the UK does not exist here.

But in the context of global flows, creolization, hybridity, and transnationalism, it is increasingly apparent that the self-evident nature of the nation-state is being undermined. For many, Britain too is increasingly a multi-ethnic society. What is the role of archaeology in these new diverse and globalized spheres? In many ways, Edmonds's book moves us toward a response to such questions. In particular, the use of two texts, the one "serious" and the one "fictional," opens up his book to wider interpretation. This move is parallel to the many experiments in ethnographic writing, and Edmonds's version is particularly successful. My only worry here is that the distinction between the two types of text is not great enough. In fact the "serious" chapters become so imaginative that they become scarcely distinguishable from the "fictional" accounts. Both chapter 4, which gives a fictional account of making a wooden track, and chapter 6, which is a story about flint quarrying, seem little more imaginative than the "serious" accounts which precede them. The end result is again homogenization. Critique and diversity could have been engendered by placing references in the serious chapters, and by having careful consideration of the evidence on which the fictional accounts were based. This would have both opened the Neolithic up, and allowed the entry of other critical voices.

An opening up of the text is also achieved by the popular and accessible writing style. As Edmonds states in his preface, he had felt frustrated at the gap between theory and evidence in British prehistory. Theory was often too abstract, turgid, impenetrable. Written accounts missed the humanity of daily life. So he tried to write in a way that is less determined and more open. "I wanted to write a less 'academic' book" (p. 157). Chapter 4 does give a wonderful sense of "being there" as Neolithic tracks were constructed. It makes the reader see that the tracks were more than wooden structures; they are set within a social context. Similarly, the mundane acts of quarrying flint are set within social memories of landscape in chapters 5 and 6.

The book is very successful in giving a sense of a landscape with people in it, a lived landscape. Edmonds is good at giving particular, rather than a general, sense of place and time. The account often emphasizes diversity and difference. Women are described doing tasks often stereotypically associated with men. Different social groups are seen using the tombs and causewayed enclosures in different ways. The same landscape is seen as being used differently in different periods through time (e.g., p. 80). As already noted, British prehistorians have not sufficiently critiqued their notions of how people lived in Neolithic landscapes, but at least Edmonds pushes us toward some degree of diversity and specificity.

CONCLUSION

The postscript dialogue is perhaps the most obvious point at which diversity, critique, and reflexivity can enter into the book. Bender usefully prises open many of the taken-for-granted assumptions that underlie the book. But I found it odd that she did not push farther in this direction since it is her own book on Stonehenge (Bender 1998) that most directly challenged the one-nation tenor of British prehistory. In her exploration of alternative perspectives on Stonehenge, in her traveling exhibit dealing with conflicting claims on the site, in her use of dialogue and debate, she produces a past which seems diametrically opposed to the comfortable certainty of the phenomenological accounts of Neolithic daily life. She directs us towards a world in which nation is not taken-for-granted, and in which the rights and interests of a diversity of groups are explored.

Another account which opens up "British" prehistory is provided by Parker Pearson and Ramilisonina (1998). Here, parallels with Madagascar are used to provide an alternative reading of Stonehenge and its landscape. In an increasingly globalized world, as nation-states become cross-cut by processes as diverse as migration and media, archaeologists will increasingly need to respond to a diversity of competing claims on the past. The response will involve new perspectives and new methodologies. Edmonds in this book is to be congratulated on both presenting an older perspective, and moving in significant ways toward the new.

14

Daily Practice and Social Memory at Çatalhöyük

IAN HODDER AND CRAIG CESSFORD

It is often argued that some form of sedentism emerges during the Natufian of the Near East (e.g. Belfer-Cohen and Bar-Yosef 2000). Some of the following PPNA (approximately 9300 to 8300 B.C.) and PPNB (8300 to 6800 calibrated B.C.) pre-agricultural and early agricultural sites in the Near East and equivalent sites in Anatolia are large and/or densely occupied. By the time of the PPNB there are sites as large as Abu Hureyra (11.5 ha, but possibly as large as 16 ha; Moore et al. 2000: 269-70), 'Ain Ghazal (12 to 13 ha; Rollefson et al.1992:444), Aşıklı Höyük (4 ha; Esin and Harmanakaya 1999:118), and Çatalhöyük (13 ha; Hodder 1996). For several decades, archaeologists working on the early prehistoric villages of the Near East have referred to the idea that agglomeration of sedentary settlement is associated with conflicts that need regulation by centralizing or coordinating functions such as ranking, rituals, symbolism and public space (e.g., Byrd 1994; Flannery 1972 and 1993; Hole 2000; Wright 1984). For example, Rosenberg and Redding (2000) argue that as storage, sedentism and group size increase, sociopolitical structures are needed that can resolve conflicts—these structures include increased hierarchy, feasting, public rituals, common symbols etc. Or in the PPNB (the major phase of village agglomeration) in the Near East, "the emergence of incipient social hierarchies and ritual ideologies were necessary to regulate and codify increasingly complex interpersonal,

intragroup and intergroup relationships" (Goring-Morris 2000:106).

Certainly there is much evidence that in general terms the emergence of large settled villages in the period between the eleventh and seventh millennia B.C. is associated with these centralizing and coordinating functions. Early sites such as Hallan Çemi in eastern Anatolia have public open space and perhaps feasting in the late tenth millennium calibrated B.C. (Rosenberg and Redding 2000), and there are public structures from the PPNA and PPNB such as the tower and wall at Jericho, the skull house at Çayönü and the "temples" at Göbekli Tepe and Nevali Çori (Bar-Josef 1986; Hauptmann 2002; Özdoğan and Özdoğan 1998; Schmidt 2001). The general increase in symbolism has been documented by Cauvin (1994). The evidence for ranking is more debated. Wright (1978) saw social stratification in Natufian burials in El-Wad, but this was questioned by Belfer-Cohen (1995) and Byrd and Monahan (1995) (see also Weinstein-Evron 1998). For PPNA and PPNB there is perhaps wider acceptance of some degree of ranking in the Near East (though see below for a different regional argument for central Anatolia), if often crosscut by strong leveling or egalitarian processes (see Kuijt 2000 for a full review of the debate).

Such harguments appear to imply that power or centralization came about in order to deal with the need for regulation or coordination. These types of argument have been widely critiqued in the social sciences and the debate in archaeology has also been well developed (McGuire 1992; Miller, Rowlands and Tilley 1989; Miller and Tilley 1984). At a theoretical level, one problem with such arguments is that they do not explain how power is accepted—how it is understood, made sense of, legitimated within non-elite groups or in society as a whole. An alternative view argues that power is always embedded within meaning, knowledge or discourse (Foucault 1977; Miller and Tilley 1984). According to this approach, focus switches to the ways in which increased power and centralized coordinating functions are produced or made possible within discourse (modes of communication and understanding).

More recent debate in archaeology and the social sciences has tended to move still further from power/knowledge wielded by dominant groups towards a consideration of daily practices (Barrett 1994; Bourdieu 1977; De Certeau 1984; Giddens 1984). Rather than focusing on discursive meanings constructed in relation to power, the emphasis is placed on the way that social rules, meanings and relations of power are in tune with, or are embedded within, the mundane practices of daily life. So, rather than ask why centralized coordinating functions emerge, the concern is to explore how changes in the social practices of everyday life make centralized coordinating functions possible. Recent work on the household as the fundamental economic and social unit in society in the PPNA and PPNB of the Levant has done much to focus attention on the daily practices of life and how they relate to the centralization of power (Byrd 1994; Goring-Morris 2000; Kuijt 2000).

As one of the main champions of practice theories, Bourdieu (1977, 1990, 1991) has shown how daily routines in eating, sitting, sleeping, moving in domestic space can be the mechanisms by which people are socialized into particular rules and orientations. As people go about their daily tasks, they may learn rules and constraints through the movements of the body. The rules become "embodied." By this term we refer to the idea that social rules and dispositions become embedded within mundane bodily practices, often non-discursively. As a child grows up within routinized domestic space, it learns that particular practices, movements, ways of holding oneself, deferential gestures and so on are positively valued while others are not. The child learns social rules in the practices of daily life within the house. In this way daily practices become social practices—they have a dimension which relates to social structuring and restructuring. Archaeologists have taken from this the notion that by exploring how bodies would have moved around spaces within houses, as well as within monuments and landscapes, we can examine changing ways in which daily practices are linked to particular forms of relationship between people, and to particular forms of power (Barrett 1994; Thomas 1996; Tilley 1994).

So far we have referred to studies of social practice that have a spatial focus. But another component of the experience of daily life is temporality, and rhythm. An important dimension of social practices is relationships with the past, and the extent to which practices repeat earlier practices as a form of memory of them. There has recently been an increased engagement with time and memory in archaeology (e.g., Alcock et al. 2003; Bradley 2002; Hamann 2002), often responding to related debates in the social sciences (Connerton 1989; Le Goff 1992). The key themes of the Neolithic of the Near East, such as sedentism, agglomeration and domestication, as well as more specific themes such as the treatment of the dead and the veneration of ancestors, all involve changes in temporality, memory and relationships with the past. It is often argued (e.g., Bradley 2002; Byrd and Monahan 1995; Goring-Morris 2000; Kuijt 2001; Shanks and Tilley 1982; Tringham 2000; Whittle 1996) that early forms of power in the Neolithic of the Near East and Europe were linked to delayed return systems, links to ancestors, repetitive practices at monuments to the dead, and the construction of greater temporal depth to activities (as in the construction of lineages). To understand the daily social practices of the Neolithic we need to examine both their spatial and temporal dimensions.

The purpose of this paper is to stimulate a discussion of changing daily social practices and embodiment associated with the formation of settled villages in Anatolia and the Near East. We do not intend to conduct a summary of the relationship between sedentism, aggregation, centralized and coordinating functions, and mundane daily social practices as in our view such a summary would be premature given a lack of widely available relevant data. Rather, our aim is to use the example at Çatalhöyük to explore some of the ways in which daily practices might be studied, in both the spatial and temporal dimensions. Only then will it be possible examine whether long-term change in social practices is part of, or even the precondition for, centralization, sedentism, agglomeration and domestication.

In turning to the particular case of Çatalhöyük in central Anatolia, it is important to recognize that the site is the product of a long period of domestication and settlement agglomeration. Dated from 7400 to 6200 calibrated B.C., it occurs at the end of the Aceramic Neolithic (PPNB in the Near East) and the four earliest (Pre-XII) levels at Çatalhöyük appear to be without pottery. But most of the sequence (Level XII upwards) is in the Ceramic Neolithic (for dated sequence see Fig. 14.1). Throughout the sequence, cereals and sheep and goat are domesticated but there is some dependence on wild resources, and cattle and pig appear not to be domesticated (Fairbairn et al. 2004; Russell and Martin 2004). Within Anatolia, and particularly within central Anatolia, there are local sequences which lead up to and prefigure Çatalhöyük. In southeast Turkey, the villages of Çayönü (Özdoğan and Özdoğan 1990) and Göbekli Tepe (Schmidt 2001) already show substantial agglomeration and elaborate symbolism in Aceramic Neolithic contexts (Bıçakçı 1998). In central Anatolia (for a definition of the Aceramic Neolithic here see Gérard and Thissen 2002), Aşıklı

Höyük has dense packed housing in a 4 ha site in Aceramic levels dated from 8400 B.C. to 7400 cal B.C. (Esin and Harmanakaya 1999). There are many other sites contemporary, or partly contemporary with Çatalhöyük that are known in central Anatolia and the adjacent Burdur-Lakes region (Duru 1999; French 1972; Gérard and Thissen 2002).

The central Anatolian region in which Çatalhöyük is located has a number of distinct characteristics. In a recent review comparing the 'origins of farming' sequences in the Levant, eastern Anatolia and the upper Euphrates, and central Anatolia, Özdoğan (2002) has pointed to several social differences between central Anatolia and sites to the east in Upper Mesopotamia. One of the clear differences is that in central Anatolia there is less craft specialization and little in the way of specialized ritual. In addition, the degree of packing of houses (at Aşıklı Höyük, Çatalhöyük, and Can Hasan) is often rather greater than is found to the east. There are few streets and at Çatalhöyük access to houses and animal pens was over roofs of houses. The rules and constraints regulating the lives of the inhabitants in such dense agglomerations may have been particularly marked. These rules dealing with access to resources, the build up of refuse, sanitation, social relations, ritual practices and so on might have been particularly complex in such densely packed settlements. Such sites are at least partly dependent on delayed agricultural systems (as defined by Woodburn 1980) and all houses have some storage. There was thus the potential for conflict. But the conflict must have been well regulated in some way since these central Anatolian settlements were occupied over long periods of time and there is remarkable continuity in their organization. At Aşıklı Höyük the dated deep sounding sequence, which is over six meters deep, covers 250 to 530 years (68% probability) or 180 to 600 years (95% probability), excluding level 3 which is undated. (Analysis of dating was undertaken using BCal (Buck et al. 1999)). Through this time period there are six rebuildings of a house in exactly the same

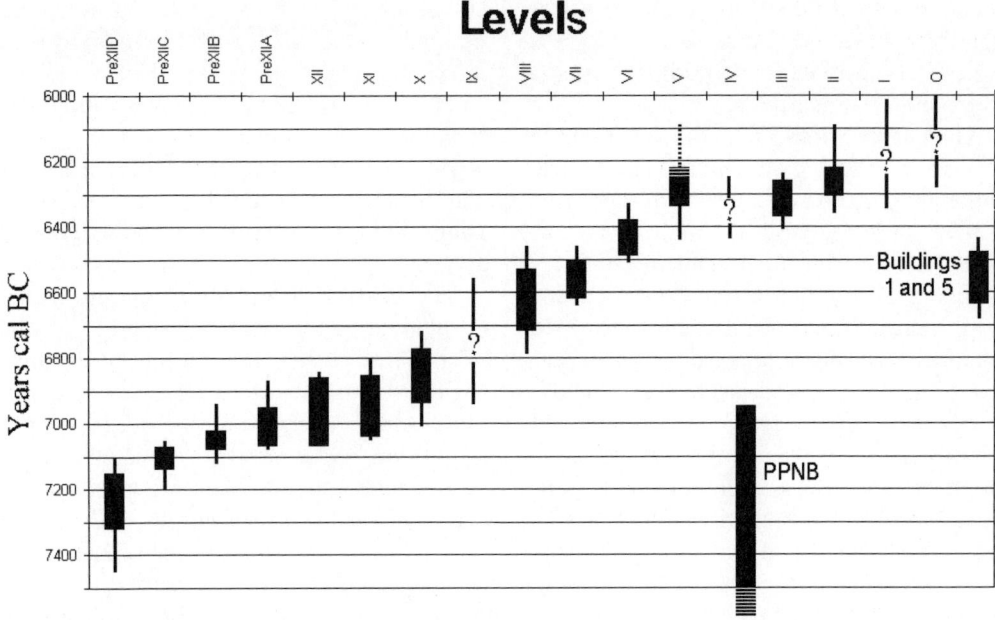

Figure 14.1. Radiocarbon dates for the levels at Çatalhöyük (Cessford 2004b).

location and with the same location of hearths and midden (Esin and Harmanakaya 1999, figure 9). At Çatalhöyük there is evidence of repetition of buildings, and of repetition of internal arrangements of buildings (hearth, platform location for example) over 500 to 1000 year time spans. This evidence suggests practices (cf Sommer 2001) that were particularly rule-bound in central Anatolia. We wish to argue that people were socialized into social roles and rules in central Anatolia and Çatalhöyük by two primary mechanisms: first through the bodily repetition of practices and routines in the house, and second through the construction of memories in which the bodily practices were embedded. The evidence from Çatalhöyük may also be relevant to the study of the long-term process of settlement agglomeration and village formation that precedes it throughout Anatolia and the Near East, although confirmation of such a claim will have to await further studies.

DAILY REPETITION OF PRACTICES WITHIN THE ÇATALHÖYÜK HOUSE

In terms of the question of how people were socialized or routinized into social roles,

Hodder (1990, 1998) elsewhere emphasized the importance of the house in the Neolithic of the Near East and Europe—as metaphor and mechanism, linking the domestication of plants and animals with the domestication of people. He argued that the house acted as a symbolic focus which domesticated people through the *domus*—that is the idea and practice of domesticating the wild (the *agrios*). That argument was based in part on a reconsideration of Çatalhöyük. We wish in this paper to consider again the importance of the house at Çatalhöyük, but to accept the criticism (Parker Pearson and Richards 1994) that the importance of the house or *domus* does not need to be based on an opposition with the wild. In this paper we will discuss two aspects of socialization in the house—repetitive daily practices and social memory.

Çatalhöyük was first excavated by James Mellaart from 1961 to 1965 (Mellaart 1967), and renewed fieldwork began in 1993 (Hodder 1996, 2000). The mound is 21 meters high and contains probably 18 levels of occupation with well preserved mud-brick houses densely packed together. The dates of the levels are shown in Figure 14.1. Each level a varying number of houses (e.g., 59 in Level

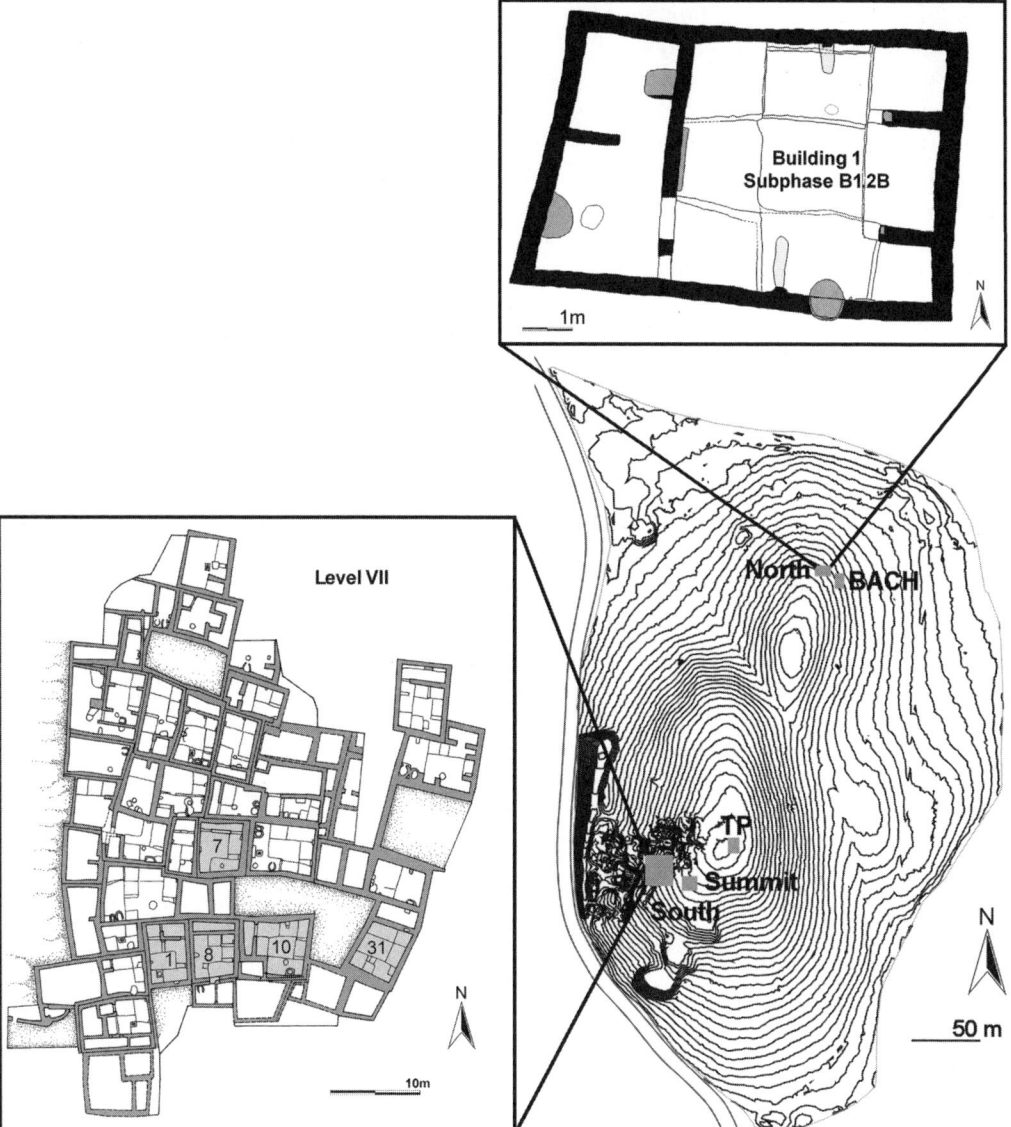

Figure 14.2. Excavated areas at Çatalhöyük and the locations of the buildings most referred to in the text. The buildings identified as "shrines" 1, 7, 8, 10, and 31 in Level VII are indicated. Buildings 6 and 17 occur in Levels VIII and IX respectively beneath "shrine" 10. Buildings 18 and 23 occur in Level X below "shrines" 8 and 1 respectively. Building 5 lies directly below Building 1.

VI.B), depending on the area of the mound excavated by Mellaart at each level. There are few or no streets, and entry to the house is through the roof. At the height of its occupation perhaps 3,500 to 8000 people lived at the site, based upon extrapolations from the 4% of the site that has been excavated, and various forms of surface sampling (including geophysical techniques) in order to assess building density over the site as a whole (Cessford 2004c; R. Matthews 1996). During the Ceramic Neolithic occupation of Çatalhöyük (Level XII and above), regional survey has shown that there were no other large sites on the same alluvial fan in the Konya plain and that even small sites are probably rare (Baird 2002).

The importance of the house as an

economic, social and ritual unit has been amply demonstrated in the recent work at the site. Mellaart (1967:77–130) had distinguished "shrines" from "houses." But the more recent work has included systematic micromorphological analysis of the deposits on floors (W. Matthews 1996), and there is clear evidence that even the most elaborate of "shrines" contained a wide range of activities associated with food preparation, consumption, obsidian working and bone tool production etc. All buildings acted as domestic houses with varying degrees of symbolic elaboration, and production, exchange and consumption at Çatalhöyük seem to be largely organized at the domestic scale. For example, there is evidence for in situ obsidian working within houses (Carter et al. 2004), and most houses have their own cache of obsidian (Conolly in press) traded from Cappodocia (Carter et al. 2004). Brick composition shows remarkable degrees of variation between houses, suggesting that clay and temper acquisition were organized at the house level (W. Matthews 1996; Tunc 2004). Every house has its own storage capacity in the form of small clay bins and baskets. Each house has its own oven, hearths and basins for food preparation (Fig 14.2).

A primarily domestic mode of production and consumption (Sahlins 1974) operated at Çatalhöyük, although there is some evidence of more specialized production of obsidian and figurines in some houses (Conolly 1996; Hamilton 1996). But the house was also an important social unit. Many houses contain the burials of a range of individuals (often up to 6, but sometimes as many as 60). The broad representation of ages and sexes of these individuals placed below the platforms of the house during its use suggests a possible relationship between those buried beneath the floors and those occupying the building (or a group of related buildings). The houses are also foci of art and ritual (Last 1998), although some burial activity took place off site and there may have been bucrania on house roofs (Stevanovic and Tringham 1999). All houses have some evidence of art or ritual. Even the least elaborate houses contain some paintings, as in the case of the geometric paintings found in the small and simple house Building 2 (Farid 2004). The amount of variation in the symbolism between houses suggests the possibility of house-based production and reproduction.

So the house is an important social, productive and symbolic unit at Çatalhöyük, and we now want to argue that it was also the main mechanism for creating social rules. We have already noted a degree of centralization of power in Neolithic societies in Anatolia and the Near East, but nowhere is the degree of centralization of power well developed. Indeed, there is little evidence of large-scale public gatherings or rituals. Apart from Jericho, where the massive tower and walls may have had some public ritual or symbolic function, ritual buildings at Göbekli Tepe, Nevali Çori, Çayönü (Özdoğan and Özdoğan 1998), 'Ain Ghazal, and elsewhere are too small to accommodate gatherings of more than 20 to 30 people. Apart from the Plaza at Çayönü there is little evidence of public space other than these ritual buildings.

Instead of social rules being imposed by centralized authorities manipulating public rituals, we argue that at Çatalhöyük the reproduction of dominant groups (e.g., elders or lineage heads) was intimately tied to the construction of bodily routines that were repeated in daily house practices over days, months, years, decades, centuries, and even millennia. Since these practices involved productive, consumptive, social and ritual spheres of life they constituted a *habitus* (Bourdieu 1977) and a set of social codes. There is much evidence for repetitive practice throughout the Ceramic Neolithic levels at Çatalhöyük (no buildings have so far been excavated in the Aceramic levels; only midden deposits have so far been encountered in these levels). For example, all central rooms in Çatalhöyük houses in all Ceramic Neolithic levels show repetitive replastering of walls, floors and platforms. Most buildings are used for 50–100 years before being rebuilt. In recent work, Matthews (2004) has used micromorphology to identify up to 700 "washes" and replasterings on one wall, over a period of 70

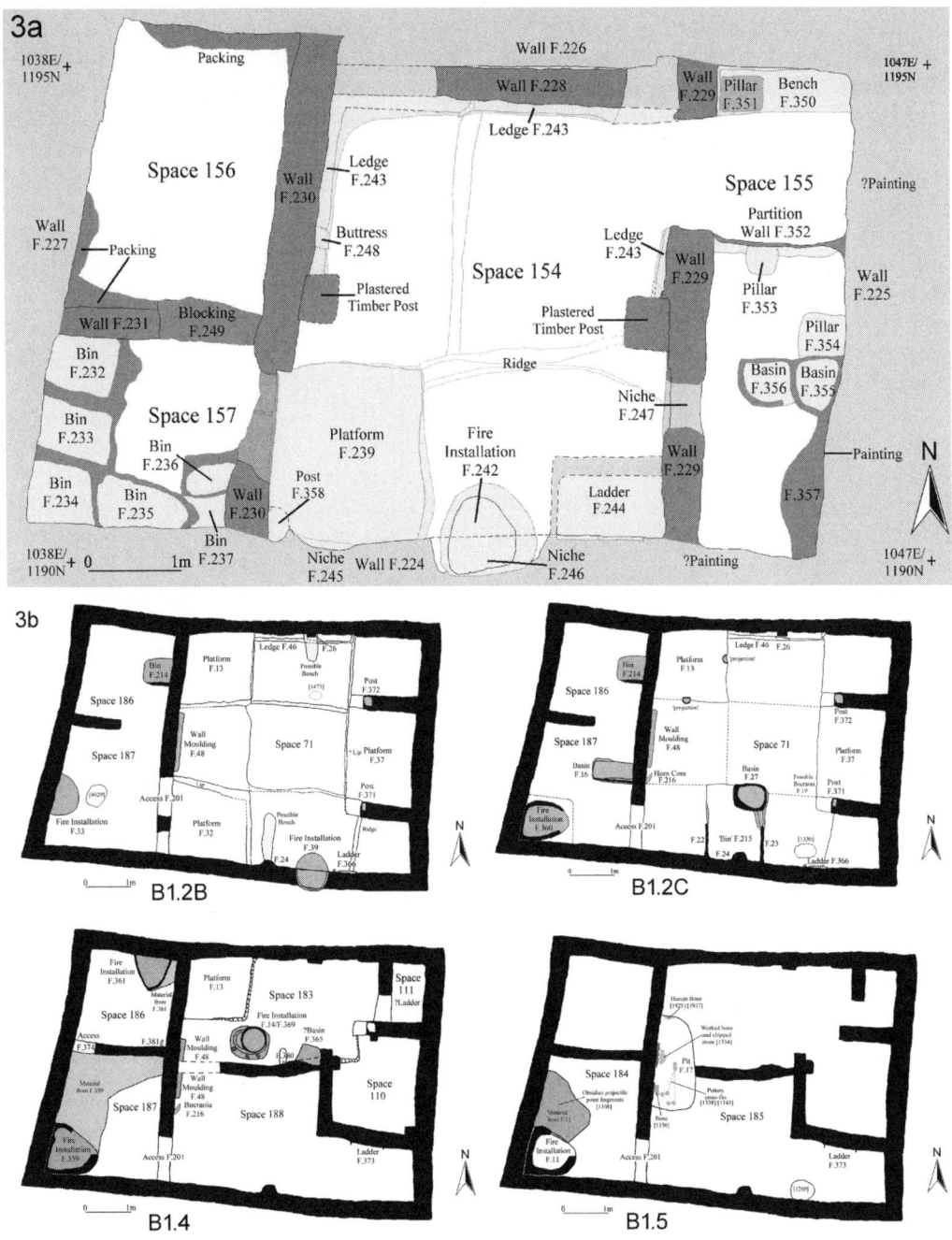

Figure 14.3. Phases of occupation of Building 5 (Fig. 3a) and the house immediately above it, Building 1 (Fig. 3b) at Çatalhöyük.

years. Annual replasterings made up of foundation and surface coatings occur routinely up to 50 to 100 times (Mellaart 1964:116–17 and 1967:50). Certainly there are changes in oven and bin locations in houses through time, and sometimes wall plasters are painted. But the degree of repetition of plastering practices is remarkable. Platform and burial locations are remarkably constant through the replastering of buildings and their rebuilding. Ovens and hearths are usually in the south part of buildings, with art and burials to the north. The ladder is usually near the oven and major bucrania (plastered cattle skulls) are usually placed on west walls. Obsidian caches always occur near hearths and ovens; pottery is never placed in graves. The burial platforms use different types of plaster and are whiter than other platforms and floor areas. All these spatial distinctions are experienced in the bodily practices of frequent repetitive replastering (as well as in other activities such as sweeping floors).

Movement around the houses at Çatalhöyük must always have involved care and restriction. The main rooms are rarely more than 5 by 5 m, and yet they are always divided by platforms, raised edges and changes in height into 1.0–1.5 m squares (Fig. 14.3). All these differences in floors restrict ease of movement. And the different areas also have different social meanings. There is a tendency for different categories of people to be buried under different platforms. For example, in Building 1 there are more young people buried beneath the northwest platform, F.13, and more older individuals under the central east platform, F.37, (Cessford 2004a). The distribution of "art" and symbolism in the house also respects spatial divisions. Painting and sculpture are rarely found in the southern area of the house, and large relief sculptures are especially common on west walls of main rooms. In Building 1 there is a possible spatial and temporal link between geometric art and burial, especially of younger people and children. In these socially and symbolically divided spaces, one activity that was carefully regulated was discard. In general terms, the floors at Çatalhöyük are remarkable clean. Apart from the last floor on which artifacts may be deposited during abandonment, it is rare to find artifacts of any size at all. On the other hand, the midden areas between houses, and within abandoned houses, contain the small sweepings and rake-out from houses and are artifact rich (W. Matthews 1996).

Given that the floors are kept so scrupu-lously clean, can variation in activities across floors be identified? Do the actual patterns of activity seem constrained by the highly segregated and compartmentalized space? In answering these questions, attention was focused on microartifacts that might have been trampled into soft plaster floors, so escaping sweeping activities. There is also much evidence from impressions and phytoliths of woven reed mats on at least some of the platforms and floors. These would have restricted the incorporation of all but the smallest artifacts into floor plasters. Studies of microartifact patterning are often based on the premise that microartifacts are more likely to represent traces of in-situ activity than larger artifacts (Dunnell and Stein 1989; Fladmark 1982; Goldberg et al. 1993; Rainville 2000; Schiffer 1987). It is postulated that "depositional sets" are more directly related to "activity sets and areas" (Carr 1984:114) at the micro level than the macro level. Largely because of different conditions at different sites, there is no agreed methodology with regard to appropriate sample sizes, what sizes constitute upper and lower ranges of microartifacts, and which material types to consider (Dunnell and Stein 1989; LaMotta and Schiffer 1999).

The premise that microartifacts in and on floors relate to activities that took place on those surfaces needs to be rigorously investigated and critiqued on a site by site basis, rather than simply assumed (for a fuller discussion see Cessford 2003). At Çatalhöyük, all deposits excavated are sampled for wet screening/flotation, usually with a single 30-liter sample, although floors are often sampled more extensively to look for evidence of spatial patterning. The heavy fraction or "heavy residue" (the material which does not float) from this process is then separated into 4 size ranges: greater than 4mm (henceforth 4mm), less than 4 mm and greater than 2 mm (henceforth 2 mm), less than 2 mm and greater than 1 mm (henceforth 1 mm) and less than 1 mm. The three larger fraction sizes are then sorted by hand and various types of material culture collected, mainly chipped

Table 14.1. Density (grams per liter) of Bone and Chipped Stone in White Clay Floors and Wall Plaster in the North and South Areas at Çatalhöyük

	North Area White Clay Floor (48 samples)	North Area Wall Plaster (12 Samples)	South Area White Clay Floor (34 Samples)	South Area Wall Plaster (40 samples)
Bone 4 mm	0.210	0.262	0.329	0.138
Chipped Stone 4 mm	0.001	0.000	0.005	0.000
Bone 2 mm	0.026	0.038	0.018	0.020
Chipped Stone 2 mm	0.002	0.003	0.002	0.001
Bone 1 mm	0.017	0.011	0.004	0.015
Chipped Stone 1 mm	0.000	0.000	0.001	0.000

stone (obsidian and flint), bone and charred plant material. These are then weighed to provide density figures expressed as grams per liter.

Because all deposits are sampled in this way, it is possible to contextualize the patterning on floors by comparing with densities in other types of deposit. The white plaster floors found at Çatalhöyük are visually similar to white plasters found on walls, and micromorphological examination indicates that both are made of similar white calcareous clay sediments (W. Matthews 1996:304). Given that microartifacts in wall plasters are unlikely to relate to in situ activities taking place on vertical surfaces, a comparison of these two deposit types should prove useful. Results from two excavation areas, North and South, are shown in Table 14.1, indicating the median densities (grams per liter) of chipped stone and bone at the three different fraction sizes. The wall plasters contain densities of material often similar to or even higher than those found in the white clay floors. This shows that at the very least a substantial percentage of such materials in floors are unlikely to relate to in situ activities.

Further information concerning this patterning can be obtained from a consideration of the material found in the wall and floor plasters. Detailed analysis of the faunal material in the wall plasters indicates in general low densities and small fragments, usually not exceeding 2 cm although sometimes as large as 5 cm. Beyond this general pattern there is much variation, with some wall plasters having digested bone indicative of dog feces. Some have very fresh bone while others have worn pellets. The profiles of the different wall plasters variously resemble assemblages from "clean" floors, "dirty" floors, "low traffic" floors, and "empty" fills, as well as other constructional material such as mudbrick, mortar and packing. The general conclusion is that much of the material in the "floor assemblages" derives from the floor construction material. In other words, it is "background noise" that gets into most construction material and has little to do with activities taking place on floors.

The relationship between microartifacts in floor deposits at Çatalhöyük and in situ activities is thus a problematic one. It could be argued that in excavation the microartifacts on floors should be separated from those in floors. The floors at Çatalhöyük are generally about 2 to 10 mm thick and within 5 cms of floor thickness there may be 10 to 20 floors—these are the replasterings referred to earlier. Under the microscope it may be possible to discern microartifacts lying on, rather than in floors, and micromorphology has been used extensively to explore such patterning. W. Mathews (1996) used micromorphology to discern two types of floors in buildings based on the presence or absence of finishing coats of white plaster on the floors. Where such finishing coats occur, overlying occupation deposits are very thin or absent. Where there are no laid white plaster layers on the

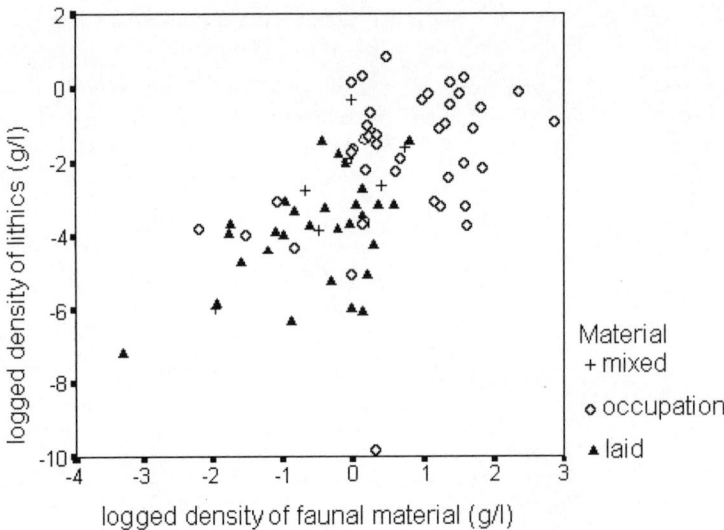

Figure 14.4. The densities of lithic and faunal material in relation to different types of floor at Çatal-höyük (Cross 2004).

floors, the overlying occupation deposits, while still only a few millimeters thick, are generally thicker and include a wider range of material such as burnt and unburnt organic and inorganic aggregates, small fragments of bone, charred cereal grain fragments, silicified plant remains, melted silica, charred wood, and calcitic ashes. But given the thinness and multiplicity of floors noted above, it is often impossible during excavation to separate individual floors from overlying lenses of occupation material. Thus the archaeological category "floor" includes clean plastered floors which may or may not have some use residues trampled into them, and floors without white plaster finishes that contain makeup and perhaps trample, but that also include thin occupation lenses above the floors. As a result, if we compare in Figure 14.4 the overall densities of lithic and faunal material (and the same is found with botanical material) in the laid white plastered floors and in the "occupation" floors without white plaster finishes, clear differences in density are observed (Cross 2004).

The densities in Figure 14.4 derive from all

Table 14.2. The Densities of Heavy Residue Material in Floors of Different Types in the North Area at Çatalhöyük

	White Clay Floors (48 Samples)		Nonwhite Laid Floors (20 Samples)		Occupation Floors (42 Samples)		All Floors (176 Samples)	
Bone 4 mm	0.210	0.73	0.241	0.84	0.653	2.28	0.287	1.00
Chipped Stone 4 mm	0.001	0.24	0.006	1.38	0.004	1.02	0.005	1.00
Bone 2 mm	0.026	0.65	0.059	1.50	0.053	1.32	0.040	1.00
Chipped Stone 2 mm	0.002	0.65	0.008	2.60	0.005	1.63	0.003	1.00
Bone 1 mm	0.016	1.00	0.013	0.82	0.020	1.20	0.016	1.00
Chipped Stone 1 mm	0.000	n/a	0.000	n/a	0.001	n/a	0.000	n/a

Note: All densities are expressed in grams per liter. For ease of comparison the overall median density value for all units can be expressed as a nominal value of 1.00 and the median values for specific types of units can be expressed as a second figure.

Table 14.3. Density of Bone and Chipped Stone in General Floors of Different Material Types in the South Area

	Baked Floor (71 Samples)		White Clay Floor (34 Samples)		Nonwhite Laid Floor (97 Samples)		Occupation Floor (188 Samples)		Mixed Floor (85 Samples)		All Floors (576 samples)	
Bone 4 mm	0.186	0.33	0.261	0.46	0.500	0.88	1.062	1.86	0.415	0.73	.570	1.00
Chipped Stone 4 mm	0.00	0.00	0.00	0.00	0.00	0.00	0.035	5.84	0.025	4.09	.006	1.00
Bone 2 mm	0.040	0.30	0.038	0.29	0.193	1.46	0.290	2.19	0.080	0.60	.132	1.00
Chipped Stone 2 mm	0.00	0.00	0.003	0.46	0.002	0.29	0.020	2.89	0.010	1.39	.007	1.00
Bone 1 mm	0.011	0.19	0.010	0.18	0.070	1.17	0.140	2.33	0.040	0.67	.060	1.00
Chipped Stone 1 mm	0.00	0.00	0.000	0.19	0.002	0.80	0.005	2.08	0.005	2.00	.002	1.00

artifacts found in the excavation trench and in dry screening, as well as the > 4 mm artifacts from the wet screen. By studying only the heavy residue data from the wet screen, we can explore further differences between categories of floor amongst the microartifacts. Figure 14.5 and Table 14.2 make the same distinction between white laid floors and occupation floors but add laid plastered floors without white plaster finishes. The differences in microartifact density between the laid floor categories probably result from both construction and use activities, and micromorphology is less frequently able to distinguish lenses of occupation on such floors. Differences in microartifact density are also shown for other categories of floors in Table 14.3 and Figure 14.6.

There are very marked differences between the surfaces of the different platforms and floors in any one building. Near the ovens the floors ("occupation" floors) are rich in charcoal and a wide range of residues from obsidian knapping debris to animal bone scatter to potsherds and charred wood and basketry. Away from the hearths and ovens there are various types of laid, whiter, higher and cleaner floors. It is probable that a large part of this variation derives from the use of different forms of construction material (containing different amounts and types of microartifact), although at least in the case of the denser "occupation" floors the on-floor material is sometimes thick enough to be distinguishable, at least under the microscope. As an example, in Figure 14.7 the "dirtier" occupation deposits could be distinguished in two areas associated with ovens (in the normal southern location and in an unusual northern location). The material in these dense and thicker occupation deposits on some floor areas allows us to argue that a wide range of activities from obsidian knapping to bone tool production, cooking and food preparation took place in the house. But it remains prudent to argue that for microartifacts in other floors the clear overall spatial differences found within buildings may relate primarily to construction and secondarily to use.

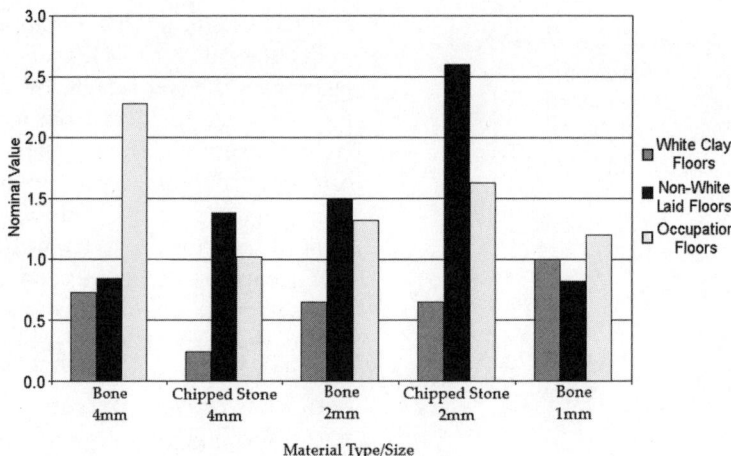

Figure 14.5. Median densities of bone and chipped stone in different types of floor in the north area at Çatalhöyük.

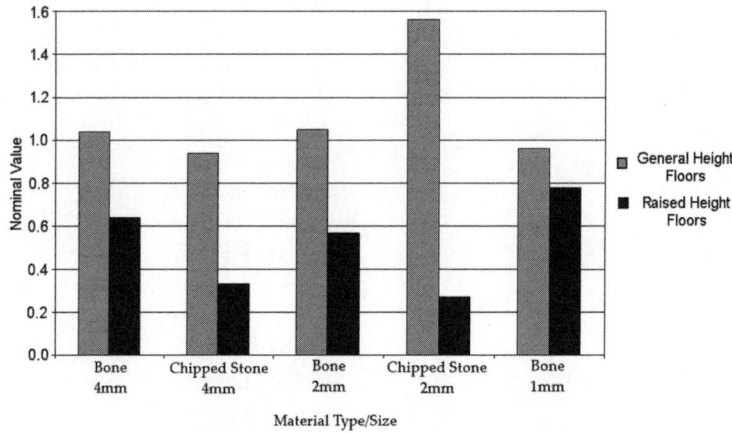

Figure 14.6. Densities of bone and chipped stone in general and raised height floors in the north area at Çatalhöyük.

The argument can be clarified by examining specific density variation in houses in relation to features such as hearths, ovens, and burials. As an example, patterning of micro-artifacts from heavy residues from individual buildings is shown for Building 1 (Subphase B1.2C) in Figure 14.8. The higher densities of small bone in food preparation and storage areas such as the western room and the south of the main room around a grinding installation and storage bin contrast with the lower densities in other parts of the main room including the platforms used for burial. The platforms and floor segments associated with art (the western and northwestern) and bur-ial (the northwestern, north central, and central east) all have low densities of small bone. Even if the patterning of heavy residues is partly the result of the use of different flooring materials, the distinctions in construction or use have a clear social significance. If we cannot talk with surety of repetitive social practices in terms of discard-producing activities for all floor types, we can talk of repetitive replastering activities with particular types of plaster chosen for different parts of floors, and we can talk of repetitive practices involving burial and the location of art, and we can certainly talk of repetitive sweeping practices.

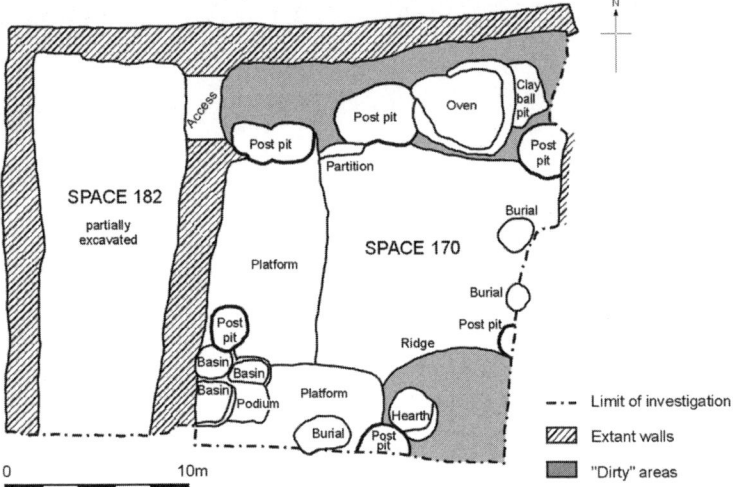

Figure 14.7. Two areas with "dirty" occupation floors in Building 17 at Çatalhöyük. These areas are well bounded and there is little "scuffing" onto adjacent floors (Farid 2004).

Inductively coupled plasma atomic emission spectrometer analysis of the elemental composition of floor deposits (Akyol and Demirci 2004; Middleton et al. 2004) shows clear differences between different floor areas (e.g., Fig. 14.9). A multi-elemental characterization of floor sediments was undertaken, for example in Building 5. Multivariate numerical classification yielded spatially coherent groups. In particular, the northwest platform in the central room of Building 5 was distinctive, probably as the result of both the use of different floor materials in the construction of different areas, and as a result of differential use of different parts of the floor.

There is some evidence that these practices extended into the wider world. Fragments of roof in the fill of Building 5, probably derived from the structure itself, revealed mixed floor types, similar to those found inside buildings, and water laid crusts indicate at least partial exposure to the elements. Charred plant remains and organic staining probably relate to domestic activities and fragments of oven plaster imply the presence of fire installations. A more complete roof discovered collapsed into Building 3 in the BACH Area showed clear evidence of spatial distinctions between cleaner and more residue rich areas, rather like the floors within the houses (Stevanovic and Tringham 1999).

But there are also contrasts as we move away from the house. The midden areas between houses and the middens in abandoned houses show a dense build up of a variety of materials including a wide range of macro and microartifacts, ash and charcoal. Traces of wall plaster and the overall nature of many of the small concentrations of discarded material suggest that some of this may be hearth sweepings and other sweepings from the house. Analysis of the bile acids of dung in the midden revealed a suite of fecal biomarkers indicative of a human origin (Bull et al. 2004). The midden is thus the end-product of the very careful regulation of daily practices inside the house, and it appears as its inverse—dense, artifact rich and spatially unsegregated. There is sometimes evidence in the middens for spatially defined activities in the form of fire spots and rare burials, but these are not repeated in the same place over time. There are other areas outside the house which also suggest less disciplined behavior. Some of the art shows ritual baiting and hunting scenes in which human figures are shown jumping, leaping, beneath and over bulls and stags, their arms raised and their bodies active. Some of these scenes show rows of people, but others show little order. If these paintings depict actual activities, they must have taken place outside the settlement

Building 1 subphase B1.2C, 2 mm bone

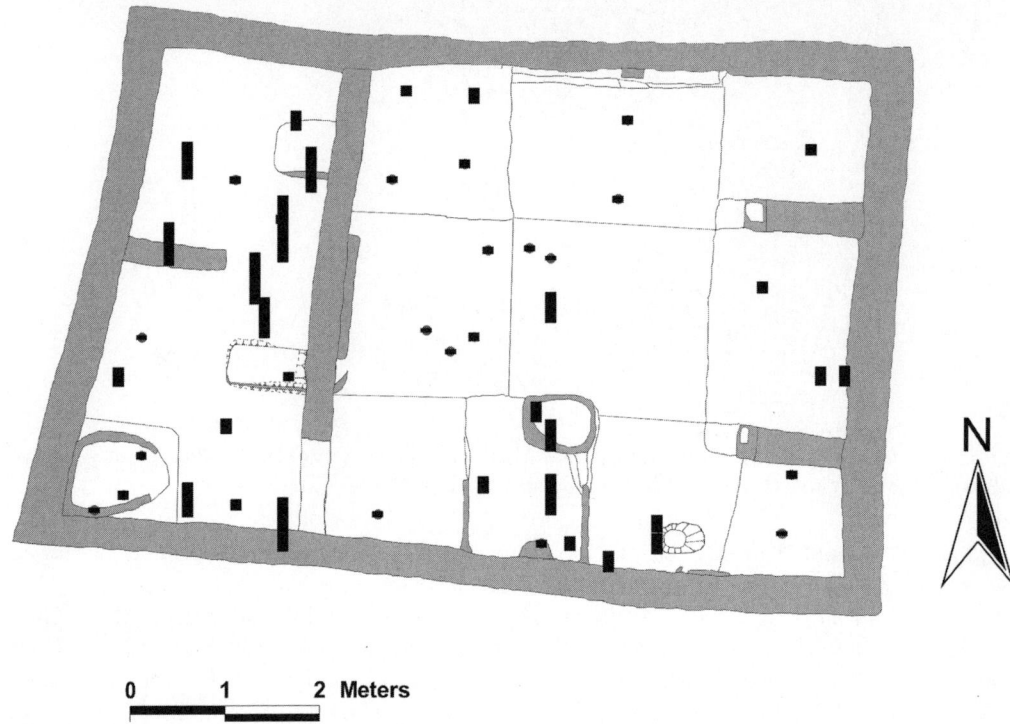

N

0   1   2 Meters

Figure 14.8. An example of heavy residue plots for microartifacts in and on floors in Building 1 at Çatal-höyük.

as they involve large animals and many people in open spaces. If we take "shrine" F.V.1 as an example we see cattle, deer, wild asses, boars, bears, wolves and lions, often associated with groups of twenty to forty people (Mellaart 1966:184–91). The regulated practices in the house are very different from these glimpses of non-house activities.

We have identified repetitive patterning in the construction and use of buildings at Çatalhöyük. Our best evidence comes from Buildings 1 and 5, but we have referred to site-wide patterns in the 15 buildings in which floors have been excavated by the present project. Repetitive patterning in, for example, the location of art, burials, obsidian hoards, ovens, and ladder-entries was identified in the over 200 houses excavated by Mellaart in the 1960s, but data were not collected at that time which would allow the study of artifact patterning on floors. Taking

the past and present excavations together, there is evidence to suggest that as a child grew up in a house at Çatalhöyük, it would have learned that different types of people were buried beneath certain platforms, that different plasters were used for different platforms, that refuse was swept up more carefully from some areas. Different symbols are often placed in different parts of the house. Because of the burial associations between different types of people and different parts of the house, it seems reasonable to assume that different people may have sat, eaten, and slept in different parts of the house. Social rules would have been learned through daily practice involving the movements of the body in the house. This is one way in which each individual would have learned and incorporated social rules.

Of course, all societies have rules to deal with the organization of space and discard,

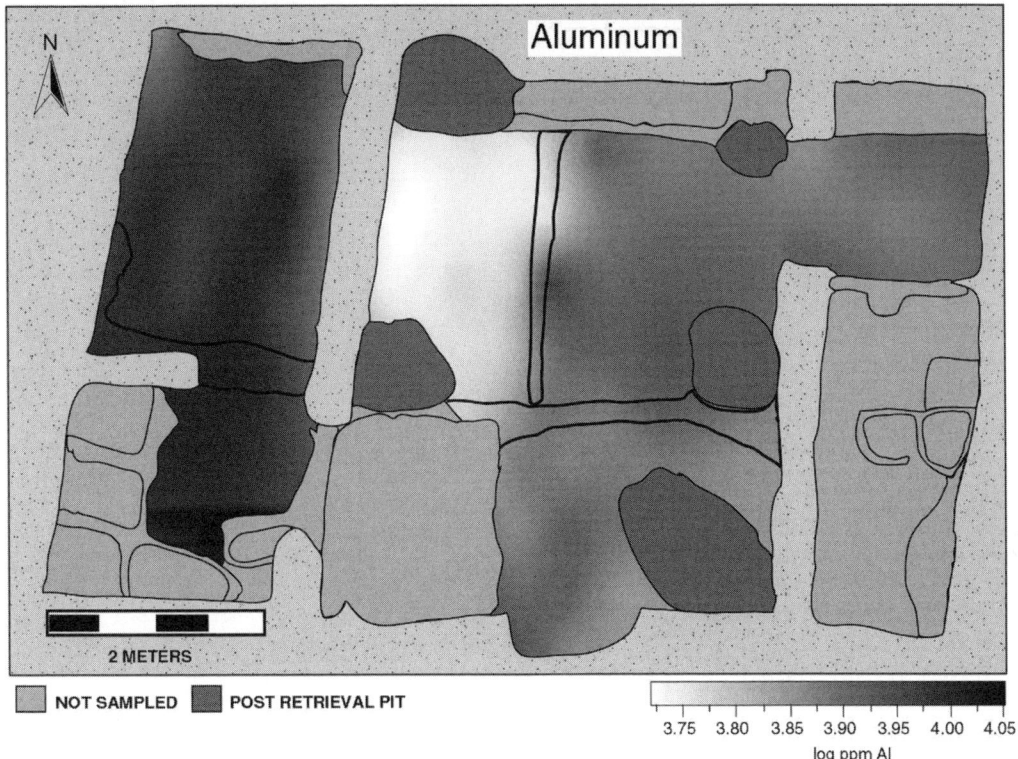

Figure 14.9. Example of plot of ICP AES analyses of the elemental composition of floor deposits from Building 5 (Middleton et al. 2004).

and it could be argued that the inhabitants of Çatalhöyük simply cleaned out their houses in order to prevent build-ups of refuse. Indeed, it is partly the arrangement of daily living practices at the site, with long-term re-use of buildings in the same location, and a high density of such buildings, that necessitates repeated cleaning out practices. The social regulation is already there in the practical need to clean out houses so thoroughly and consistently. But at Çatalhöyük, there is more than just the regular dumping out of refuse. As with other activities in the house, refuse sweeping took place within a highly divided social space, marked and fragmented by platform edges, pillars, ledges and so on. The body moved around this space cleaning up; but also replastering floors, burying the dead, painting the walls, moving up and down from platform to platform, preparing and cooking food, knapping obsidian, eating,

sleeping. All these movements of the body were constrained by platforms, edges, delicate ledges and pillars and relief sculptures sticking out from walls. All societies have rules about movement and discard in space and in houses, but at Çatalhöyük there is a particular emphasis on segmenting space in the house and regulating movement around that space. Çatalhöyük sees a particular emphasis on repetition, with layer upon layer of replastering using similar divisions of space. The tidy ordering of domestic space and movements within that space, are repeated over decades and centuries. Buildings 5 and 1 were together occupied for over a century; both Mellaart's "shrines" 10 and 31 continued in use from Level IX to Level VIA which is a period of about 400 years. Mellaart did not excavate all levels in the same part of the mound and so only future excavation will be able to show whether some buildings at

Çatalhöyük were rebuilt for large parts of the 1200 years of occupation at the site.

But whose interests do these repetitive bodily practices serve? There is very little evidence of gender differentiation in the location and associations of burial, in diet as suggested by isotopic analysis of human bone and wear analysis of teeth (Andrews, Molleson and Boz 2004; Richards and Pearson 2004), and there is little evidence of status differentiation amongst burials. On the other hand, some houses seem more elaborate than others. These more elaborate houses were termed "shrines" by Mellaart (1967). More recently Ritchey (1996) and Düring (2001) have quantified the degree of elaboration of buildings in each level based on numbers of internal spaces, moldings, basins, pillars, posts, benches and platforms. Gradual clines of variation from less to more elaborate buildings can be seen at all levels, and the more elaborate buildings are interspersed spatially amongst less elaborate buildings. Despite the fact that all buildings are houses with a full range of domestic activity, storage and domestic production, there is some indication that fine bifacially flaked obsidian points are concentrated in the more elaborate buildings (Conolly 1996). The fact that obsidian cores also concentrate in the more elaborate buildings suggests some preferential access to or involvement in obsidian. The largest numbers of figurines come from very elaborate buildings (Hamilton 1996). But the notion that the more elaborate buildings were in some sense "dominant" is best supported by the evidence of burial. In the case of Building 1, around 60 individuals were interred in the structure during its construction and occupation. Of these at least 30 individuals must have been alive at the same point in time. This is too many to have actually lived in the building on a day-to-day basis, as it is unlikely that this exceeded 10 individuals based on the size of the building and probable sleeping arrangements. This suggests that Building 1 acted as a focus for burial for a number of buildings. Building 1 could be defined as elaborate in terms of its bucrania, paintings, posts, numbers of platforms, and

moldings. Some elaborate buildings excavated by Mellaart in the 1960s also contained large numbers of burials, although the records are imprecise (Hamilton 1996). The two buildings with most burials from the 1960s are "shrine" 10 which had 32 skeletons in Level VI, and "shrine" 31 which had 58 skeletons in Level VII. "Shrine" 10 occurs second in terms of Ritchey's (1996) ranking of 59 buildings in Level VIB. "Shrine" 31 is the second most elaborate building in his ranking of the 45 buildings in Level VII. At the other end of the scale, there are non-elaborate buildings such as Building 2 which have no burials. Overall it seems probable that certain buildings became preferential sites for burial. In this way they had a "dominance" in relation to access to previous lineage members.

There is some evidence that the dominant houses were more invested in the regulation of repetitive bodily practices. The more elaborate buildings such as Building 17 (this is a renumbering of Mellaart's "shrine" 10 in Level IX, the first full level that could be excavated in this building by the present project) placed more emphasis on the maintenance of the internal floor scheme identified in this paper (Farid 2004). The distinctiveness of platforms and the degree of separation between floors with cleaner plasters and those with high densities of charcoal and hearth sweepings seem stronger in more elaborate buildings with burials, such as Buildings 1, 3 and 17 (see Fig. 14.7) than in smaller buildings without burials such as Building 2 (and perhaps 18, 23 and 5). In Building 2, the ridges between the area near the oven and the more northerly whiter floors are ill-defined and there is overspill of charcoal-rich deposits across the ridges. This type of "scuffing" is less common in the more elaborate houses.

But the degree of dominance is slight, and could even be reversed if one considered alternate criteria. Building 2 for instance had two caches of chipped stone deposited in its foundations, totaling over 50 pieces. As already noted, Özdoğan (2002) sees much more evidence for social differentiation in eastern as opposed to central Anatolia. It is difficult to explain the overall emphasis on repetitive practices in central Anatolia solely by referring to centralized power or the use of force. The overall repetition of practices must have been embedded in a wider discourse for it to have been so pervasive. People accepted the regulated and repetitive practices, presumably because they enabled social life. The rules would have enabled practical living in confined spaces and the carrying out of a multiplicity of tasks in those spaces. The practices created rules and a *habitus* (such as deference to elders) that could have helped in the negotiation of disputes over movement, access, rights in the settlement as a whole. The regulation and the habituation would have allowed the growth of the long-term dependencies which are necessary for delayed-return economic systems (Woodburn 1980).

SOCIAL MEMORY

What was the social context in which the repetition of practices was made possible at Çatalhöyük, and what role did the more elaborate houses play? While it might be suggested that daily practice and social memory are distinct topics, we would argue that in this context they are inseparable in that regulation is not simply imposed at Çatalhöyük but is constructed through the habituation of practices. In societies without any form of writing, an important mechanism of social reproduction is through the construction of social memory. We use the term memory to take the discussion away from "tradition" and towards an active process of memorizing that is socially embedded. We do not just remember biologically (Ebron 1998). What we remember is selective, and can thus be socially constructed and contested (Connerton 1989). So how were memories constructed at Çatalhöyük and how were they used in the interests of social regulation? We will argue that one important mechanism was again the house.

The notion that the house can act as a site for social memory has been widely recognized ethnographically and archaeologically (e.g., Carsten and Hugh-Jones 1995; Joyce

and Gillespie 2000). In Levi-Strauss's (1982: 174) definition of "house societies" we see a move away from kinship classificatory models towards the "house" as a corporate body holding an estate which reproduces itself through the transmission of its name, goods and titles. Particularly in more recent research (Carsten and Hugh-Jones 1995; Joyce and Gillespie 2000), the materiality of the house, its practices and heirlooms are foregrounded. The transmission of houses and of objects kept in houses, forges social memory and constitutes social units (Joyce 2000a). In Polynesia, for example, an important component of the reproduction of the corporate group is the burial of ancestors and the transformation of houses into ritual temples (Kirch 2000).

The continuity in the layout of houses through time in the Neolithic tells of the Levant and southeastern Anatolia has been identified as relevant to the discussion of social memory by Kuijt (2001; see also Banning and Byrd 1987; Kirkbride 1968:94). The construction of social memory has also been related to the widespread Near Eastern practice of removing and circulating skulls, including the plastering of facial features (Cauvin 1994; Garfinkel 1994; Goring-Morris 2000; Kuijt 2000; Stordeur et al. 1977). The specific social context of this activity seems to vary between individualized and collective memory construction (Kuijt 2001). Clearly not all mortuary ritual is about ancestral cults (Morris 1991), but equally, ancestral rituals may refer to both generic and specific ancestors (Whitley 2002).

We can see the importance of creating social memories at Çatalhöyük in that burial in houses is more prevalent here than in other sites in Anatolia and the Near East. But are we dealing here with specific or general ancestors (see also Parker-Pearson 1999b:164)? We need to be able to demonstrate specific links to argue that particular house-based corporate groups are being constructed. We also have to distinguish habituated behavior, involving the repetition of acts, from commemorative events involving specific social memories (Connerton 1989). In the former case, ritual and other acts may become routinized and codified but there is no specific memory of events and histories, while in the latter case a link is remembered to a specific event or person. There may also be community wide memories embedded in daily practices and rules (everyone knows that the hearth is in the south of the house) without there being any specific memory of an individual house in which the hearth was in the south. So the onus is on us to demonstrate specificity of memory construction if we wish to argue that memory was used to reproduce regulatory codes through the practices in the house.

We have already described how the continuity of houses is seen in the exact building of one house on the walls of the preceding house. We have also noted the remarkable degree of continuity of platforms and floor divisions through successive replasterings and rebuildings. Change does occur in the location of ovens and hearths etc, and in terms of the overall cultural assemblage, but it is gradual and incremental. Earlier in this paper we described the sequences at Aşıklı Höyük and Çatalhöyük showing the repetition of house, platform, hearth and midden location over hundreds of years. But all this evidence could be produced by habituated practices at the level of the site as a whole. What is the evidence of house-based memory construction?

All fifteen houses excavated by the current project at Çatalhöyük show some form of founding or abandonment practices and rituals. An enormous emphasis is placed at abandonment on scouring out bins, filling in ovens, cleaning floors, dismantling timbers and filling in rooms. It is important to recognise that these abandonment processes may have been set within a thoroughly practical logic. Structural timbers were probably removed so that they could be reused in a later house. Dendrochronology appears to support the idea that some posts were reused (Newton and Kuniholm 1999). Scouring of bin floors, house floors and moldings may have occurred so that the fine plaster could be reused in later houses, especially if some

forms of lime-rich muds and clays were difficult to obtain. The packing of ovens with clean soil and the filling in of rooms may also reflect a concern with attempting to provide as stable a base as possible for the next structure to be constructed. While this is true, the degree of "cleaning up" that occurs is remarkable, and the deliberate placing of artifacts (such as the upturned grinding stone placed on the floor in one phase of Building 1's abandonment, and the cattle scapulae placed on top of or near hearths in the final Building 1 abandonment and in Buildings 23 and 17) are less easy to explain fully in this way. In a number of cases foundation deposits have been found, such as the burial of three individual neonates, an adult woman with neonate and an old man in Building 1. Evidence of possible feasting (concentrations of large animal bones from large animals) has been found beneath some walls. In Building 17 in the southeast corner of the main room, a hearth was found which had been rebuilt several times. In the sealing deposit of one of the hearths a broken figurine was placed with both head and torso present, but separate. The deliberateness of this act is reinforced by the faunal remains from the same context (locus) which suggest a single event consumption of a young sheep. Two sub-phases of hearth reconstruction later, a broken figurine head was again deposited—directly over the earlier example. This head was very similar in appearance and size to the earlier one, and both were quite different from other figurines found at the site. This evidence of closure and reenactment strongly suggests specific house-based memories.

One place where we have moderately good evidence for replacement of one house by another at Çatalhöyük is Building 1 and the house immediately beneath it, Building 5, although we did not excavate beyond the latest phase in Building 5 (Fig. 14.3). In general terms the similarities between the successive buildings are striking and exceed what might be anticipated simply from general similarities between buildings at a site wide level. It was immediately clear as we dug through below the floors in Building 1 that the main walls of the building continued down and were more or less continuous with the building below. In fact, it was often difficult to determine a boundary between the two buildings in time; they formed part of a continuous process of replacement.

The overall plan of Building 1, especially in its earliest phases, follows very much that of the earlier Building 5. The placing of the western rooms, and the entrance into them in the south are the same. The oven is in much the same place in Building 1 Subphase B1.2B. The ladder emplacement is in the same location as before. Of course, some of these continuities result from the technical preference for locating later walls on the solid foundations of earlier walls rather than on softer fill. Other continuities (such as the oven and ladder locations) are part of a site-wide pattern. But there are also acts too specific to be explained in this way, as in the Building 17 example just provided.

An example of specific commemorative memory in the Building 5 to 1 sequence may be represented by the retrieval pits against the walls in the western parts of the main rooms. In Building 5, F.240 is a retrieval pit dug to remove a post from the eastern face of the west wall in Space 154. The retrieval pit contains two bone points and an obsidian projectile point. This is one of only two Building 5 retrieval pits with substantial artifacts. F.240 is directly beneath Building 1 retrieval pit F.17. The latter was dug to remove or retrieve relief sculpture (only traces of which remained on the wall) from the east face of the west wall in the main room. This again contained "offerings" of three bone points, a bird bone and eight assorted pieces of obsidian and flint placed in a group in its fill. So there is perhaps a specific repetition of retrieval and closure acts involving bone and obsidian objects.

The retrieval pit just described in Building 1 (F. 17) provides an example of commemorative memory maintained at both house and larger scales. The pit is dug down from the filled-in building, subphase B1.5B. And yet, whatever was on the west wall of this room

had already been disturbed or even partially destroyed in phases B1.3 and B1.4 by the construction of wall F.18. Indeed, the sculpture on the west wall could only have been an integrated part of the room in Building 1 back in subphase B1.2C. Phases B1.3 to B1.5B probably lasted decades, based on the relative criteria of numbers of floors and oven bases. And so the retrieval pit implies a memory going back for some time. It might be seen to imply a precise social memory. However, there are difficulties beyond the uncertainty about the lengths of phases. We do not know what the relief sculpture was on the west wall of the main room in Building 1; and we do not know how the wall F.18 affected the sculpture although it is likely that it did damage it in some way. Both the relief sculpture and its relation to wall F.18 were destroyed by the retrieval pit itself. All we can say with certainty is that retrieval pit F.17 was dug down very carefully against the correct wall, in exactly the place where the sculpture was located. Given the large amount of erosion off the top of the mound that occurred in the millennia after the Neolithic occupation, we cannot know how deep these Neolithic 'archaeologists' had to dig, but it was at least 0.7 m and probably substantially more. We do know that Building 1 had been filled and that any digging down implies a precise historical memory even if embedded within wider knowledge about where important sculptures were generally placed. Not all houses have major relief sculptures on the west walls of main rooms. Specific memory is also implied by certain burials in Building 1. Whilst in some instances it was clearly permissible for later interments to disturb earlier bodies, there are clear indications that the precise locations and nature of earlier burials were remembered years or even decades later.

Can we estimate how much overlap in population there could have been between Buildings 5 and 1? Were any of the nearly 60 people buried in Building 1 alive during the time of Building 5? Detailed AMS dating of these buildings based on 40 dates has allowed

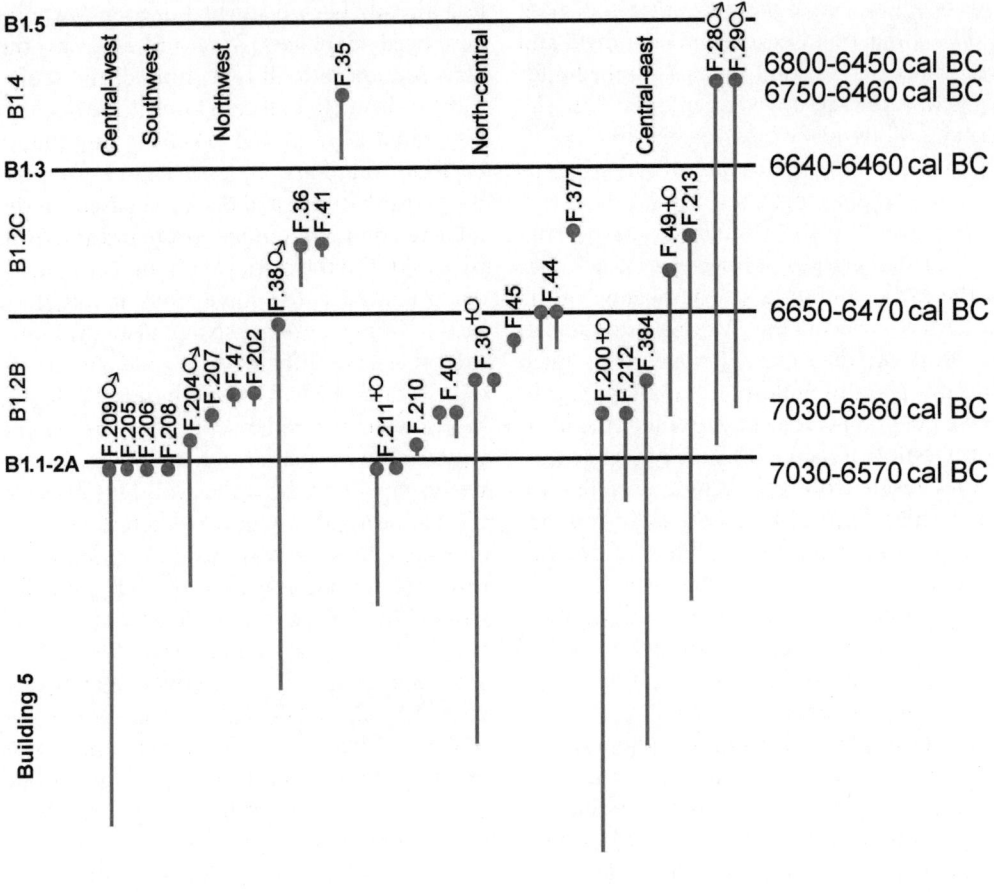

Figure 14.10. Lifespans of individuals buried in Building 1 in relation to selected absolute dates of phases of Buildings 1 and 5 (to two standard deviations)(Cessford 2004a).

precise evaluation of the duration of occupation phases and dates of burials (Cessford 2004b, and Fig. 14.10). Assessing phasing has also been helped by the apparent yearly replastering of main walls (corroborated in general terms against AMS and dendrochronology; see Newton and Kuniholm 1999). Amongst some of the earliest burials in Building 1 were several old individuals who must have been alive for most of the lifespan of Building 5. An old man (F.209) buried during the construction of Building 1 was at least 50 years old and an elderly woman (F.200) buried during the earliest occupational subphase was around 60 years old. Although we

cannot be certain how long Building 5 was occupied, wall plaster suggests that it may be around 70 years, which is broadly compatible with the overall site dating sequence. This suggests that individuals F.209 and F.200 were alive for most if not all of the occupation of Building 5. A similar phenomenon can be observed for Building 1, where two males F.28 and F.29 buried towards the end of the building's occupation were at least nearly as old as the structure itself.

The fact that the relief sculpture in Building 1 was not removed immediately, but after the house had been filled in, may suggest that time had to pass before it could be removed.

This memory across several phases is seen in other examples. For example, Mellaart (1964: 70), discussed the depiction of a bull in his "shrine" 8 in Level IX. "Once again the presence of a bull on the north wall of "shrines" in this position should be noted, for this is the third in succession ("shrines" VI.8, VII.8, and IX.8)." Bulls are found elsewhere on northern walls, as in VI.10, but not on the eastern part of the north wall as in the "shrine" 8 sequence. What is also remarkable is that this specific memory in "shrine" 8 was retained across phases in which a totally different form of wall art was used. Despite a period in Levels VIII and part of VII with vulture paintings, the distinctive bull motif was returned to in Levels VII and VI. Memory was retained of an earlier arrangement of the house and was returned to.

There is much evidence that not only the heads of wild animals, but also of people were used as part of the construction of specific social memories. In Building 2, there is evidence of removal of something large from the west wall of the main room, possibly linked to a large wild bull horn found on the floor nearby. We have already noted the removal of sculpture from the west wall in the main room in Building 1, where remnants of its mudbrick core and a separate bull horn had been left in the wall. Mellaart (1967:Figure 16) records a frequent pattern of the destruction of the west walls of main rooms in order to remove sculpture. We do not know what exactly the bucrania represented, but in the art the baiting of bulls and other wild animals is linked to group activities and probably represents initiation or other rituals. A possibly similar instance may be the placement of at least 13 wild goat horns from a minimum of eight animals in a group in Building 1. Such groups of wild animal skeletal elements are paralleled from the excavations by Mellaart in the 1960s. For example, 13 lower boars' jaws were mounted in VIA.8 (Mellaart 1967:69) and must either represent curated assemblages or material specifically obtained by a reasonably sized group at some distance from the site. It is possible to suggest

that the heads and other cranial elements of such animals when placed in houses created memories of significant events in the life cycles of the houses or the people in them.

In the same way that a pit was dug down to retrieve sculptures in Building 1 and other buildings (see above), so pits were also dug to retrieve the heads of selected humans. In both Building 1 and Building 6 a skeleton was found buried beneath the house floors with its head removed and with traces of cut marks on the upper vertebrae. Andrews et al. (2004) suggest, on the basis of the completeness of the skeletons and the condition of the bones, that the bodies were buried with their flesh on, and that the head was cut off after a period of decay. Headless human corpses are frequently shown in the wall art, but so far only two headless skeletons have been excavated by the current project. Most skeletons were found with head intact. It is possible that some special status was associated with the headless burials as the skeletons have been treated in distinctive ways (in Building 6 an unusual layout of the body and the placing of a cloth and plank over the torso). How were these heads reused? In the recent excavations, detached human skulls were found in foundation deposits, in a post retrieval pit in Building 17, and in structured abandonment deposits in Building 3 (Stevanovic and Tringham 1999). The removal and reuse of human heads suggests some attempt to construct links between social groups and specific ancestors, since heads were (perhaps a year) later removed from individuals who had been treated in special ways at death. It is the heads of these particular individuals that were chosen for head removal. It is these particular locations that were remembered.

The plastered skulls from Kösk Höyük (Silistreli 1991) are broadly contemporary with the later levels at Çatalhöyük and indicate a related but probably rather different phenomenon in central Anatolia. As in the Levant the plastering of features on skulls may reinforce the idea of specific memories. There is abundant evidence from Çatalhöyük of the construction of social memories, although many of these may be general and site-wide and be embedded in practices and routines rather than being conscious, specific and commemorative. But there is some evidence that the politics of memory were at least partly based in the house at Çatalhöyük and that the house was central to the construction of social memory.

What was the role of the dominant, more elaborate houses in the politics of memory? There is some evidence that these dominant houses were particular guardians of the archive of memories, alongside their particular investment in the regulation of daily practices that we saw earlier. We have already seen that they have concentrations of burials, suggesting that the archive of lineal and/or affinal relations was constructed preferentially in the dominant house. There is also a clear link between houses with large numbers of burials and houses which are replaced through many levels. The current project has so far only excavated one building (Building 5) below Building 1 which has 62 burials, but deeper sequences were excavated by Mellaart. From his data, the two buildings with most burials ("shrines" 10 and 31, see above) in Levels VI and VII, were both rebuilt through 5 levels (IX to VIA). Other buildings with many burials ("shrines" 1, 7, 8 in Level VI) also continued across 3 to 5 levels. Adjacent less elaborate buildings with few or no burials (such as Building 2 by "shrine" 10) are not replaced from level to level. The floors of "shrine" 10 (Buildings 17 and 6) in Levels VIII and IX are lower than surrounding buildings, suggesting that this more elaborate building may have been modified and rebuilt at a slower rate than surrounding buildings. Thus domestic houses used for large numbers of burials, and those houses which are more elaborate, may have been more closely tied to continuity and the preservation of a collective memory.

All this indicates that the politics of memory at Çatalhöyük were house based, and perhaps that dominant houses invested particularly in the construction and control of social memory. The construction of longer term memories, both specific and general,

would have been the basis for the social, ritual and economic practices involved in delayed return societies. The social memories helped create the repetition in which daily practices were embedded.

CONCLUSIONS

We have argued that at Çatalhöyük the house was an important mechanism for regulating daily practice, the embodiment of social rules, and the construction of social memory. We do not argue that the processes discussed here need be found outside the areas considered. Indeed, we have seen differences even between central and eastern Anatolia. For example, Özdoğan (2002:254) notes that architectural change in eastern Anatolia and Upper Mesopotamia is much faster (at sites like Hallan Çemi and Çayönü) than in central Anatolia (Aşıklı Höyük and Çatalhöyük), although these comparisons are made across large distances and expanses of time. Architectural change is also apparently more pronounced at sites to the west of Çatalhöyük in the Lake District (Duru 1999), on the Mediterranean coast and in Northwest Anatolia (Matthews 2002:96–97). Certainly there are a number of sites in central Anatolia that show long-term occupation with little change (Aşıklı Höyük 8400–7400 B.C., Can Hasan III 7650–6600 B.C.). This suggests that central Anatolia was particularly distinctive in terms of the maintenance of regulatory codes through daily practice and house based memory. There may thus be a link between the great emphasis on internal divisions of space, the dense packing of houses, and the great continuity of house-based practices in central Anatolia, although more work is needed to see how internal activities were organized at sites other than Çatalhöyük.

The general themes of repetitive practices and social memory may be discussed as relevant to many delayed return, early agricultural societies. In the central Anatolian Neolithic, the socialization and regulation allowed people to deal with the economic, social, sanitation, crowding, access problems associated with living in particularly tightly packed agglomerations with limited centralization of power. The practices were productive, providing mechanisms to deal with these problems and to create longer term social relationships and memories, and delayed return economic systems. But they also served the interests of dominant groups and the structures that supported them. Even if further work at Çatalhöyük discovers larger-scale centralization than so far identified, the question of how that power was embedded within daily practice will remain.

Acknowledgements

We are grateful to all the members of the Çatalhöyük project on whose work all the above is based. In particular we thank Shahina Farid, Duncan Lees for Figure 14.7 and Slobodan Mitrovic for his work on the heavy residue patterning. We also wish to thank Dušan Boriç, Bleda Düring and various anonymous reviewers for specific comments on this paper. The abstract was translated into Spanish by Dante Angelo.

15

The Lady and the Seed:
Some Thoughts on the Role of Agriculture in the "Neolithic Revolution"

It was Burcu Tunc who found it. She was working on the top of the Neolithic east mound at Çatalhöyük, excavating the shallow foundation trenches for a large shelter that we had decided to build over the area excavated by Mellaart in the 1960s. This "south" area had also been one of the foci of our own excavations since the mid 1990s. But in our work we had concentrated on the lower levels of the site, especially Levels VI and below, and we had conducted little excavation in the upper levels. In the lower levels we rarely found female figurines of the type made famous by Mellaart. We found figurines certainly—of animals and humanoid or birdlike forms, but not the distinctive rounded female figurines with clear breasts, arms, and legs. Mellaart had mainly found the latter type in Levels I–IV (Hamilton 1996).

So when Burcu shouted my name across the south area, I was not thinking in terms of finding female figurines, though the huddle of excited people peering at something very small should have given me a clue. In her hand Burcu held an extremely small figurine with its head, as usual, broken off. Tiny though it was, it had clear breasts and a swollen stomach or abdomen. The arms were distinct, although crudely modeled, in the position that is formulaic for such figurines at Çatalhöyük—resting on the stomach or upper legs. The bottom of the figurine did not have clear legs, but looked rather like the base of the "bird" or "humanoid" figurines (Fig. 15.1a).

The figurine had been found right at the top of the mound. Like many of the figurines we had found lower down, it was in midden deposits of ash, bone, ceramics, obsidian, and shell—rich layers of refuse. It was impossible to give an exact level since we did not have stratigraphic links between this foundation trench and other parts of the mound. But the figurine was probably in Level III or IV. We dry-sieved the surrounding soil carefully, looking for the missing head, but this was never recovered. The vast majority of female figurines found by Mellaart and by us had their heads missing.

So the figurine was taken down to the dig house and put into the finds processing and cataloguing system. I thought little of it after that, for a time at least. After all, the aim of the new excavations at Çatalhöyük is the scientific recovery of information about social processes. Our aim is to understand the environmental, economic, social, and ideological organization, as well as to respond to the different communities interested in the site. We were not hunting art or nice objects in an antiquarian way. We wanted to understand things in their context, not as isolated objects. But then something else happened that forced me to turn back to this particular figurine.

In cleaning the figurine a small opening was found in its back (Fig. 15.1b). And

Figure 15.1. (a–b) Views of the figurine discussed in the text. The white bar at the base of the frontal view provides a 1-cm scale. Photographs: Michael Ashley-Lopez.

through the aperture one could see a small seed. I asked Meltem, a member of the archaeobotany team, to have a careful look at the seed. She showed me what she could see under the microscope. With a small brush you could move the seed around in its hole in the back of the figurine. Identification was still difficult, and the hole in the seed seemed to be a break. What one could say with absolute certainty was that the object in the back of the figurine was a seed, and from its size one could be sure that it was a wild seed.

Could the seed have got there by accident? Perhaps the seed just happened to be in the clay used to make the figurine, and then in the firing of the figurine the seed had shrunk, making it appear as if it was in a small cavity. This interpretation did not persuade any of the people I talked to about it. The seed was too precisely placed—exactly in the middle of the back. It was almost as if the whole tiny figurine had been modeled, rather quickly and crudely, around this small seed. Also arguing against the accidental hypothesis is the fact that in all the hundreds of figurines we had previously found we had never seen a similar seed cavity, in any part of any figurine body. Of course, one could not rule out the "accidental" hypothesis, and the argument which follows in this paper is based on other evidence. But it remains my view that the

seed is more likely to have been specifically inserted into the back of the figurine and partially or completely covered over before it was accidentally or intentionally fired.

When I was first told about the seed in the figurine I had immediately assumed the seed would be a cereal grain. After all, here we were, well into the ceramic Neolithic, in the second half of the seventh millennium B.C., long after the origins of agriculture. And how could one not be influenced by the mass of literature arguing for the centrality of fertility symbolism in the Neolithic of Anatolia and the Near East—all the ideas about women, reproduction, cycles of birth and death, the renewal of the crops, etc.? For many people, from Cauvin (1994), Mellaart (1967), and my own work (Hodder 1990) to the Goddess followers, the whole point about early representations of women was that they were linked to agricultural as well as to human fertility. The seed should be a cereal. It should represent the crops on which the whole of settled life depended after the Neolithic Revolution.

But there was no doubt. The seed in the tiny figurine was wild. There were other examples of a link between female figurines and agriculture, such as the famous "Mother Goddess" figurine found by Mellaart in a Level III "shrine" in a grain bin. But this new figurine suggested a more general relationship between female figurines and plants rather than specifically with domesticated plants. There is an ambiguous painting which possibly shows women gathering, though neither the gender nor the activity are clear, and there is certainly no specific evidence in the art of women being associated with cultivated plants—indeed there is very little plant symbolism in the art at all.

The association between the tiny female figurine and a wild seed reminded me of something I had been thinking for some time. The more we excavated at Çatalhöyük, the more I had become struck by the lack of symbolism related to domesticated plants and animals. The pattern was clearest for animals, perhaps because animal symbolism is much more prevalent at Çatalhöyük. The work by Louise Martin and Rissa Russell (Hodder 2004) had shown that there was a high proportion of domesticated sheep and goats in all levels at the site. But all other animals seem morphologically to be wild, including the cattle. And it is wild animals that dominate in the painting and relief sculpture. The art is centered round bulls, bears, deer, boars, leopards, vultures, foxes, weasels, and so on. There are certainly some rams' heads placed on walls although these could be wild. None have been found by the present project. In recent excavations of Building 1, six horn cores of morphologically wild goats were found in the collapse or abandonment deposits in a bin containing burned lentils. There is one painting from the excavations in the 1960s apparently showing goats, which again could be wild, associated with possible trees.

These examples do little to lessen the impression that the dominant symbolism at Çatalhöyük deals with wild animals. There are scenes of people hunting, teasing, and baiting wild bulls, deer, bears, and boars. There are the pairings of relief leopards. There are the bucrania which in all cases examined by us are made from the skulls and horns of wild bulls. There are the cutouts and paintings of bulls, and of vultures and cranes. This relative avoidance of domesticated

sheep and goats in the symbolism, despite their massive dominance in the faunal remains, is remarkable. There are large numbers of animal figurines, but they are not carefully modeled and it is usually difficult to assign them to species (is this a dog or an equid or a bull?) never mind to decide whether they are wild or domestic. There are no scenes of people herding large flocks of small domestic ruminants. The bones of sheep and goats show much evidence of intensive use, having been broken up for cooking and marrow extraction. They clearly provided a central resource. But they are not prominent in the symbolism. Similarly, there are no scenes of people cutting, harvesting, or winnowing cereal crops, even though domesticated cereals contributed the major component to the archaeobotanical assemblage. There are no images of people grinding grain, cooking, or engaged in other domestic activities. Indeed the whole world of "the domesticated" is underrepresented in the art. Of course, the domestic spaces, the buildings at Çatalhöyük which all have "domestic" functions of food preparation and storage and tool production, form the arena for the symbolism at the site. In this sense the domestic world is the center of the art and symbolism at Çatalhöyük. But on the other hand, that art and symbolism look outwards and away from the domestic world. The symbolism studiously ignores what we might have thought would be the main area of interest in the millennia after the famed "agricultural revolution." Why is this?

I intend to suggest two answers to this question. The first concerns the role of agriculture in the "agricultural revolution" and the second concerns the role of women in that transformation and at Çatalhöyük.

First, then, was agriculture very important in the "agricultural revolution"? It has long been argued, from Rousseau, Marx and Engels onwards, that the revolutionary nature of the domestication of plants and animals was that agricultural intensification and storage led to social differentiation, concentrations of power, specialization of production, sedentism, and ultimately urbanism. Over recent decades, the picture has become more nuanced and complex. The process was clearly very slow, from the Natufian and earlier onwards. Different crops and animals were domesticated at different times, and there is much evidence of regional variability throughout the Near East and Anatolia (Özdoğan 2002). Few would now speak of a "revolution" at all, but of a slow process in which morphological changes in plants and animals are only a component. The evidence of early large agglomerated sites with ritual buildings but still dependent on wild resources (as at Göbekli, Schmidt 2001) or with a limited use of domesticated plants and animals suggests that the social processes of sedentism and the economic processes of intensification were not heavily dependent on the rise of domesticated plants and animals. Even when a full suite of domestic plants is present, as at Çatalhöyük, there is little evidence that it always led to specialization and centralization. At Çatalhöyük, the organization of production and subsistence remains stubbornly domestic. Each building at the site is a house with its own storage, hearths, oven, and basins. The amount of storage in each house, large or small, seems quite similar and there is no evidence of large-scale or centralized storage. There is some degree of specialization seen in finer obsidian production, for example, but most production activities are present in most houses. The storage of plants and crops seems small scale and domestic. There is no evidence that the storage of cereals was used to create major differences in wealth and status. Specialized ritual buildings are found to the east in Anatolia, and the variability between central and eastern Anatolia is described by Özdoğan (2002).

As we worked in recent years on the post-excavation analysis of the data from the 1995–99 seasons, we all became puzzled by some intriguing information. On the one hand, Neil Roberts and the team working on palaeoenvironmental reconstruction, were certain that the area around the site had been a wetland with severe seasonal flooding. On the other hand, Arlene Rosen, working on

the plant phytoliths, was equally clear that the cereal crops had been grown on dry land. The nearest dry land to the site 9,000 years ago would have been 10–12 km away! For the faunal team, too, it made no sense to locate the site in a wetland, far from good grazing for sheep and goats. So why was the site located where it was? It seemed that domesticated plants and animals were not central to the decision-making process about the location of Çatalhöyük. The site may have been placed in the plain, in a wetland area, because this allowed easy access to the suite of clays and marls needed in the construction of mud-bricks and different types of plaster. It at least seemed likely, that once again agriculture and domesticated animals did not seem to have been uppermost in people's minds.

If we take a broad, global, view, it can be argued that sedentism, intensification, and some degree of social consolidation or differentiation occur very widely in the early Holocene. This point has recently been re-stated by Diamond (2002). He notes that many areas of the world show these traits. Some are associated with agricultural origins—in the Fertile Crescent, China, Mesoamerica, Andes/Amazonia, eastern United States, Sahel, tropical West Africa, Ethiopia, and New Guinea. But in many other areas, the same or similar effects are produced through the intensive use of wild resources. In the Holocene, hunter-gatherers developed sedentary village life with increased population densities, complex material culture, and in some cases pottery, and ranked societies in several areas such as Mesolithic Europe, Japan and maritime Far East Asia, the North American High Arctic, the Pacific Coast of northwest North America, interior California's oak woodlands, the California Channel Islands, the Calusa of Florida, the coast of Ecuador, and the Murray-Darling Basin of southeast Australia. There is a broad social process which happens to involve early agriculture in some areas.

Such a broad perspective takes us a long way from the tiny figurine that Burcu found at Çatalhöyük in 2002. But I think this wider context helps to make sense of my wonder that the seed was wild. It is as if people at Çatalhöyük were not really interested in agriculture. It is as if they hardly noticed it. It played such a small role in their symbolic and social lives. There is little evidence for revolutionary impact deriving from domestication itself. Their concerns seem to have been elsewhere—with wild animals, and with wild plants.

Of course, there comes a time, much later on in the fifth and fourth millennia in the Near East and Europe, when agricultural symbolism (images of ploughs, carts, wheels, domesticated cattle, and so on) becomes prevalent in cultural, social, and economic life. By this time the use of secondary animal products had taken hold, and it is easy to argue that agricultural products were central to marked social differentiation, specialization, and social complexity. But in the ninth to seventh millennia, agriculture and domestication had yet to have a full social impact.

If indeed the adoption of agriculture in the Near East and Anatolia was as significant as is often claimed, we might expect a rapid spread of agriculture. And certainly there are those who argue for movements of people into Europe at this time (Renfrew 1996). However, my own view is that both the linguistic and genetic data are far from convincing. As for the archaeological data, there is much evidence of local sequences and local development (Zvelebil 1995). The slow spread and the long periods of stasis, for example at the edges of the loess in Europe, seem to be related to the development of fairly sedentary, socially complex societies based on gathering and hunting. It is remarkable how long it takes for agriculture to spread to such societies. This is perhaps because in its early stages agriculture offered fewer advantages —it did not make a big difference. As Diamond (2002) points out, some areas just happened to have domesticable plants and animals. Later on the domesticates derived from these animals conferred considerable advantages on the populations in those areas. But initially there would have been little to differentiate those societies with and without what we call domesticated plants and animals.

Thus, for many centuries after the adoption of domesticated plants and sheep and goats, the inhabitants of Çatalhöyük continued to focus their social lives on wild plants and resources. In such a context the wild seed in the back of the tiny figurine is unremarkable.

But perhaps this response is naive. After all, during the industrial revolution in England and France in the nineteenth century, much art, such as fine painting, continued to dwell on rural scenes and pastoral idylls. Much of the art ignored or erased the smoke stacks, factories, and railway lines. Perhaps the symbolism at Çatalhöyük is part of an attempt to deny new forms of life and power. Perhaps it is a misrepresentation that masks emerging social differentiation based on domesticated plants and animals.

For example, perhaps the whole symbolic scheme at Çatalhöyük celebrates male power and hides or misrepresents female contributions and female labor. After all, we have seen some evidence for a symbolic link between women and plants. A number of authors (e.g., Watson and Kennedy 1991) have argued that since ethnographically women are often centrally involved in wild plant collecting and processing, they were probably often key to the domestication of plants. Perhaps this was so at Çatalhöyük, and perhaps this role was downplayed and denied in the symbolism. In some of the animal baiting scenes all the figures are bearded. So perhaps there was a social and economic link between men and wild animals, and perhaps too they controlled the symbolism in such a way as to deny the role of women and agriculture.

In fact this line of argument is difficult to substantiate. The work of the recent project at Çatalhöyük has been unable to identify clear differences between the roles of men and women. For example, if women were centrally involved in plant processing and cooking in the house we might have expected some clear spatial differentiation between such activities and those associated with men. It is often assumed that men would have made obsidian tools, or at least obsidian projectile points. But at Çatalhöyük we have found that most houses have obsidian caches near the hearth and oven, and that there is clear evidence of flint knapping debris in these same areas. There are many ways of interpreting such evidence, but it is at least clear that there is no support for distinct gendered activity areas. Other evidence is less ambiguous. Stable isotope studies of human bone at the site has shown no clear dietary differences between males and females (Richards and Pearson 2004), and the same is true of teeth wear studies (Andrews et al. 2004). We have found no systematic differences in the location and layout of male and female bodies and graves. A few individuals at Çatalhöyük had their heads removed after burial. These heads were later used in foundation and abandonment ceremonies, and it is reasonable to suppose that they were involved in relations of inheritance or affiliation. If so, it is of interest that both male and female skulls were removed and deposited in this way. It was as important to establish social relations through women as it was through men.

None of this suggests that the existence of agriculture had led to radical gender inequality at Çatalhöyük. It is thus difficult to argue that women's real roles in agriculture or domestic production were being masked or hidden in the symbolism. Rather it seems as if, regardless of whether men and/or women were involved, domestic plants and animals had limited social significance.

But, as already noted, we have been excavating the lower part of the mound. While this bias is being rectified in new excavations, for the moment our data about the roles of men and women come from the earlier levels (up to VI). On the other hand, the figurines of which Burcu's tiny new find is an example, come mainly from Level IV and above. It is in these upper levels that the more clearly gendered painting occurs—such as the baiting scenes with bearded men. Perhaps there are changes in gender relations through time at Çatalhöyük.

Certainly there is evidence of greater specialization of production in the upper levels, seen in more varied and differentiated ceramic and lithic production. There are also large ovens which appear to be more than simply domestic. It is possible that through time gendered roles became more marked as specialization in various forms of production took place. Men and women may have gradually moved into separate roles as complexity increased. At this stage, then, the masking hypothesis might become relevant. But it remains a hypothesis that future work will have to explore.

What we are left with is the possibility that the lack of emphasis on domesticated themes in the symbolism at Çatalhöyük is a product of the relative lack of social and economic importance of domesticated plants and animals in these early communities. The hypothesis regarding the masking and hiding of such activities seems to work less well although more work needs to be done. Certainly for animals, it seems difficult to argue for a social masking of the role of sheep and goats. Sheep and goats clearly played an important part in the economy but social life seems to have been based on rituals and feasting involving wild animals. Domesticated plants too were important in the subsistence economy, and they must, with sheep and goats, have contributed to social standing and the ability to give feasts, etc. But they had yet to play a major social role.

The question then arises, if agriculture itself does not play a full revolutionary social role until later millennia, what then does cause the changes observed in the Near East, Anatolia, and globally in the Holocene? Of course, climatic factors have some impact, but I would concur with Diamond (2002) that a longer-term social and economic process beginning in the Upper Palaeolithic led to greater sedentism, intensification, and greater social consolidation and complexity. These processes, often "accidentally," caused domesticated plants and animals to emerge in some areas. The "Neolithic Revolution" was perhaps primarily social. The economic changes built up and had their major effects later on.

It is for these reasons that we should not be surprised that the seed in the tiny figurine was wild. Even in the second half of the seventh millennium B.C., the symbolism of domesticated plants and animals still had little effect. Great changes were taking place in the formation of social groups and in their corporate relations to ancestors, but agriculture as yet had not become so socially important that it was represented in symbolism. Social rituals and relationships were largely worked out with wild plants and animals.

The tiny figurine found at Çatalhöyük has led to a train of thought involving large-scale issues. This is thus a fitting paper to honor a small figure of enormous importance to our understanding of the Neolithic of Anatolia. It is to Ufuk Esin that the Çatalhöyük project owes a special debt for her support. Inspired by her work at Aşıklı, we plan to excavate larger areas of Çatalhöyük in the hope of placing figurines like the one described here in a fuller context.

Conclusion

16

Setting Ethical Research Agendas at Archaeological Sites: The Attempt at Çatalhöyük

How should archaeologists decide which questions to ask about the sites they are excavating? Normally, we consider questions that arise within the academy of scientists. In order to get research funding we ask questions that are topical and which are sanctioned by the scientific community. Or we may respond to the interests of donors, while at the same time trying to retain academic integrity and independence. In all these ways, the agenda-setting process is top-down; it comes from the archaeologists themselves, perhaps in collaboration with their funders.

But in a globalized world, is this sufficient? Is it adequate to focus on the testing of hypotheses set by the academy—an academy always steeped in its own interests and directions? On most if not all archaeological sites there are multiple communities with an interest in the site. They are "stakeholders" such as local inhabitants, tourists, the media, politicians, and so on. And there may be different interested communities with conflicting interests. Is it socially and ethically responsible to conduct archaeological research without taking account of the questions they might be interested in asking? The usual response to such concerns is to build a museum, or provide an exhibit in an information center, and so on. Local communities then have to accept or comment on what has been done by the archaeologists—their contribution is minimized. A fuller response is to en-

gage the different stakeholder interests in the setting of agendas in the first place.

In this paper I intend to discuss some of the ways in which the archaeological research at Çatalhöyük responds to and integrates questions set by a variety of communities. In my view, to understand what these communities are, and to understand the questions they would most like to have answered, is a specialist area of research. For this reason, there are several ethnographers who work on the Çatalhöyük project, and who assist in the dialogue with different communities. This paper is, then, especially indebted to Ayfer Bartu, David Shankland, and Nurcan Yalman who have worked on the various communities discussed here. In more general terms, the ethical need for closer interaction between archaeologists and the communities they serve leads to a demand for closer collaboration between archaeologists and ethnographers. While there are many groups with some form of interest in Çatalhöyük, I intend to concentrate on four broad groupings: politicians, local residents, New Age Goddess followers, and artists.

In discussing the way that research questions can be set within a collaboration and negotiation of interests, I do not mean to argue that the archæologists themselves should have no questions of their own. Clearly they have a duty to respond to questions set by the academy, and to act in accord with best disciplinary practice. But rather than imposing questions from outside, they also have a duty, in my view, to engage in research that seeks compromise and bridges between a variety of different interests. A post-colonial solution involves dialogue and hybridity rather than imperial imposition of outside agendas (Appadurai 1996; Bhabha 1994).

INTRODUCTION TO ÇATALHÖYÜK

Some of the reasons that Çatalhöyük is the focus of so much interest from diverse communities can be found in its history of discovery and research. It was first excavated by James Mellaart in the 1960s (Mellaart 1967), and he successfully publicized its enormous importance. At an early date, now known to be 7400 to 6200 B.C., its great size (13 ha) is impressive, as are the 16 or so levels of occupation in a 21-m-high mound. The site showed that large early sites existed outside the "Fertile Crescent" in the Near East. But it was especially the art that caught the scholarly and public interest. The wall paintings and relief sculpture were unique, and even today, after the discovery of parallel sites in southeast Anatolia with elaborate art, it remains the densest concentration of symbolism so far found in the Eastern Mediterranean at this time. Internationally, the site became widely known through Mellaart's publications in the *Illustrated London News* and elsewhere. Within Turkey the site took on a special significance as the origin of Anatolian civilization.

New research at the site under my direction began in 1993, after decades of inactivity. But it was clear from our earliest press days, that the site had not lost its hold on the public imagination, at least in Turkey. Our sponsors started organizing press days in order to attract publicity for their contributions, and frequently 50 or more press and media representatives turned up at the site, eager to get the latest news. Most of these have been national and local media, but we also get coverage from the international press and television.

THE POLITICIANS

For the first group which has an interest in Çatalhöyük, this media interest is crucial. The politicians have come to show a special engagement with the site since, at press events, they are able to gain wide media coverage. Of course, they each have their different claims to make, but for all, the pay-off is publicity in the context of an international project working at one of the most important early sites in Turkey. I wish to limit this discussion to two contrasting groups of politicians—the local regional politicians and the European politicians. As we will see, they use the site in very different ways. To what extent can the archaeology engage in a dialogue with such political interests? To what extent can it respond to the questions the politicians raise?

Çatalhöyük is situated 1 hour east of Konya, in a region known for its religious fundamentalist and/or nationalist politics. In recent years the region has been the stronghold of the nationalist MHP party, and it is also a center for Islamic companies and traditional rural Islamic attitudes towards women regarding social and economic behavior. When politicians such as the local mayor (from Çumra, the local town), or governor, give talks in front of the press at the site, they talk about the importance of the locality and the region. They say that the presence of Çatalhöyük demonstrates the special nature of the region. Of course, they admit that the site is pre-Turk and pre-Islamic, but they nevertheless say that it shows the importance of the land and its traditions. They point also to the international character of the project and the visitors it attracts. Again this shows the importance of the region. Some try at times to make links to the migrations of the Turks themselves, but most are content with rather vaguer connections between past and present.

There is undoubtedly a political and local interest in the question "who were the people that lived at Çatalhöyük?" Local people ask us this question all the time. "Were they related to us?" To what extent can archaeologists respond to this question? One obvious contemporary method is through ancient

DNA analysis (e.g., Jones 2001). The human burials discovered in the excavations at Çatalhöyük have been the subject of two ancient DNA projects. The first was undertaken by the Leeuwen laboratory in Belgium, and the second by Stanford University (Malhi et al. 2004). So far this work has only been able to suggest that there may be some ancient DNA present in the human bones. Much more and very intensive study will be needed before anything can be said about the similarities between the ancient and modern populations in central Turkey.

There clearly is considerable local interest in trying to understand the genetic links between Çatalhöyük and present-day populations, and so the project will continue to try to find ways of continuing this ancient DNA research. Another response would be to focus on historical studies which show how the local villages in the Çatalhöyük-Çumra area are made up of migrants from the Balkans, and such research is part of ethnoarchaeological work being carried out by Nurcan Yalman. Yet another response is to show ways in which Çatalhöyük is part of a regional tradition. It has long been assumed that the agricultural revolution spread through Anatolia and Europe after originating in the Fertile Crescent. Contemporary versions of this view will be discussed below. But recent comparative research by Özdoğan (2002) has suggested the importance of regional continuities in central Anatolia. Certainly the evidence from Çatalhöyük shows connections across a wider zone reaching into the Levant and middle Mesopotamia. The use of lime plaster in the earliest levels is parallel to its use in the PPNB in the Levant. The figure with upraised arms and legs is found at Göbekli and Kösk Höyük (Öztan 2002; Schmidt 2001). And of course more generic traits such as the bull heads and female figurines and burials beneath floors are widely found. Plastered skulls from Kösk Höyük recall those from the Levant (Öztan 2002). On the other hand, Özdoğan points to distinctly regional traits in central Anatolia such as the lack of centralized authority. There are undoubtedly distinctive characteristics of the Çatalhöyük

evidence that suggest a local process of development, even if influenced by the Near East.

Such evidence says nothing, of course, about the continuity between the past and the present, but it reinforces the interests of local politicians in the distinctive contributions of their region. As archaeologists we have to resist, however, those politicians that wish to take the evidence towards an extreme interpretation in terms of cultural or racial superiority. The archaeological and historical evidence indicates a long period of cultural mixing between local traditions and outside influence. Even the DNA evidence will not resolve the issues of "who we are," since answers to that question are as much social, cultural, and historical as they are genetic. The important point is that archaeologists are able to enter into a debate with local politicians about issues in which they show a prime concern.

From time to time, a very different type of politician visits Çatalhöyük. For example, the Ambassador of the European Union makes very different speeches when he speaks to the press at the site. His aim is to speak to those in Turkey who, in contrast to the nationalist politicians, wish to take Turkey into the European Union. The Ambassador talks of the fact that there was no boundary between Europe and Asia at the time of Çatalhöyük. He refers to the evidence we have discussed with him for cultural contacts between central Anatolia and southeast Europe in the Neolithic. He is fascinated when we describe to him the work of Colin Renfrew (1987) on the spread of Indo-European languages and on the relationship between that language dispersal and the spread of farming from Anatolia into Europe. He takes this as proof of his view that "originally" Turkey was part of Europe, and he seems less interested when we say that many archaeologists take the view that there are difficulties with the notion of a large-scale spread of Indo-Europeans associated with the spread of agriculture. We point out the evidence described above, for regional sequences, but he looks at the evidence through his own political lenses.

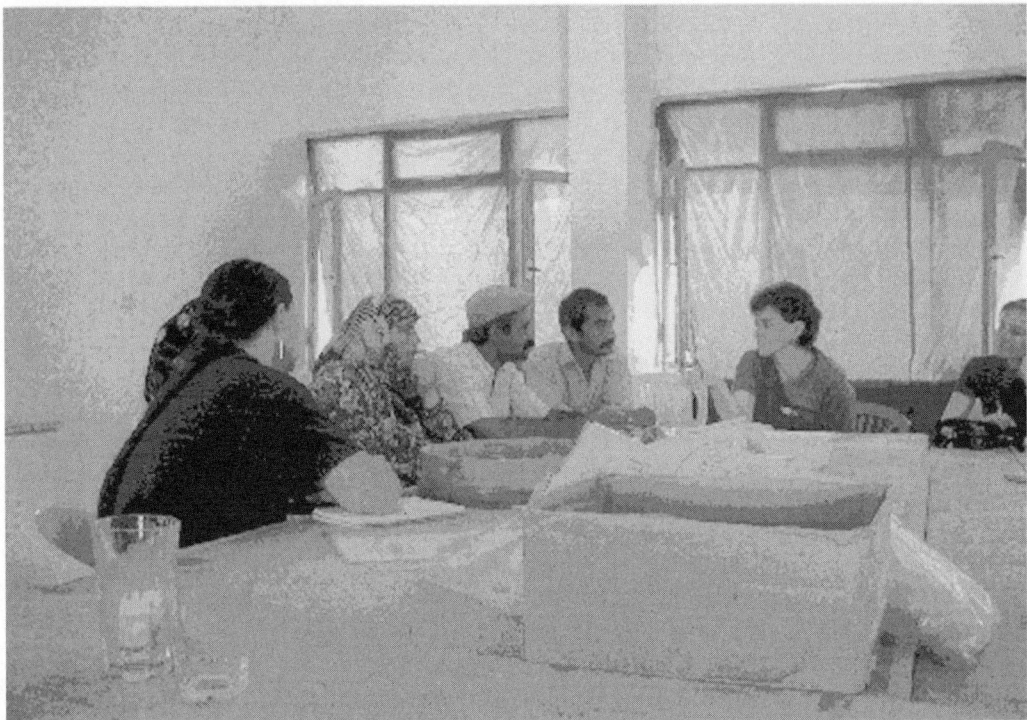

Figure 16.1. Members of the local village community contributing to laboratory discussions about the interpretation of analytical results from Çatalhöyük.

It does seem possible, then, to direct archaeological research so that it responds to issues raised by local politicians. Indeed, I would claim an ethical duty to respond not simply because of responsibility towards one's hosts, but also because the politicians use the distant past to make claims about origins and identities. These claims need to be tempered by the archaeological evidence, or at least the archaeologist needs to provide the opportunity for competing points of view to be taken up. The site and the data that are made known by the archaeologist will be used in one way or another to support political claims—in my view it is unethical for the archaeologists to wash their hands of this process and to remain disengaged.

THE LOCAL COMMUNITIES

The Turkish men and women who work on the project come mainly from the local village of Kuçukköy (1 km from the site) and from the local town (15 km from the site) of Çumra. They work in a variety of capacities

from laborers, to guards and guides, to flotation assistants and heavy-residue sorters. Increasingly the site has been visited by local people from other neighboring villages and towns and from the regional center at Konya. What types of questions are these stakeholders interested in, and how can we contribute to their interests in and understanding of the site?

Many of the local rural inhabitants are farmers with low incomes and limited education. Their knowledge about the site is obtained from primary school and from folk traditions. In general, they have little detailed knowledge of the history and prehistory of Turkey and the Konya region. Their interests in the site thus include more practical concerns, such as how to benefit economically from the project, the site, and its tourists. Up to 40 or 50 people are employed by the project for a few months every year. A villager from Kuçukköy has built a café and shop outside the entrance to the site, and the women from the village sell embroidered cloth at the dig house. The project has also contributed to the digging of a new well and the provision of a new water supply, it has helped to persuade regional officials to build a new school in the village, and it has contributed a library to the village.

As already noted, finding out what the local communities want to know about the site is a specialized task and the ethnographers who work with us have been involved in various schemes to educate and engage the local communities in the site and the project. For example, Ayfer Bartu has given talks about the project in the village. She has also assisted the women from the village to set up a community exhibit in the Visitor Center at the dig house. In this exhibit, the women chose to concentrate on the plants that grow on the mound—these are important as herbs and medicines.

In 2001, a group of men and women from the village were asked to take part in our post-excavation studies (Fig. 16.1). They were paid to contribute to discussions about the interpretation of the site, based on the most recent analytical results that were explained to them. These discussions were put on video and their comments will be transcribed and used as verbatim quotes in the publication texts. The types of question to which they could most effectively contribute were those that related to the practices of living in the central Anatolian environment. Thus they were able to contribute to issues of how ovens of different shape and made of different clays could be used. They knew the effect of the dominant winds on the location of fireplaces in houses. They contributed to issues regarding the difficulties of life in the winter.

One question that most interested them was "why here?" They were particularly interested in why this particular bit of land was chosen for the site. They were interested in the specifics of the locality, and how it was used for agriculture and food. In fact, it has proved difficult to answer the question "why here?" Much work on establishing the landscape and palaeoenvironment has been done by a team led by Neil Roberts, based on the

sedimentology and pollen of cores taken from around the site and in the region. It is clear that at the time of the site's occupation there was severe seasonal flooding and wetlands in the vicinity of the site. This location is reflected in the number of water birds found at the site. It was therefore surprising to find that the cereal phytoliths being studied by Arlene Rosen indicated dry-land farming. The archaeobotanical team also found an association between cereals and dry-land weeds. At the time, the nearest dry land was 10–12 km away. Most data specialists agreed that the site would have been better located up the local river system towards higher and drier land. For example, a wetland is not an ideal environment for domestic sheep. Why was the site located where it was, in a wetland? One possible answer is that we have much evidence now that the plastering of houses and the use of mud for building at Çatalhöyük were very elaborate. Particularly in the early levels we have evidence of considerable lime burning to make high quality lime floors which were painted. The location of the site low down within the plain gives easy access to the wide range of lime-rich clays and marls needed for the plastering and sculpture within the buildings. These factors, as much as subsistence resources, may have determined the location of the site.

Much of the evidence that we have considered shows that, at least in the earlier levels of the site, the subsistence economy was diverse and small scale. There were domesticated cereals and sheep and goats, but these were only part of a patchwork of resources used, some obtained from great distances, such as the hackberry. There is much evidence also that in the early levels these resources were largely collected within a domestic mode of production. Storage evidence is small scale and within-house. There are only small containers (pots, baskets, wooden bowls) and small grinding stones. At least in the early levels these domestic units collected a wide range of resources over a complex seasonal round. There was undoubtedly cooperation at supra-house levels, but much of daily subsistence was carried out at a small-scale level.

We can, then, attempt to answer some of the local questions about the site. But it is also important not to promote the view that somehow the local communities are "lost in time," leftovers from prehistory. It is not surprising, perhaps, that the local community is most interested in locality and land use. But it would be wrong to assume that there is some continuous connection between past and present. Historically there has been much in and out migration. There has been massive social and cultural change over the last nine millennia. It would be wrong to assume that the local communities are an "other" that is somehow closer to prehistory than "we" are (Fabian 1983). The local communities contribute to the project and ask questions of it that relate to their knowledge of the environment and its soils. They do not have some privileged knowledge based on cultural continuity. To claim that would be to "museumize" the local communities.

THE GODDESS COMMUNITIES

Another set of communities interested in the work of the project at the site is defined by an interest in the Goddess. Groups on Goddess tours regularly visit the site from the USA, Germany, Istanbul, and elsewhere. They come to pray, hold circle dances, feel the power of the Goddess, and even eat the earth of the mound! There is a great diversity of such groups from Gaia groups, to Ecofeminists, to Goddess New Age travelers. Individuals are often visibly moved by the experience of visiting and it is undoubtedly the case that for many the existence of the Goddess at Çatalhöyük is important for their personal sense of identity. The project has entered into dialogue with some members of the varied Goddess groups on its Website, and some of the research directions being taken result from these interactions.

One specific offshoot of the interest in the site from women's movements was a fashion show staged in Istanbul by Bahar Korçan, a Turkish/international dress designer. She based an exhibition on the theme of Çatalhöyük and "women of other times." The clothes were inspired by the site, the catwalk was "in" a model of Çatalhöyük, and slides of the site and its art were shown in the background as part of a multimedia experience. In fact, the show was a major press and TV event, with the top popular singer at the time, Tarkan, making an appearance. The press coverage extended globally, to France, Japan, and beyond.

The varied Goddess groups with an interest in Çatalhöyük ask different questions of the site. Some take a strong line regarding the role of women in the past, arguing that women were dominant and that the society was peaceful and without violence. Others want simply to engage in the site from a spiritual and religious point of view. Others have an educated interest in the evidence for the role of women at the site 9,000 years ago.

It is not possible for archaeologists to contribute to the religious view that the goddess is present at Çatalhöyük. But it is possible to try and respond to those women's groups that want to know about the role of women at the site. Was Gimbutas (1982) right in arguing for a powerful position for women, even a matriarchy, at these early sites? Can we identify the roles of men and women?

The work of the recent project at Çatalhöyük has been unable to identify clear differences between the roles of men and women in their daily lives. For example, if women were centrally involved in plant processing and cooking in the house we might have expected some clear spatial differentiation between such activities and those associated with men. It is often assumed that men would have made obsidian tools, or at least obsidian projectile points. But at Çatalhöyük we have found that most houses have obsidian caches near the hearth and oven, and that there is clear evidence of knapping debris in these same areas. There are many ways of interpreting such evidence, but it is at least clear that there is no support for distinct gendered activity areas. Other evidence is less ambiguous. Stable isotope studies of human bone at the site has shown no clear dietary differences between males and females

(Richards and Pearson 2004), and the same is true of teeth wear studies (Andrews et al. 2004). We have found no systematic differences in the location and layout of male and female bodies and graves (Hamilton 2004). A few individuals at Çatalhöyük had their heads removed after burial. These heads were later used in foundation and abandonment ceremonies, and it is reasonable to suppose that they were involved in relations of inheritance or affiliation. If so, it is of interest that both male and female skulls were removed and deposited in this way. It was as important to establish social relations through women as it was through men.

So there is nothing to suggest that men and women lived very different gendered lives at Çatalhöyük. There is no evidence that in practice, gender was very important in assigning social roles. However, there are some clear differences in the art, and some symbolic associations between women and plants. The famous figurine of a woman sitting on a seat of felines was found in a grain bin, and recently the project has found a small clay figurine of a woman with breasts, in the back of which was a cavity containing a small wild seed. Women are more often shown in a seated position. In the art, there are scenes of bearded figures involved in animal baiting and hunting and dancing. These clear differences in the depiction of men and women in the art may not relate to gendered differences in the practices of daily life. Rather, they may be metaphorical and idealized. But, in my view, there are no unambiguous depictions of women giving birth, or suckling or tending children. In other words, there is little evidence of the "Mother." Women are certainly depicted in powerful positions, such as sitting on felines with their hands resting on the heads, but there is no good evidence that this symbolic power derived from the "Mother" idea, rather than from other attributes of women such as their sexuality or their productive capacities.

These arguments, that women may not have had clearly gendered roles in practice, and that their symbolic significance is not necessarily related to the "Mother" idea, has angered many in the Goddess communities, but it would be unethical to carry on supporting arguments for which there appears to be little evidence. Many followers of the Goddess have engaged in dialogue and have been able to see that the new evidence can be incorporated into a revised perspective—for example, one in which women were powerful for reasons other than mothering and in which some equality existed in practice. Thus it is possible to ask questions that are of interest to particular groups, and then to enter into a dialogue that can contribute to changed perspectives.

ARTISTS

One of the most surprising components of the renewed research at Çatalhöyük has been the way in which the site attracts a variety of artists. These again vary in terms of specific motivation and interest. They include those who create works or performances about the site at other venues, and those involved in installation art at the site. There is also some overlap with the Goddess groups as several of the artists are inspired by the notion that women at Çatalhöyük had a more powerful role than in contemporary society.

One example is Jale Yılmabaşar, an artist working in Istanbul. She recently held an exhibit of paintings in Istanbul that referred to the paintings that Mellaart has argued come from the site. Originally known in Turkey as a ceramicist, she has recently turned more to oil paintings, and her canvases are large, bold, and colorful. She is not particularly interested in the site itself; more with the ways in which the project, and I as its director, can provide an extra dimension and validation to her work. Thus, I have been asked to name the paintings for her, and have been pictured in catalogues holding conversations with her in front of the paintings.

The pianist and composer Tuluyhan Uğurlu gave a concert in Istanbul inspired by Çatalhöyük. His music is popular and it mixes a variety of styles including Turkish motifs. He was trained as a concert pianist

Figure 16.2. Adrienne Momi working on her art spiral at Çatalhöyük.

and composer mainly in Austria and describes himself as ethnic, classical, and New Age. He decided to write music about Çatalhöyük because of its global and New Age associations, but also because he came from Konya. One of the main parts of the concert centered on a poem written by Reşit Ergener, a Turkish economist and tour guide, and co-organizer and leader of many of the Goddess tours to Çatalhöyük. The concert also used slides and images, taken from the project website. The music acted as a "frame" around the slides, which he watched as he played and partly improvised to.

Örge Tulga, who had a gallery exhibit of her gold and silver jewelery on display in Istanbul in 2002, explained how her designs were inspired by and based on the art of Catalhoyuk, especially the Goddess imagery. She also said how much she wanted to visit the site: "I want to come and feel the atmosphere. I want to live there a little." The "atmosphere" referred to here is partly spiritual.

This linking of performance, art, and spirituality at the site itself is seen particularly in the work of Adrienne Momi. Again an organizer of Goddess tours, and based in California, she has constructed installation art at a number of prehistoric sites in Europe. In 2001 she made a spiral on the site itself (Fig. 16.2). She worked closely with the archaeological team, learning about the current interpretations of the site. She engaged local people and school children in her art—which involved making paper on site, then making stamps based on the art from the site, and then printing these designs onto the paper and sticking the paper on a large paper spiral laid out on the grass slope of the Neolithic mound. She was careful to get official permission and throughout worked in a consensual way. The spiral and the art were meant to provide a channel of communication with the subconscious of the site. She called her installation "Turning Through Time: Communication with the Distant Past at Çatalhöyük."

Figure 16.3. Reconstruction by John Swogger of the interior of Building 1 as seen from the entrance ladder, looking north into the main room with paintings around the northwest platform under which there is a concentration of young people buried.

There are various ways in which artists can be engaged in the archaeological project. Another example involves the artists employed by the project itself to illustrate the finds and architecture. John Swogger has been working as an on-site archaeological illustrator at Çatalhöyük since 1998. He adamantly identifies himself as an illustrator rather than an artist, but as an illustrator who is pushing the rigid boundaries of archaeological illustration (Swogger 2000). By defying the strict, but what he sees as artificial, boundaries between the media considered to be the domain of the "artists" and the domain of the "the archaeological illustrators," he suggests that all these media can be seen as a "tool—a mechanism or process for recording and presenting archaeological information in visual form." He also argues that such an expansion and broadening of the definition of what archaeological illustration is gives the illustrator the freedom to embrace

different types of media and styles that will enable exploration of different aspects of archaeological information. What he does is to create reconstructions based on the evidence provided by different specialists at the site. These sketches, drawings, and reconstructions provide means of visualizing various findings, interpretations, hypotheses, and theories (e.g., Fig. 16.3). As Swogger points out, "combined with a process of exploring new modes of visual expression and looking carefully at the way 'art' can illustrate the data of 'science,' there could be here the potential for creating a powerful and important tool for managing on-site interpretation and analysis" (Swogger 2000:149). His illustrations and reconstructions have been integrated within the recording, analysis, and public presentation of the findings from the site.

Another artist, Nessa Leibhammer, also works as an illustrator, but she uses more straightforward artistic conventions and

Figure 16.4. Nessa Leibhammer doing an 'artistic' drawing of the same feature that is being drawn using archaeological conventions.

does not attempt to use detailed measured drawings. She feels that the "scientific" codified drawings do not capture the full sense of what is seen. Her more interpretive and aesthetic drawings complement the more scientific depictions (Leibhammer 2000; Fig. 16.4). In contrast to Swogger's illustrations, Leibhammer's images are artistic and personal interpretive drawings that focus on the visible, physical aspects of archaeology such as walls, rooms, and spaces, rather than reconstructions that attempt to incorporate all the evidence from the site. But her drawings have also enriched and become part of the archaeological archive of Çatalhöyük. Her drawings and paintings provide a fuller sense of depth and volume in the complex wall plasters, and they are more successful at this than the measured line drawings.

So, one way of involving artists in the archaeological project is to engage them in the process of recording and expression. But another response is to attempt to answer the questions they ask about the role of "art" at Çatalhöyük 9,000 years ago. The artists bring their contemporary assumptions about aesthetics, framing, and specialist production. And yet can we talk about the symbolism at Çatalhöyük in these terms. Was this "art" at all? And what was the role of the "art"—how can we interpret it?

I wish to suggest first of all that there are many different types of "art" at Çatalhöyük, and that explanations will vary for the different types. I want here to restrict my comments to two particular classes of "art" at the site. The first is the relief sculpture. This is installed and remains as part of the house over a long time. The second is the geometric paintings. These occur on some wall plasters, but in any one house there may be over 100 yearly replasterings of the walls in the main room. Few of these are ever painted. The paintings are transient and probably have a different explanation from the relief sculptures.

Let us take the relief sculptures first. These are incorporated into the architecture of the buildings. For example, bull horns may be set deeply into bricks in the walls, and plastered bucrania may be set on the upright posts that hold up the roof. The bucrania and relief leopards often have evidence of repeated painting, and may have lasted throughout the lifetime of a house. In addition, during the abandonment of the house, as in Building 2 (Farid 2004), bucrania and other sculpture were removed from western walls in the main rooms. In the case of Building 1, the building was filled up with soil on abandonment, and then some decades later a trench was dug down to remove sculpture from the western wall (Cessford 2004a). This suggests a clear memory of the location of these bucrania, and their retrieval, perhaps to use in later houses. The retention of animal heads in this way recalls the removal of heads from human skeletons buried below floors. It seems feasible that the plastered animal heads acted as mnemonics of important events in the history of households, and that they acted as markers of lineage and ancestry. They were incorporated into the fabric of the house, literally holding it up.

The geometric paintings are very different in their social roles. Through most of the life of any particular house, the walls were white. But for short periods of time they became transformed into a blaze of color and activity, either as figurative or geometric paintings. The paintings were then plastered over and the walls reverted to their plain form. Here I can only comment on the geometric painting as we have not found figurative narrative scenes in the recent excavations. But in Building 1, a clue as to the function of these paintings has been found (Fig. 16.3). Here there is a spatial and temporal link between geometric painting and the burial of mainly young people. It is the northwest platform in the main room that is surrounded by painting during part of the occupation of the house. It is this platform under which young people were preferentially buried. But there is also a temporal link. It is always difficult to assess which wall plaster goes with which floor

plaster, and only approximate correlations could be made in Building 1. But in general terms the phases of painting corresponded to the phases of burial under this platform. One possible interpretation of this link is that the geometric painting acted in some way to protect or to communicate with the dead below the platform. Gell (1998) has discussed the apotropaic use of art, and this seems a reasonable interpretation in the case of Building 1. A comparable association has been found in the adjacent Building 3 (Stevanovic and Tringham 1999), where again the northwest platform contained most of the burials in the main room, and red paint concentrated (or was best preserved) on the walls around this same northwest platform.

So in both cases the "art" is not "art" in the sense of something simply to be contemplated with aesthetic sensibilities. Rather, art at Çatalhöyük does something (Gell 1998). It can be interpreted as playing a social role in relation to lineage and in relation to interaction with the dead. In this sense it perhaps contrasts with the activities of the contemporary artists at Çatalhöyük. At one level too, their art, especially the installation art, is designed to do something. And yet it remains an aesthetic expression somewhat removed from daily practice. It can be argued that the 9,000-year-old "art" at Çatalhöyük is closer to science than it is to contemporary art, in the sense that it aims to intervene in the world, to understand how it works, to change it. Thus the dialogue between ancient and contemporary artists can lead to changes of perspective both for artists and archaeologists. The dialogue challenges the tendency among contemporary artists to appropriate the art into their own perspective. The archaeological evidence can contribute to an understanding of the "otherness" of prehistoric art.

CONCLUSION

In a globalized world, archaeologists increasingly work with multiple communities. I have tried to provide examples of some of the problems and issues that are raised in such a context. I have tried to suggest that rather than just setting our own agenda, it is possible to negotiate research questions with a number of groups. It is possible to collaborate with these groups in relation to the answers given and the interpretations made.

Çatalhöyük is perhaps an extreme site in that so many stakeholder groups are involved. On the other hand, in many parts of the world archaeologists work in the context of contested pasts. I have tried to argue here that archaeologists have an ethical responsibility to ask questions about the past that resonate with stakeholder communities. But it is also clear that the answers to such questions may be uncomfortable for specific stakeholder groups. They may involve the archaeologist taking a stance with regard to how the data can be used to support arguments that are made by interested parties. Archaeology becomes reflexively part of the social process.

Acknowledgments

I am grateful to all the members of the Çatalhöyük Project for the work on which this paper is based, and to the Turkish Ministry of Culture, The British Institute of Archaeology at Ankara, and all our sponsors. This article is the revised version of a lecture delivered at the W. F. Albright Institute of Archaeological Research in Jerusalem in March 2002, when the author was the third Trude Dothan Lecturer in Ancient Near Eastern Studies. This series, which also includes lectures at Al-Quds and the Hebrew Universities, was sponsored by the Albright Institute and endowed by the Dorot Foundation.

References Cited

Adams, M.
2000   The Optician's Trick: An Approach
        to Recording Excavation Using an
        Iconic Formation Process Recogni-
        tion System. In *Interpreting Stratig-
        raphy. Site Evaluation, Recording
        Procedures and Stratigraphic Analy-
        sis. Papers Presented to the Inter-
        preting Stratigraphy Conferences
        1993–1997*, edited by S. Roskams,
        pp. 91–101. BAR International Se-
        ries 910. Oxford.

Akyol, A. A., and Ş. Demirci
2004   Phosphorus Analysis of Sediments.
        In *Inhabiting Çatalhöyük: Reports
        from the 1995–1999 Seasons*, edited
        by I. Hodder. McDonald Institute
        for Archaeological Research and
        British Institute of Archaeology at
        Ankara, Cambridge. In press.

Alcock, S. E., R. Van Dyke, and N. H. Keeble
(eds.)
2003   *Archaeologies of Memory*. Black-
        well, Oxford.

Andrén, A.
1993   Doors to Other Worlds. *Journal of
        European Archaeology* 1:33–56.

Andrews, G., J. Barrett, and J. Lewis
2000   Interpretation not Record: The Prac-
        tice of Archaeology. *Antiquity*
        74:525–530.

Andrews, P., T. Molleson, and B. Boz
2004   The Human Burials at Çatalhöyük.
        In *Inhabiting Çatalhöyük: Reports
        from the 1995–1999 Seasons*, edited
        by I. Hodder. McDonald Institute
        for Archaeological Research and
        British Institute of Archaeology at
        Ankara, Cambridge. In press.

Anyon, R., T. J. Ferguson, L. Jackson, and
L. Lane
1996   Native American Oral Traditions
        and Archaeology. *Society for Ameri-
        can Archaeology Bulletin*
        14(2):14–16.

Appadurai, A
1996   *Modernity at Large*. University of
        Minnesota Press, Minneapolis.

Arnold, B.
1993   Lake Constance Yields Breast
        Reliefs. *Archaeology* 46(2):23.

Australia ICOMOS
1981   *The Australia ICOMOS Charter for
        the Conservation of Places of Cul-
        tural Significance (Burra Charter)*.
        Canberra, Australia.

Avrami, E., M. Demas, R. Mason, G. Palumbo,
J. M. Teutonico, and M. de la Torre
2000   *A Methodological Approach for
        Conservation Planning*. Getty Con-
        servation Institute, Los Angeles.

Bailey, D.
1990   The Living House: Signifying Conti-
        nuity. In *The Social Archaeology of
        Houses*, edited by R. Samson, pp.
        17–48. Edinburgh University Press,
        Edinburgh.

Baird, D.
2002   Early Holocene Settlement in Cen-
        tral Anatolia: Problems and
        Prospects as Seen from the Konya
        Plain. In *The Neolithic of Central*

Anatolia, edited by F. Gerard and L. Thissen, pp. 139–152. L Ege Yayınları, Istanbul.

Banning, E. B., and B. F. Byrd
1987   Houses and the Changing Residential Unit: Domestic Architecture at PPNB 'Ain Ghazal, Jordan. *Proceedings of the Prehistoric Society* 53:309–325.

Bapty, I., and T. Yates
1990   *Archaeology after Structuralism.* Routledge, London.

Bar-Yosef, O.
1986   The Walls of Jericho, an Alternative Interpretation. *Current Anthropology* 27:157–162.

Barfield, L.
1994   The Iceman Reviewed. *Antiquity* 68:10–26.

Barker, P.
1977   *Techniques of Archaeological Excavation.* Batsford, London.

Barrett, J.
1994   *Fragments from Antiquity: An Archaeology of Social Life in Britain, 2900–1200 B.C.* Blackwell, Oxford.
2000   A Thesis on Agency. In *Agency in Archaeology,* edited by M.-A. Dobres and J. Robb, pp. 61–68. Routledge, London.

Barth, F.
1987   *Cosmologies in the Making.* Cambridge University Press, Cambridge.

Barthes, R.
1973   *Mythologies.* Paladin, London.

Beaudry, M., L. J. Cook, and S. A. Mrozowski
1991   Artifacts and Active Voices: Material Culture as Social Discourse. In *The Archaeology of Inequality,* edited by R. H. McGuire and R. Paynter, pp.150–191. Blackwell, Oxford.

Beck, A., and M. Beck
2000   Computing, Theory and Practice: Establishing the Agenda in Contract Archaeology. In *Interpreting Stratigraphy. Site Evaluation, Recording Procedures and Stratigraphic Analysis. Papers Presented to the Interpreting Stratigraphy Conferences 1993–1997,* edited by S. Roskams, pp. 173–181. BAR International Series 910. Oxford.

Bekaert, S.
1998   Multiple Levels of Meaning and the Tension of Consciousness. *Archaeological Dialogues* 5:7–29.

Belfer-Cohen, A.
1995   Rethinking Social Stratification in the Natufian Culture: The Evidence from Burials. In *The Archaeology of Death in the Ancient Near East,* edited by S. Campbell and A. Green, pp. 9–16. Oxbow Monograph 51, Oxford.

Belfer-Cohen, A., and O. Bar-Yosef
2000   Early Sedentism in the Near East: A Bumpy Ride to Village Life. In *Life in Neolithic Farming Communities. Social Organization, Identity, and Differentiation,* edited by I. Kuijt, pp. 19–38. Kluwer Academic/ Plenum Publishers, New York.

Bell, C.
1992   *Ritual Theory, Ritual Practice.* Oxford University Press, Oxford.

Bender, B.
1978   Gatherer-Hunter to Farmer: A Social Perspective. *World Archaeology* 10:204–222.
1998   *Stonehenge: Making Space.* Berg, Oxford.

Bender, B., S. Hamilton, and C. Tilley
1997   Leskernick: Stone Worlds; Alternative Narratives; Nested Landscapes. *Proceedings of the Prehistoric Society* 63:147–178.

Berggren, Å.
2001   Swedish Archaeology in Perspective and the Possibility of Reflexivity. *Current Swedish Archaeology* 9:9–23.
2003   Between Structure and Individual— Reflexive Approaches to Archaeological Fieldwork in Malmö, Sweden. *Interpreting Stratigraphy Meeting 2001.* In press.

Bhabha, H.
1994   *The Location of Culture.* Routledge, London.

Bıçakçı, E.
1998   An Essay on the Chronology of the Pre-Pottery Neolithic Settlements of the East-Taurus Region (Turkey). In *Light on Top of the Black Hill. Studies Presented to Halet Çambel,* edited by G. Arsebuk, M. Mellink, and W. Schrimer, pp. 137–150. Ege Yayınları, Istanbul.

Binford, L. R.
1962   Archaeology as Anthropology. *American Antiquity* 28:217–225.
1989   *Debating Archaeology*. Academic Press, New York.

Binford, L. R., and J. A. Sabloff
1982   Paradigms, Systematics and Archaeology, *Journal of Anthropological Research* 38:137–153.

Blinkhorn, P. W., and C. G. Cumberpatch
1998   The Interpretation of Artifacts and the Tyranny of the Field Archaeologist. *Assemblage* 4. University of Sheffield. (http://www.shef.ac.uk./assem/4/4bln_cmb.html)

Borič, D.
2003   'Deep Time' Metaphor: Mnemonic and Apotropaic Practices at Lepenski Vir. *Journal of Social Archaeology* 3(1).

Bourdieu, P.
1977   *Outline of a Theory of Practice*. Cambridge University Press, Cambridge.
1990   [1987] *In Other Words: Essays Towards a Reflexive Sociology*. Polity Press, London.
1991   [1984] *Language and Symbolic Power*. Harvard University Press, Cambridge, Massachusetts.

Bradley, R.
1990   *The Passage of Arms*. Cambridge University Press, Cambridge.
1993   *Altering the Earth: The Origins of Monuments in Britain and Continental Europe*. Society of Antiquaries of Scotland, Edinburgh.
2002   *The Past in Prehistoric Societies*. Routledge, London.

Braithwaite, M.
1982   Decoration as Ritual Symbol: A Theoretical Proposal and Ethnographic Study in Southern Sudan. In *Symbolic and Structural Archaeology*, edited by I. Hodder, pp. 80–88. Cambridge University Press, Cambridge.

Brill, D.
2000   Video-Recording as Part of the Critical Archaeological Process. In *Towards Reflexive Methods in Archaeology: The Example at Çatalhöyük*, edited by I. Hodder, pp. 229–234. McDonald Institute for Archaeological Research and British Institute of Archaeology at Ankara, Monograph 289. Cambridge.

Brumfiel, E.
1996   Figurines and the Aztec State: Testing the Effectiveness of Ideological Domination. In *Gender and Archaeology*, edited by R. P. Wright. University of Pennsylvania, Philadelphia.

Buck, C. E., J. A. Christen, and G. N. James
1999   BCal: An On-line Bayesian Radiocarbon Calibration Tool. *Internet Archaeology* 7. (http://intarch.ac.uk/journal/issue7/buck_toc.html)

Bull, I. D., M. E. Elhmmali, V. Perret, W. Matthews, D. J. Roberts, and R. P. Evershed
2004   Biomarker Evidence of Faecal Deposition in Archaeological Sediments at Çatalhöyük, Turkey. In *Inhabiting Çatalhöyük: Reports from the 1995–1999 Seasons*, edited by I. Hodder. McDonald Institute for Archaeological Research and British Institute of Archaeology at Ankara, Cambridge. In press.

Butler, J.
1990   *Gender Trouble: Feminism and the Subversion of Identity*. Routledge, New York.

Byrd, B. F.
1994   Public and Private, Domestic and Corporate: The Emergence of the Southwest Asian Village. *American Antiquity* 59(4):639–666.

Byrd, B. F., and C. M. Monahan
1995   Death, Mortuary Rituals and Natufian Social Structure. *Journal of Anthropological Archaeology* 14:251–287.

Carr, C.
1984   The Nature of Organization of Intrasite Archaeological Records and Spatial Analytic Approaches to Their Investigation. *Advances in Archaeological Method and Theory* 7:103–222.

Carsten. J., and S. Hugh-Jones (eds.)
1995   *About the House: Lévi-Strauss and Beyond*. Cambridge University Press, Cambridge.

Carter, T., J. Conolly, and A. Spasojevię
2004   The Chipped Stone. In *Changing Materialities at Çatalhöyük: Reports*

from the 1995–1999 Seasons, edited by I. Hodder. McDonald Institute for Archaeological Research and British Institute of Archaeology at Ankara, Cambridge. In press.

Carver, M.

1989   Digging for Ideas. *Antiquity* 63:666–674.

1990   Digging for Data: Principles and Procedures for Evaluation, Excavation and Post-Excavation in Towns. *Theory and Practice of Archaeological Research* 2:255–302. Institute of Archaeology and Ethnology, Polish Academy of Sciences.

Castañeda, Q.

1996   *In the Museum of Maya Culture: Touring Chichén Itzá.* University of Minnesota Press, Minneapolis.

Castells, E.

1996   *The Rise of the Network Society.* Blackwell, Oxford.

Cauvin, J.

1994   *Naissance des Divinités, Naissance de l'Agriculture.* CNRS, Paris.

Cessford, C.

2003   Microartifactual Floor Patterning: The Case at Çatalhöyük. *Assemblage* 7. (http://www.shef.ac.uk/asem/issue7/cessford.html)

2004a   Neolithic Excavations in the North Area, East Mound, Çatalhöyük 1995–1998. In *Excavating Çatalhöyük: South, North and KOPAL Area: Reports from the 1995–1999 Seasons,* edited by I. Hodder. McDonald Institute for Archaeological Research and British Institute of Archaeology at Ankara, Cambridge. In press.

2004b   Absolute Dating at Çatalhöyük. In *Changing Materialities at Çatalhöyük: Reports from the 1995–1999 Season,* edited by I. Hodder. McDonald Institute for Archaeological Research and British Institute of Archaeology at Ankara, Cambridge. In press.

2004c   Estimating the Neolithic Population of Çatalhöyük. In *Inhabiting Çatalhöyük: Reports from the 1995–1999 Season,* edited by I. Hodder. McDonald Institute for Archaeological Research and British Institute of

Archaeology at Ankara, Cambridge. In press.

Chadha, A.

2002   Visions of Discipline: Sir Mortimer Wheeler and the Archaeological Method in India (1944–1948). *Journal of Social Archaeology* 2(3).

Chadwick, A.

1998   Archaeology at the Edge of Chaos: Further Toward Reflexive Excavation Methodologies. *Assemblage* 3. (http://www.shef.ac.uk/assem/3/3chad.htm)

2003   What Have the Post-Processualists Ever Done for Us? Towards an Integration of Theory and Practice, and a Radical Field Archaeology. *Interpreting Stratigraphy Meeting 2001.* In press.

Childe, V. G.

1925   *The Dawn of European Civilisation.* Kegan Paul, London.

1939   *Man Makes Himself.* Oxford University Press, Oxford.

1949   *Social Worlds of Knowledge.* Oxford University Press, Oxford.

1952   *New Light on the Most Ancient East.* Routledge and Paul, London.

1960   *What Happened in History.* Max Parrish, London.

Clark, G.

1934   Archaeology and the State. *Antiquity* 8:414–428.

1957   *Archaeology and Society.* 3rd edition. Methuen, London.

Clarke, D.

1968   *Analytical Archaeology.* Methuen, London.

1972   A Provisional Model of an Iron Age Society and its Settlement System. In *Models in Archaeology,* edited by D. Clarke, pp. 801–870. Methuen, London.

Cleere, H.

1989   *Archaeological Heritage Management in the Modern World.* Unwin Hyman, London.

Clifford, J., and G. Marcus (eds.)

1986   *Writing Culture: The Poetics of Ethnography.* University of California Press, Berkeley.

Coles, B., and J. Coles

1989   *People of the Wetlands.* Thames and Hudson, London.

Collingwood, R. G.
1946   *The Idea of History.* Oxford University Press, Oxford.

Condori, C. M.
1989   History and Pre-history in Bolivia: What about the Indians? In *Conflicts in the Archaeology of Living Traditions,* edited by R. Layton, pp. 46–59. Unwin Hyman, London.

Conkey, M.
1989   The Structural Analysis of Paleolithic Art. In *Archaeological Thought in the Americas,* edited by C. C. Lamberg-Karlovsky, pp. 135–154. Cambridge University Press, Cambridge.

Conkey, M., and R. Tringham
1995   Archaeology and the Goddess: Exploring the Contours of Feminist Archaeology. In *Feminisms in the Academy: Rethinking the Disciplines,* edited by A. Stewart and D. Stanton, pp. 199–247. University of Michigan Press, Ann Arbor.

Connerton, P.
1989   *How Societies Remember.* Cambridge University Press, Cambridge.

Conolly, J.
1996   The Knapped Stone. In *On the Surface: Çatalhöyük 1993–95,* edited by I. Hodder, pp. 173–198. McDonald Institute for Archaeological Research and British Institute of Archaeology at Ankara Monograph 22. Cambridge.
2003   The Çatalhöyük Obsidian Hoards: A Contextual Analysis of Technology. In *Lithic Studies for the New Millennium,* edited by N. Moloney and M. Shott. Archetype Books/Institute of Archaeology, London. In press.

Cross, S.
2004   Statistical Integration of Contextual Data. In *Changing Materialities at Çatalhöyük: Reports from the 1995–1999 Seasons,* edited by I. Hodder. McDonald Institute for Archaeological Research and British Institute of Archaeology at Ankara, Cambridge. In press.

Daniel, G.
1962   *The Idea of Prehistory.* Penguin, Harmondsworth.

Daniel, G., and C. Renfrew
1988   *The Idea of Prehistory.* Edinburgh University Press, Edinburgh.

Dean, P. A., and C. F. Marler
2001   Shoshone Spirituality and Enhancing Archaeological Interpretation in Southeast Ohio. *SAA Archaeological Record* 1(2):34–36.

de Certeau, M.
1984   *The Practice of Everyday Life.* University of California Press, Berkeley.

Deetz, J.
1977   *In Small Things Forgotten.* Anchor Books, New York.

de la Torre, M. (ed.)
1997   *The Conservation of Archaeological Sites in the Mediterranean Region.* The Getty Conservation Institute, Los Angeles.

Denzin, N. K., and Y. S. Lincoln
1994   *Handbook of Qualitative Research.* Sage, London.

Derrida, J.
1976   *Of Grammatology.* Johns Hopkins University Press, Baltimore, Maryland.

Diamond, J.
2002   Evolution, Consequences, and Future of Plant and Animal Domestication. Circulated manuscript.

Diaz-Andreu, M., and T. Champion
1996   *Nationalism and Archaeology in Europe.* UCL Press, London.

Dobres, M.-A.
2000   *Technology and Social Agency.* Blackwell, Oxford.

Dobres, M.-A., and J. Robb (eds.)
2000   *Agency in Archaeology.* Routledge, London.

Donley, L. W.
1982   House Power: Swahili Space and Symbolic Markers. In *Symbolic and Structural Archaeology,* edited by I. Hodder, pp. 63–73. Cambridge University Press, Cambridge.
1987   Life in the Swahili Town House Reveals the Symbolic Meaning of Spaces and Artefact Assemblages. *African Archaeological Review* 5:181–192.

Douglas, M.
1970   *Natural Symbols.* Vintage, New York.

Dowdall, K., and O. Parrish
2003   A Meaningful Disturbance of the Earth. *Journal of Social Archaeology* 3(1).

Downer, A.
1997   Archaeologists–Native American Relations. In *Native Americans and Archaeologists. Stepping Stones to Common Ground,* edited by N. Swidler, K. Dongoske, R. Anyon, and A. Downer, pp. 23–34. Alta-Mira Press, Walnut Creek, California.

Duke, P., and D. J. Saitta
1998   An Emancipatory Archaeology for the Working Class. *Assemblage 4.* (http://www.shef.ac.uk/assem/4/)

Dunnell, R. C., and J. K. Stein
1989   Theoretical Issues in the Interpretation of Mmicroartifacts. *Geoarchaeology* 4:31–41.

Düring, B. S.
2001   Social Dimensions in the Architecture of Neolithic Çatalhöyük. *Anatolian Studies* 51:1–18.

Duru, R.
1992   Höyücek Kazıları 1989. *Belleten* 61:551–566.
1999   The Neolithic of the Lake District. In Neolithic in Turkey, edited by M. Özdoğan and N. Başgelen, pp. 165–192. Arkeoloji ve Sanat Yayınları, Istanbul.

Dymond, M.
1998   Not Just a Day Out! Archaeology and Education on the Gardom's Edge Project. *Assemblage 4.* (http://www.shef.ac.uk/assem/4/)

Ebron, P.
1998   Enchanted Memories of Regional Difference in African American Culture. *American Anthropologist* 100:94–105.

Edgeworth, M.
1990   Analogy as Practical Reason: The Perception of Objects in Excavation Practice. *Archaeological Review from Cambridge* 9(2):14–23.

Edmonds, M.
1999   *Ancestral Geographies of the Neolithic: Landscapes, Monuments and Memories.* Routledge, London.

Eiland, M. L.
1993   The Past Re-made: The Case of Oriental Carpets. *Antiquity* 67: 859–863.

Emele, M.
2000   Virtual Spaces, Atomic Pig-Bones and Miscellaneous Goddesses. In *Towards Reflexive Methods in Archaeology: The Example at Çatalhöyük,* edited by I. Hodder, pp. 219–228. McDonald Institute for Archaeological Research and British Institute of Archaeology at Ankara, Monograph 289. Cambridge.

Esin, U.
1991   Salvage Excavations at the Pre-Pottery Site of Aşıklı Höyük in Central Anatolia. *Anatolia* 17:123–174.

Esin, U., and S. Harmanakaya
1999   Aşıklı in the Frame of Central Anatolian Neolithic. In *Neolithic in Turkey,* edited by M. Özdoğan and N. Başgelen, pp. 115–132. Arkeoloji ve Sanat Yayınları, Istanbul.

Estabrook, R., and C. Newman.
1996   The Deltona Project: Cultural Resource Management in the Hillsborough River Basin. *The Florida Anthropologist* 49(4):179–187.

Fabian, J.
1983   *Time and the Other: How Anthropology Makes its Object.* Columbia University Press, New York.

Fagette, P.
1996   *Digging for Dollars. American Archaeology and the New Deal.* University of New Mexico Press, Albuquerque.

Fairbairn, A., J. Near, and D. Martinoli
2004   Macrobotanical Investigation of the North, South and KOPAL Area Excavations at Çatalhöyük East. In *Excavating Çatalhöyük: South, North and KOPAL Area: Reports from the 1995–1999 Seasons,* edited by I. Hodder. McDonald Institute for Archaeological Research and British Institute of Archaeology at Ankara, Cambridge. In press.

Farid, S.
2004   The South Area. In *Excavating Çatalhöyük: South, North and KOPAL Area: Reports from the 1995–1999 Seasons,* edited by I. Hodder. McDonald Institute for

Archaeological Research and British Institute of Archaeology at Ankara, Cambridge. In press.

Faulkner, N.

2002   The Sedgeford Project, Norfolk: An Experiment in Popular Participation and Dialectical Method. *Archaeology International* 5:16–20. Institute of Archaeology, University College, London.

Featherstone, M.

1991   *Consumer Culture and Postmodernism*. Sage, London.

Featherstone, M., S. Lash, and R. Robertson (eds.)

1995   *Global Modernities*. Sage, London.

Feinman, G.

2000   New Perspectives on Models of Political Action and the Puebloan Southwest. In *Social Theory in Archaeology*, edited by M. B. Schiffer, pp. 31–51. University of Utah Press, Salt Lake City.

Fladmark, K. R.

1982   Microdebitage Analysis: Initial Considerations. *Journal of Archaeological Science* 9:205–220.

Flannery, K. V.

1972   The Origins of the Village as a Settlement Type in Mesoamerica and the Near East: A Comparative Study. In *Man, Settlement and Urbanism*, edited by P. J. Ucko, R. Tringham, and G. W. Dimbleby, pp. 23–53. Duckworth, London.

1993   Will the Real Model Please Stand Up: Comments on Saidel's 'Round House or Square?' *Journal of Mediterranean Archaeology* 6(1):109–117.

Forte, M., and A. Siliotti

1997   *Virtual Archaeology*. Thames and Hudson, London.

Fotiadis, M.

1993   Regions of the Imagination: Archaeologists, Local People, and the Archaeological Record in Fieldwork, Greece. *Journal or European Archaeology* 1:151–170.

Foucault, M.

1977   *Discipline and Punish*. Vintage Books, New York.

1979   *Discipline and Punish: The Birth of the Prison*. Penguin, London.

1981   *The History of Sexuality*, vol. 1: *An Introduction*. Penguin, Harmondsworth.

French, D.

1972   Excavations at Can Hasan III. In *Papers in Economic Prehistory*, edited by E. Higgs, pp. 181–190. Cambridge University Press, Cambridge.

Friedman, J., and M. Rowlands

1978   *The Evolution of Social Systems*. Duckworth, London.

Galison, P.

1997   *Image and Logic. A Material Culture of Microphysics*. University of Chicago Press, Chicago.

Garfinkel, Y.

1994   Ritual Burial of Cultic Objects: The Earliest Evidence. *Cambridge Archaeological Journal* 4(2):159–188.

Gathercole, P., and D. Lowenthal

1989   *The Politics of the Past*. Unwin Hyman, London.

Geertz, C.

1973   *The Interpretation of Cultures*. Fontana, London.

Gell, A.

1998   *Art and Agency: An Anthropological Theory*. Clarendon, Oxford.

Gérard, F., and L. Thissen

2002   *The Neolithic of Central Anatolia. Internal Developments and External Relations during the 9th–6th Millennia CAL B.C.* Ege Yayınları, Istanbul.

Gero, J.

1991   Who Experienced What in Prehistory? A Narrative Explanation from Queyash, Peru. In *Processual and Postprocessual Archaeologies*, edited R. Preucel, pp. 126–189. Southern Illinois University, Carbondale.

1996   Archaeological Practice and Gendered Encounters with Field Data. In *Gender and Archaeology*, edited by R. Wright, pp. 251–280. University of Pennsylvania Press, Philadelphia.

Gero, J. M., and M. W. Conkey (eds.)

1991   *Engendering Archaeology: Women and Prehistory*. Blackwell, Oxford.

Giddens, A.

1979   *Central Problems in Social Theory*. MacMillan, London.

1984   *The Constitution of Society: An Outline of the Theory of Structuration.*

Cambridge Polity Press, Cambridge, and the University of California Press, Berkeley.

1992   *The Transformation of Intimacy.* Stanford University Press, Stanford, California.

Gimbutas, M.
1982   *The Goddesses and Gods of Old Europe.* Thames and Hudson, London.

Glassie, J.
1975   *Folk Housing of Middle Virginia.* University of Tennessee Press, Knoxville.

Glob, P. V.
1977   *The Bog People.* Faber, London.

Goldberg, P., D. T. Nash, and M. D. Petraglia (eds.)
1993   *Formation Processes in Archaeological Context.* Monographs in World Archaeology 17.

Goring-Morris, N.
2000   The Quick and the Dead: The Social Context of Aceramic Neolithic Mortuary Practices as Seen from Kfar HaHoresh. In *Life in Neolithic Farming Communities: Social Organization, Identity, and Differentiation,* edited by I. Kuijt, pp. 13–36. Kluwer Academic/Plenum Publishers, New York.

Gosden, C.
1994   *Social Being and Time.* Blackwell, Oxford.

Gramsch, A.
1993   Death and Continuity. Unpublished M.Phil. diss. Department of Archaeology, University of Cambridge, Cambridge.
1995   Death and Continuity. *Journal of European Archaeology* 3(1):71–90.

Gupta, A., and J. Ferguson (eds.)
1997   *Anthropological Locations: Boundaries and Grounds of a Field Science.* University of California Press, Berkeley.

Hamann, B.
2002   The Social Life of Pre-Sunrise Things: Indigenous Mesoamerican Archaeology. *Current Anthropology* 43(3):351–382.

Hamilakis, Y.
1999   La Trahison des Archéologues? Archaeological Practice as Intellectual Activity in Postmodernity. *Journal of*

Mediterranean Archaeology 12(1): 60–79.

Hamilton, N.
1996   Figurines, Clay Balls, Small Finds and Burials. In *On the Surface: Çatalhöyük 1993–1995,* edited by I. Hodder, pp. 215–264. McDonald Institute for Archaeological Research and British Institute of Archaeology at Ankara Monograph 22. Cambridge.
2004   Social Aspects of Burial. In *Inhabiting Çatalhöyük: Reports from the 1995–1999 Seasons,* edited by I. Hodder. McDonald Institute for Archaeological Research and British Institute of Archaeology at Ankara, Cambridge. In press.

Handler, R., and E. Gable
1997   *The New History in an Old Museum: Creating the Past at Colonial Williamsburg.* Duke University Press, Durham, North Carolina.

Harris, E. C.
1989   *Principles of Archaeological Stratigraphy.* 2nd edition. Academic Press, London.

Harris, E. C., M. R. Brown III, and G. J. Brown
1993   *Practices of Archaeological Stratigraphy.* Academic Press, London.

Hassan, F.
1997   Beyond the Surface: Comments on Hodder's "Reflexive Excavation Methodology," *Antiquity* 71:1020–1025.

Hauptmann, H.
2002   Upper Mesopotamia in its Regional Context during the Early Neolithic. In *The Neolithic of Central Anatolia,* edited by F. Gérard and L. Thissen, pp. 263–271. Ege Yayınları, Istanbul.

Hawkes, C.F.C.
1954   Archaeological Theory and Method: Some Suggestions from the Old World. *American Anthropologist* 56:155–168.

Hayden, B.
1990   Nimrods, Piscators, Pluckers, and Planters: The Emergence of Food Production. *Journal of Anthropological Archaeology* 9:31–69.

Helskog, K.
1995   Maleness and Femaleness in the Sky

and the Underworld—and in Between. In *Perceiving Rock Art:
Social and Political Perspectives*,
edited by K. Helskog and B. Olsen,
pp. 247–262. The Institute for
Comparative Research in Human
Culture, Oslo.

Hesse, M.
1995   Past Realities. In *Interpreting
         Archaeology*, edited by I. Hodder,
         M. Shanks, and others, pp. 45–47.
         Routledge, London.

Hester, T., H. Shafer, and K. Feder (eds.)
1997   *Field Methods in Archaeology*. 7th
         ed. McGraw-Hill, New York.

Hill, J., and J. Gunn
1977   *The Individual in Prehistory*. Acade-
         mic Press, New York.

Hobsbawm, E.
1994   *The Age of Extremes*. Michael
         Joseph, London.

Hodder, I.
1982   *Symbols in Action*. Cambridge
         University Press, Cambridge.
1986   *Reading the Past* Cambridge
         University Press, Cambridge.
1990   *The Domestication of Europe*.
         Blackwell, Oxford.
1992   *Theory and Practice in Archaeology*.
         Routledge, London.
1993   The Narrative and Rhetoric of
         Material Culture Sequences. *World
         Archaeology* 25:268–282.
1997   "Always Momentary, Fluid and
         Flexible": Towards a Reflexive Ex-
         cavation Methodology. *Antiquity*
         71:691–700.
1998   The *Domus*: Some Problems Re-
         considered. In *Understanding the
         Neolithic of North-western Europe*,
         edited by M. Edmonds and
         C. Richards, pp. 84–101. Cruithne
         Press, Glasgow.
1999a   *The Archaeological Process. An
         Introduction*. Blackwell, Oxford.
1999b   British Prehistory: Some Thoughts
         Looking In. *Cambridge Archaeolog-
         ical Journal* 9:376–380.

Hodder, I. (ed.)
1996   *On the Surface: Çatalhöyük
         1993–95*. McDonald Institute for
         Archaeological Research and British
         Institute of Archaeology at Ankara.
         Monograph 22. Cambridge.

2000   *Towards Reflexive Methods in
         Archaeology: The Example at
         Çatalhöyük*. McDonald Institute
         for Archaeological Research and
         British Institute of Archaeology at
         Ankara, Monograph 289. Cam-
         bridge.

Hodder, I., and C. Evans
n.d.   *On the Edge*. English Heritage and
         McDonald Institute for Archaeolog-
         ical Research. Cambridge. In press.

Hodder, I., and P. Shand
1988   The Haddenham Long Barrow:
         An Interim Statement. *Antiquity*
         62:349–353.

Hodder, I., M. Shanks, A. Alexandri, V. Buchli,
J. Carman, J. Last, and G. Lucas (eds.)
1995   *Interpreting Archaeology*. Rout-
         ledge, London.

Hole, F.
2000   Is Size Important? Function and
         Hierarchy in Neolithic Settlements.
         In *Life in Neolithic Farming Com-
         munities. Social Organization, Iden-
         tity, and Differentiation*, edited by
         I. Kuijt, pp. 191–210. Kluwer
         Academic/Plenum Publishers, New
         York.

Humphrey, C., and U. Onon
1996   *Shamans and Elders*. Clarendon
         Press, Oxford.

Hunter, J., and I. Ralston
1993   The Structure of British Archaeol-
         ogy. In *Archaeological Resource
         Management in the UK. An Intro-
         duction*, edited by J. Hunter and
         I. Ralston. Alan Sutton Publishing,
         Institute of Field Archaeologists,
         London.

Jacobs-Huey, L.
2002   The Natives are Gazing and Talking
         Back: Reviewing the Problematics of
         Positionality, Voice, and Account-
         ability among "Native" Anthropol-
         ogists. *American Anthropologist*
         104(3):791–804.

Johnson, A., and T. Earle
1987   *The Evolution of Human Societies*.
         Stanford University Press, Stanford.

Johnson, M.
1989   Conceptions of Agency in Archaeo-
         logical Interpretation. *Journal of
         Anthropological Archaeology*
         8:189–211.

Jones, M.
2001   *The Molecule Hunt: Archaeology and the Search for Ancient DNA.* Allen Lane, London.

Joukowsky, M.
1980   *A Complete Manual of Field Archaeology.* Prentice Hall, Englewood Cliffs, New Jersey.

Joyce, A., L. A. Bustamante, and M. N. Levine
2002   Commoner Power. *Journal of Archaeological Method and Theory.*

Joyce, R. A.
1994   Dorothy Hughes Popenoe: Eve in an Archaeological Garden. In *Women in Archaeology,* edited by C. Claassen, pp. 51–66. University of Pennsylvania Press, Philadephia.
1998   Performing the Body in Prehispanic Central America. *Res* 33:147–165.
2000a   *Gender and Power in Ancient Mesoamerica.* University of Texas Press, Austin.
2000b   Heirlooms and Houses. Materiality and Social Memory. In *Beyond Kinship. Social and Material Reproduction in House Societies,* edited by R. A. Joyce and S. D. Gillespie, pp. 189–212. University of Pennsylvania Press, Philadelphia.

Joyce, R. A., and S. D. Gillespie (eds.)
2000   *Beyond Kinship. Social and Material Reproduction in House Societies.* University of Pennsylvania Press, Philadelphia.

Kenyon, K.
1953   *Beginning in Archaeology.* Phoenix House, London.

Kiln, R.
1974   Archaeology as a Hobby and How to Start. In *Rescue Archaeology,* edited by P. Rahtz, pp. 256–273. Penguin Books, Harmondsworth.

Kinnes, I.
1992   *Non-Megalithic Long Barrows and Allied Structures in the British Neolithic.* British Museum, Occasional Paper 52, London.

Kirch, P.
2000   Temples as 'Holy Houses.' The Transformation of Ritual Architecture in Traditional Polynesian Societies. In *Beyond Kinship. Social and Material Reproduction in House Societies,* edited by R. A. Joyce

and S. D. Gillespie, pp. 103–114. University of Pennsylvania Press, Philadelphia.

Kirkbride, D.
1968   Beidha 1967: An Interim Report. *Palestine Exploration Quarterly* 100:90–96.

Kluth, R., and K. Munnell
1997   The Integration of Tradition and Scientific Knowledge on the Leech Lake Reservation. In *Native Americans and Archaeologists. Stepping Stones to Common Ground,* edited by N. Swidler, K. Dongoske, R. Anyon, and A. Downer, pp. 112–114. AltaMira Press, Walnut Creek, California.

Knapp, A. B., and L. Meskell
1997   Bodies of Evidence in Cypriot Prehistory. *Cambridge Archaeological Journal* 7(2):183–204.

Kohl, P., and C. Fawcett (eds.)
1995   *Nationalism, Politics and the Practice of Archaeology.* Cambridge University Press, Cambridge.

Kosso, P.
1991   Method in Archaeology: Middle Range Theory as Hermeneutics. *American Antiquity* 56:621–627.

Kramer, B., and K. Schmidt
1998   Two Radiocarbon Dates from Göbekli Tepe, South Eastern Turkey. *Neo-Lithics: A Newsletter of South-West Asian Lithics Research* 3/98:8–9.

Kristiansen, K.
1984   Ideology and Material Culture: An Archaeological Perspective. In *Marxist Perspectives in Archaeology,* edited by M. Spriggs, pp. 72–100. Cambridge University Press, Cambridge.

Kuijt, I.
1996   Negotiating Equality through Ritual: A Consideration of Late Natufian and Pre-Pottery Neolithic Mortuary Practices. *Journal of Anthropological Archaeology* 15:313–336.
2001   Place, Death, and the Transmission of Social Memory in Early Agricultural Communities of the Near Eastern Pre-Pottery Neolithic. In *Social Memory, Identity, and Death: An-*

thropological Perspectives on Mortuary Rituals, edited by M. S. Chesson, pp. 80–99. Archaeological Papers of the American Anthropological Association 10.

Kuijt, I. (ed.)

2000 Life in Neolithic Farming Communities: Social Organization, Identity, and Differentiation. Kluwer Academic/Plenum Publishers, New York.

Kus, S.

1992 Toward an Archaeology of Body and Soul. In Representations in Archaeology, edited by J.-C. Gardin and C. S. Peebles, pp. 168–177. Indiana University Press, Bloomington.

Lakoff, G., and M. Johnson

1999 Philosophy in the Flesh: The Embodied Mind and its Challenge to Western Thought. Basic Books, New York.

LaMotta, V. M., and M. B. Schiffer

1999 Formation Processes of House Floor Assemblages. In The Archaeology of Household Activities, edited by P. M. Allison, pp. 19–29. Routledge, London.

Lampeter Archaeology Workshop

1997 Relativism, Objectivity and the Politics of the Past. Archaeological Dialogues 4:166–175.

Lane, P. J.

1987 Reordering Residues of the Past. In Archaeology as Long-Term History, edited by I. Hodder, pp. 54–62. Cambridge University Press, Cambridge.

Langford, R. F.

1983 Our Heritage—Your Playground. Australian Archaeology 16:1–6.

Larsson, S.

2000 Stadens Dolda Kulturskikt. Lundaarkeologins Förutsättningar och Förståelsehorisonter Uttryckt Genom Praxis för Källmaterialsproduktion 1890-1990. Archaeologica Lundensia. Investigationes de antiqvitatibus urbis Lundae IX. Lund.

Last, J.

1998 A Design for Life. Interpreting the Art of Çatalhöyük. Journal of Material Culture 3:355–378.

Latour, B.

1988a Mixing Humans and Nonhumans Together: The Sociology of a Door Closer. Social Problems 35:298–310.

1988b 'The Prince' for Machines as well as for Machinations. In Technology and Social Process, edited by B. Elliott, pp. 20–43. Edinburgh University Press, Edinburgh.

Latour, B., and S. Woolgar

1979 Laboratory Life: The Social Construction of Scientific Facts. Sage, London.

Layton, R.

1989 Conflict in the Archaeology of Living Traditions. Unwin Hyman, London.

Leach, E.

1976 Culture and Communication. Cambridge University Press, Cambridge.

Le Goff, J.

1992 History and Memory. Columbia University Press, New York.

Leibhammer, N.

2000 Rendering Realities. In Towards Reflexive Methods in Archaeology: The Example at Çatalhöyük, edited by I. Hodder, pp. 129–142. McDonald Institute for Archaeological Research and British Institute of Archaeology at Ankara, Monograph 289.

Lemonnier, P.

1993 Technological Choices. Routledge, London.

Leone, M.

1982 Some Opinions about Recovering Mind. American Antiquity 47:742–760.

Leone, M., P. B. Potter, and P. Shackel

1987 Toward a Critical Archaeology. Current Anthropology 28:283–302.

Lévi-Strauss, C.

1968 Structural Anthropology. Allen Lane, London.

1970 The Raw and the Cooked. Jonathan Cape, London.

1982 The Way of the Masks. University of Washington Press, Seattle.

1983 The Way of the Masks. Jonathan Cape, London.

1987 Anthropology and Myth. Blackwell, Oxford.

1991 Maison. Dictionnaire de l'Ethnologie et de L'Anthropologie. Presses Universitaires de France, Paris.

Lindhé, E., P. Sarnäs, and M. Steineke
2001   *Citytunneln och Spåren i Land-skapet. Projektprogram och Under-sökningsplaner för Arkeologiska Slutundersökningar för Citytunnelns Spårsträckningar och Hotelltomten.* Malmö Kulturmiljö.

Longacre, W.
1970   *Archaeology as Anthropology.* Anthropological Papers of the University of Arizona 17, Tucson.

Lucas, G.
2001a   *Critical Approaches to Fieldwork. Contemporary and Historical Archaeological Practice.* Routledge, London.
2001b   Destruction and the Rhetoric of Excavation. *Norwegian Archaeological Review* 34:35–46.

Ludlow Collective
2001   Archaeology of the Colorado Coal Field War 1913–1914. In *Archaeologies of the Contemporary Past,* edited by V. Buchli and G. Lucas, pp. 94–107. Routledge, London.

Lynch, Michael
2000   Against Reflexivity as an Academic Virtue and Source of Privileged Knowledge. *Theory, Culture and Society* 17:26–54.

Lyotard, J.-F.
1984   *The Postmodern Condition.* University of Minnesota Press, Minneapolis.
1991   *The Inhuman.* Polity Press, Cambridge.

Lynch, M.
2000   Against Reflexivity as an Academic Virtue and Source of Privileged Knowledge. *Theory, Culture and Society* 17(3):26–54.

McDavid, C.
1997   Descendents, Decisions, and Power: The Public Interpretation of the Archaeology of the Levi Jordan Plantation. *Historical Archaeology* 31:114–131.
2000   Archaeology as Cultural Critique: Pragmatism and the Archaeology of a Southern United States Plantation. In *Philosophy and Archaeological Practice: Perspectives for the 21ˢᵗ Century,* edited by C. Holtorf and

H. Karlsson, pp. 221–239. Bricoleur, Göteborg.

McGimsey III, C., B. Lipe, and D. Seifert
1995   SAA, SHA, SOPA, AIA Discuss Register of Professional Archaeologists. *SAA Bulletin* 13(3):6–8, 14–15.

McGuire, R.
1992   *A Marxist Archaeology.* Academic Press, New York.

McGuire, R. H., and M. Walker
1999   Class Confrontations in Archaeology. *Historical Archaeology* 33(1):159–183.

Malhi, R., M. Van Tuinen, J. Mountain, I. Hodder, and E. A. Hadly
2004   Pilot project: Çatalhöyük Ancient DNA Study. In *Inhabiting Çatalhöyük: Reports from the 1995–1999 Seasons,* edited by I. Hodder. McDonald Institute for Archaeological Research and British Institute of Archaeology at Ankara, Cambridge. In press.

Marquardt. W. H.
1992   Dialectical Archaeology. *Archaeological Method and Theory* 4:101–140.

Matero, Frank
2000   The Conservation of an Excavated Past. In *Towards Reflexive Methods in Archaeology: The Example at Çatalhöyük,* edited by I. Hodder, pp. 71–88. McDonald Institute for Archaeological Research and British Institute of Archaeology at Ankara, Monograph 289.

Matthews, R.
1996   Surface Scraping and Planning. In *On the Surface: Çatalhöyük 1993–95,* edited by I. Hodder, pp. 79–100. McDonald Institute for Archaeological Research and British Institute of Archaeology at Ankara, Monograph 22.
2002   Homogeneity versus Diversity: Dynamics of the Central Anatolian Neolithic. In *The Neolithic of Central Anatolia,* edited by F. Gérard and L. Thissen, pp. 91–103. Ege Yayınları, Istanbul.

Matthews, W.
1996   Multiple Surfaces: The Micromorphology. In *On the Surface: Çatal-*

höyük 1993–95, edited by I. Hodder, pp. 301–342. McDonald Institute for Archaeological Research and British Institute of Archaeology at Ankara, Monograph 22.

2004   Micromorphological and Microstratigraphic Traces of Uses and Concepts of Space. In *Inhabiting Çatalhöyük: Reports from the 1995–1999 Seasons*, edited by I. Hodder. McDonald Institute for Archaeological Research and British Institute of Archaeology at Ankara, Cambridge. In press.

Mawson, A.N.M.

1989   The Triumph of Life: Political Dispute and Religious Ceremonial among the Agar Dinka of Southern Sudan. Unpublished Ph.D. diss., University of Cambridge, Cambridge.

Mellaart, J.

1964   Excavations at Çatal Hüyük, Third Preliminary Report, 1963. *Anatolian Studies* 14:39–119.

1966   Excavations at Çatal Hüyük, Fourth Preliminary Report, 1965. *Anatolian Studies* 16:15–191.

1967   *Çatal Hüyük: A Neolithic Town in Anatolia*. Thames and Hudson, London.

Mellaart, J., U. Hirsch, and B. Balpinar

1989   *The Goddess from Anatolia*. Eskanazi, Rome.

Merleau-Ponty, M.

1945   *Phénoménologie de la Perception* Gallimard, Paris.

Meskell, L.

1995   Goddesses, Gimbutas and New Age Archaeology. *Antiquity* 69:74–86.

1996   The Somatisation of Archaeology: Institutions, Discourses, Corporeality. *Norwegian Archaeological Review* 29:1–16.

1998   Intimate Archaeologies: The Case of Kha and Merit. *World Archaeology* 29:363–379.

1999   *Archaeologies of Social Life*. Blackwell, Oxford.

2002a   The Intersections of Identity and Politics in Archaeology. *Annual Review of Anthropology* 31:279–301.

2002b   Negative Heritage and Past Mastering in Archaeology. *Anthropology Quarterly* 75(3):557–574.

2002c   *Private Life in New Kingdom Egypt*. Princeton University Press, New Jersey.

Middleton, W. D., T. D. Price, and D. C. Meiggs

2004   Chemical Analysis of Floor Sediments for the Identification of Anthropogenic Residues. In *Inhabiting Çatalhöyük: Reports from the 1995–1999 Seasons*, edited by I. Hodder. McDonald Institute for Archaeological Research and British Institute of Archaeology at Ankara, Cambridge. In press.

Miller, D., and C. Tilley (eds.)

1984   *Ideology Power and Prehistory*. Cambridge University Press, Cambridge.

Miller, D., M. Rowlands, and C. Tilley (eds.)

1989   *Domination and Resistance*. Routledge, London.

Molleson, T.

1994   Can the Degree of Sexual Dimorphism Provide an Insight into the Position of Women in Past Populations? *Dossier de Documentation Archéologique* 17:51–67.

Moore, A.M.T., G. C. Hillman, and A. J. Legge

2000   *Village on the Euphrates. From Foraging to Farming at Abu Hureyra*. Oxford University Press, Oxford.

Moore, H. L.

1982   The Interpretation of Spatial Patterning in Settlement Residues. In *Symbolic and Structural Archaeology*, edited by I. Hodder, pp. 74–79. Cambridge University Press, Cambridge.

1986   *Space, Text and Gender*. Cambridge University Press, Cambridge.

1987   Problems in the Analysis of Social Change: An Example from the Marakwet. In *Archaeology as Long-Term History*, edited by I. Hodder, pp. 85–104. Cambridge University Press, Cambridge.

1994   *A Passion for Difference: Essays in Anthropology and Gender*. Polity Press, Cambridge.

Moran, P., and D. Shaun Hides
1990   Writing, Authority and the Determi-
          nation of a Subject. In *Archaeology
          after Structuralism,* edited by
          I. Bapty and T. Yates, pp. 205–221.
          Routledge, London.
Morris, I.
1991   The Archaeology of Ancestors: The
          Saxe/Goldstein Hypothesis Revis-
          ited. *Cambridge Archaeological
          Journal* 1:147–169.
2000   *Archaeology as Cultural History.*
          Blackwell, Oxford.
Musson, C.
1974   Rescue Digging all the Time. In *Res-
          cue Archaeology,* edited by P. Rahtz,
          pp. 79–89. Penguin Books, Har-
          mondsworth.
Nelson, M. C.
2000   Abandonment: Conceptualization,
          Representation, and Social Change.
          In *Social Theory in Archaeology,*
          edited by M. B. Schiffer, pp. 52–62.
          University of Utah Press, Salt Lake
          City.
Newton, M. W., and P. I. Kuniholm
1999   Wiggles Worth Watching—Making
          Radiocarbon Work. The Case of
          Çatal Höyük. In *Studies in Aegean
          Archaeology Presented to Malcolm
          H. Wiener as He Enters His 65th
          Year,* edited by P. P. Betancourt,
          V. Karageorghis, R. Laffineur, and
          W.-D. Niemeier. *Aegaeum* 20:527–
          537.
O'Brien, M. J., and R. L. Lyman
2000   Evolutionary Archaeology: Recon-
          structing and Explaining Historical
          Lineages. In *Social Theory in Ar-
          chaeology,* edited by M. B. Schiffer,
          pp. 126–142. University of Utah
          Press, Salt Lake City.
Onians, R. B.
1951   *The Origins of European Thought
          About the Body, the Mind, the Soul,
          the World, Time and Fate.* Cam-
          bridge University Press, Cambridge.
Özdoğan, M.
1995   Neolithic in Turkey: The Status of
          Research. In *Readings in Prehistory.
          Studies Presented to Halet Çambel,*
          pp. 41–60. University of Istanbul,
          Istanbul.
2002   Defining the Neolithic of Central

Anatolia. In *The Neolithic of Cen-
          tral Anatolia,* edited by F. Gérard
          and L. Thissen, pp. 253–261. Ege
          Yayınları, Istanbul.
Özdoğan, M., and A. Özdoğan
1990   Çayönü. A Conspectus of Recent
          Work. *Paléorient* 15(1):65–74.
1998   Buildings of Cult and the Cult of
          Buildings. In *Light on Top of the
          Black Hill: Studies Presented to
          Halet Çambel,* edited by G. Arsebuk,
          M. Mellink, and W. Schrimer, pp.
          581–601. Ege Yayınları, Istanbul.
Öztan, A.
2002   Kösk Höyük: New Contributions to
          Anatolian Archaeology. *Tüba-Ar*
          5:57–72.
Parker Pearson, M.
1982   Mortuary Practices, Society and
          Ideology: An Ethnoarchaeological
          Study. In *Symbolic and Structural
          Archaeology,* edited by I. Hodder,
          pp. 99–114. Cambridge University
          Press, Cambridge.
1999a   Food, Sex and Death: Cosmologies
          in the British Iron Age with Particu-
          lar Reference to East Yorkshire.
          Cambridge Archaeological Journal
          9:43–69.
1999b   *The Archaeology of Death and
          Burial.* Sutton, Stroud.
Parker Pearson, M., and Ramilisonina
1998   Stonehenge for the Ancestors: The
          Stones Pass on the Message. *Antiq-
          uity* 72:308–326.
Parker Pearson, M., and C. Richards (eds.)
1994   *Architecture and Order: Approaches
          to Social Space.* Routledge, London.
Patrik, L.
1985   Is There an Archaeological Record?
          *Advances in Archaeological Method
          and Theory* 8:27–62.
Patterson, T. C.
1995   *Toward a Social History of Archae-
          ology in the United States.* Harcourt
          Brace and Co., Orlando, Florida.
Paynter, R.
1983   Field or Factory? Concerning the
          Degradation of Archaeological
          Labour. In *The SocioPolitics of
          Archaeology,* edited by J. M. Gero,
          D. M. Lacy, and M. L. Blakey. De-
          partment of Anthropology, Univer-
          sity of Massachusetts, Amherst.

Pearson, M., and S. Sullivan
1999   *Looking after Heritage Places.* Melbourne University Press, Melbourne.

Petrie, W. M. Flinders
1904   *Methods and Aims in Archaeology.* MacMillan, London.

Pitt-Rivers, A.H.L.F.
1887   *Excavations in Cranborne Chase,* vol. 1. Privately printed.

Politis, G.
2001   On Archaeological Praxis, Gender Bias and Indigenous Peoples in South America. *Journal of Social Archaeology* 1:90–107.

Porter, D.
1997   *Internet Culture.* Routledge, New York.

Potter, P.
1991   Self-Reflection in Archaeology. In *Processual and Postprocessual Archaeologies: Multiple Ways of Knowing the Past,* edited by R. Preucel, pp. 225–234. Center for Archaeological Investigations, Occasional Paper 10. Southern Illinois University, Carbondale.

Preucel, R. W., and A. A. Bauer
2001   Archaeological Pragmatics. *Norwegian Archaeological Review* 34(2): 85–96.

Purdy, B.
1996   *How to do Archaeology the Right Way.* University Press of Florida, Gainesville.

Rahtz, P.
1974a   Rescue Digging Past and Present. In *Rescue Archaeology,* edited by P. Rahtz, pp. 53–72. Penguin Books, Harmondsworth.
1974b   Volunteers. In *Rescue Archaeology,* edited by P. Rahtz, pp. 274–279. Penguin Books, Harmondsworth.

Rainville, L.
2000   Microdebris Analysis in Early Bronze Age Mesopotamian Households. *Antiquity* 74:291–292.

Rathje, W. L.
2001   Archaeology and the World Trade Center Atrocity. *MSW-Management* 11(7):12–13.

Redman, C.
1987   Surface Collection, Sampling, and Research Design: A Retrospective. *American Antiquity* 52:249–265.

Renfrew, C.
1973a   *Before Civilization.* Jonathan Cape, London.
1973b   *Social Archaeology.* Southampton University, Southampton.
1984   *Approaches to Social Archaeology.* Edinburgh University Press, Edinburgh.
1987   *Archaeology and Language.* Penguin, Harmondsworth.
1996   Language Families and the Spread of Farming. In *The Origins and Spread of Agriculture and Pastoralism in Eurasia,* edited by D. Harris, pp. 70–92. University College Press, London.

Renfrew, C., and P. Bahn
1991   *Archaeology.* Thames and Hudson, London.

Renfrew, C., and E. Zubrow
1994   *The Ancient Mind: Elements of Cognitive Archaeology.* Cambridge University Press, Cambridge.

Richards, C.
1990   The Late Neolithic House in Orkney. In *The Social Archaeology of Houses,* edited by R. Samson, pp. 111–124. Edinburgh University Press, Edinburgh.

Richards, M., and J. Pearson
2004   Stable Isotope Evidence of Diet at Çatalhöyük. In *Inhabiting Çatalhöyük: Reports from the 1995–1999 Seasons,* edited by I. Hodder. McDonald Institute for Archaeological Research and British Institute of Archaeology at Ankara, Cambridge. In press.

Ricoeur, P.
1971   The Model of the Text: Meaningful Action Considered as a Text. *Social Research* 38:529–562.
1984   *Time and Narrative.* University of Chicago Press, Chicago, Illinois.

Ritchey, T.
1996   Note: Building Complexity. In *On the Surface: Çatalhöyük 1993–95,* edited by I. Hodder, pp 7–17. McDonald Institute for Archaeological Research and British Institute of Archaeology at Ankara, Monograph 22.

Robertson, J.
2002   Reflexivity Redux. *Anthropological Quarterly* 75(4):785–792.

Rollefson, G. O., A. H. Simmons, and Z. Kafafi
1992   Neolithic Culture at 'Ain Ghazal. *Journal of Field Archaeology* 19: 443–470.

Rosaldo, R.
2000   [1989] Grief and a Headhunter's Rage. In *Anthropological Theory,* edited by R. J. McGee and R. L.Warms, pp. 521–535, 2nd ed. Mayfield Publishing, Mountain View, California.

Rosenberg, M., and R. W. Redding
2000   Hallan Çemi and Early Village Organization in Eastern Anatolia. In *Life in Neolithic Farming Communities. Social Organization, Identity, and Differentiation,* edited by I. Kuijt, pp. 39–62. Kluwer Academic/ Plenum Publishers, New York.

Roskams, S.
2001   *Excavation.* Cambridge University Press, Cambridge.

Rowlands, M.
1993   The Role of Memory in the Transmission of Culture. *World Archaeology* 25:141–151.

Russell, R., and L. Martin
2004   The Çatalhöyük Faunal Remains. In *Inhabiting Çatalhöyük: Reports from the 1995–1999 Seasons,* edited by I. Hodder. McDonald Institute for Archaeological Research and British Institute of Archaeology at Ankara, Cambridge. In press.

Sahlins, M.
1974   *Stone Age Economics.* Tavistock Publications, London.
1981   *Historical Metaphor and Mythical Reality.* University of Michigan Press, Ann Arbor.

Said, E. W.
1978   *Orientalism.* Routledge and Kegan Paul, London.

Salzman, P. C.
2002   On Reflexivity. *American Anthropologist* 104(3):805–813.

Saville, A.
1990   *Hazleton North. Gloucestershire.* English Heritage Archaeological Report 13.

Schiffer, M. B.
1987   *Formation Processes of the Archaeological Record.* University of New Mexico Press, Albuquerque.
1999   *The Material Life of Human Beings.* Routledge, London and New York.

Schiffer, M. B. (ed.)
2000   *Social Theory in Archaeology.* University of Utah Press, Salt Lake City.

Schmidt, K.
2001   Göbekli Tepe, Southeastern Turkey: A Preliminary Report on the 1995– 1999 Excavations. *Paléorient* 26(1): 45–54.

Schmidt, R. A., and B. L. Voss
2000   *Archaeologies of Sexuality.* Routledge, London.

Schnapp, A.
1996   *The Discovery of the Past. The Origins of Archaeology.* British Museum Press, London. (First published in French in 1993.)

Shackel, P.
2000   Craft to Wage Labor: Agency and Resistance in American Historical Archaeology. In *Agency in Archaeology,* edited by M.-A. Dobres and J. Robb, pp. 232–246. Routledge, London.

Shankland, D.
1996   Çatalhöyük: The Anthropology of an Archaeological Presence. In *On the Surface: Çatalhöyük 1993–95,* edited by I. Hodder, pp. 349–358. McDonald Institute for Archaeological Research and British Institute of Archaeology at Ankara, Cambridge.

Shanks, M. and R. McGuire
1996   The Craft of Archaeology. *American Antiquity* 61:75–88.

Shanks, M., and C. Tilley
1982   Ideology, Symbolic Power and Ritual Communication: A Reinterpretation of Neolithic Mortuary Practices. In *Symbolic and Structural Archaeology,* edited by I. Hodder, pp. 129–154. Cambridge University Press, Cambridge.
1987   *Reconstructing Archaeology.* Cambridge University Press, Cambridge.

Sherratt, A.
1981   Plough and Pastoralism. In *Pattern of the Past,* edited by I. Hodder, G. Isaac, and N. Hammond, pp. 261–305. Cambridge University Press, Cambridge.
1995   Reviving the Grand Narrative. Archaeology and Long-Term Change.

Journal of European Archaeology 3:1–32.

Silistreli, U.
1991   1989 Köşk Höyük Kazısı. *XII Kazı Sonuçları Toplantısı* 1:95–104.

Sinclair, A.
2000   Constellations of Knowledge: Human Agency and material Affordance in Lithic Technology. In *Agency in Archaeology,* edited by M.-A. Dobres and J. Robb. Routledge, London.

Smith, C. E, L. Willika, P. Manabaru, and G. Jackson
1995   Looking after the Land: The Barunga Rock Art Management Programme. In *Archaeologists and Aborigines,* edited by I. Davidson, C. Lovell-Jones, and R. Bancroft, pp. 36–37. University of New England Press, Lebanon, New Hampshire.

Smith, C. E., and G. K. Ward (eds.)
2000   *Indigenous Cultures in an Interconnected World.* Allen and Unwin, Sydney, and University of British Columbia, Vancouver.

Sommer, U.
2001   "Hear the Instruction of the Father, and Forsake not the Law of the Mother": Change and Persistence in the European Early Neolithic. *Journal of Social Archaeology* 1:244–270.

Spector, J.
1993   *What This Awl Means: Feminist Archaeology in a Wahpeton Dakota Village.* Minnesota Historical Society Press, St. Paul.

Spindler, K.
1993   *The Man in the Ice.* Weidenfeld and Nicolson, London.

Spivak, G.
1999   *A Critique of Postcolonial Reason: Toward a History of the Vanishing Present.* Harvard University Press, Cambridge, Massachusetts.

Stanley Price, N., M. K. Talley, and A. M. Vaccaro (eds.)
1996   *Historical and Philosophical Issues in the Conservation of Cultural Heritage.* Getty Conservation Institute, Los Angeles.

Stevanovic, M.
2000   Visualising and Vocalizing Archaeol-

ogy's *Archival* Record: Narrative as Image. In *Towards Reflexive Methods in Archaeology: The Example at Çatalhöyük,* edited by I. Hodder, pp. 235–238. McDonald Institute for Archaeological Research and British Institute of Archaeology at Ankara, Monograph 289.

Stevanovic, M., and R. Tringham
1999   The Bach Area 1999. *Çatal News* 6:6–8.

Stordeur, D., D. Helmer, and G. Wilcox
1977   Jefrel Ahmar: Un Noveau Site de l'horizon PPNA sur le Moyen Euphrate Syrien. *Bulletin de la Société Préhistorique Française* 94:282–285.

Swidler, N., K. Dongoske, R. Anyon, and A. Downer (eds.)
1997   *Native Americans and Archaeologists. Stepping Stones to Common Ground.* AltaMira Press, Walnut Creek, California.

Swogger, J.
2000   Image and Interpretation: the Tyranny of Representation? In *Towards Reflexive Methods in Archaeology: The Example at Çatalhöyük,* edited by I. Hodder, pp. 143–152. McDonald Institute for Archaeological Research and British Institute of Archaeology at Ankara, Monograph 289.

Tambiah, S. J.
1969   Animals are Good to Think and Good to Prohibit. *Ethnology* 8:423–459.

Taylor, W.
1948   *A Study of Archaeology.* Southern Illinois University Press, Carbondale.

Thomas, D. H.
1998   *Archaeology.* 3rd ed. Harcourt Brace College Publishers, New York.

Thomas, J.
1987   Relations of Production and Social Change in the Neolithic of North-West Europe. *Man* 22:405–430.

1991   *Rethinking the Neolithic.* Cambridge University Press, Cambridge.

1993   Discourse, Totalization and "The Neolithic." In *Interpretive Archaeology,* edited by C. Tilley, pp. 357–394. Berg, London.

1996   *Time, Culture and Identity.* Routledge, London.

Thomas, J. (ed.)
2001   *Interpretive Archaeology: A Reader.* Leicester University Press, Leicester.

Thomas, N.
1991   *Entangled Objects.* Harvard University Press, Cambridge, Massachusetts.

Thomas, S.
1996   On-Line Hypertext in Archaeological Site Interpretation. Paper presented at TAG conference, Liverpool.

Tilley, C.
1989   Archaeology as Theatre. *Antiquity* 63:275–80.

1991   *The Art of Ambiguity: Material Culture and Text.* Routledge, London.

1994   *The Phenomenology of Landscape.* Berg, London.

Tilley, C. (ed.)
1990   *Reading Material Culture.* Blackwell, Oxford.

1993   *Interpretative Archaeology.* Berg, London.

Treherne, P.
1995   The Warrior's Beauty: The Masculine Body and Self-Identity in Bronze Age Europe. *Journal of European Archaeology* 3:105–144.

Trigger, B.
1984   Alternative Archaeologies: Nationalist, Colonialist, Imperialist. *Man* 19:355–370.

Tringham, R.
1991   Households with Faces: The Challenge of Gender in Prehistoric Architectural Remains. In *Engendering Archaeology: Women and Prehistory,* edited by J. M. Gero and M. W. Conkey, pp. 93–131. Blackwell, Oxford.

1994   Engendered Places in Prehistory. *Gender, Place, and Culture* 1(2): 169–204.

2000   The Continuous House. A View from the Deep Past. In *Beyond Kinship. Social and Material Reproduction in House Societies,* edited by R. A. Joyce and S. D. Gillespie, pp. 115–134. University of Pennsylvania Press, Philadelphia.

Tringham, S.
1996   The Use of Hypertext in Site Interpretation. Paper presented at TAG conference, Liverpool.

Tschauner, H.
1996   Middle-Range Theory, Behavioural Archaeology, and Post-Empiricist Philosophy of Science in Archaeology. *Journal of Archaeological Method and Theory* 3:1–30.

Tunc, B.
2004   Chemical Analysis of Bricks. In *Inhabiting Çatalhöyük: Reports from the 1995–1999 Seasons,* edited by I. Hodder. McDonald Institute for Archaeological Research and British Institute of Archaeology at Ankara, Cambridge. In press.

Turner, B.
1994   *Orientalism, Postmodernism and Globalism.* Routledge, London.

Turner, V.
1969   *The Ritual Process: Structure and Anti-Structure.* Routledge and Kegan Paul, London.

Ucko, P.
1987   *Academic Freedom and Apartheid: The Story of the World Archaeological Congress.* Duckworth, London.

Ucko, P. (ed.)
1995   *Theory in Archaeology: A World Perspective.* Routledge, London.

Walker, W. H., and L. J. Lucero
2000   ————. In *Agency in Archaeology,* edited by M.-A. Dobres and J. Robb, pp. 130–147. Routledge, London.

Wasson, P.
1994   *The Archaeology of Rank.* Cambridge University Press, Cambridge.

Watkins, J.
2000   *Indigenous Archaeology. American Indian Values and Scientific Practice.* AltaMira Press, Walnut Creek, California.

Watson, P. J.
1991   A Parochial Primer: The New Dissonance as Seen from the Midcontinental United States. In *Processual and Postprocessual Archaeologies: Multiple Ways of Knowing the Past,* edited by R. Preucel, pp. 265–274. Center for Archaeological Investigations, Occasional Paper 10. Southern Illinois University at Carbondale.

Watson, P., and M. Kennedy
1991   The Development of Horticulture

in the Eastern Woodlands of North America: Women's Role. In *Engendering Archaeology*, edited by J. Gero and M. Conkey, pp. 255–275. Blackwell, Oxford.

Webster, G.
1974   Training the New Archaeologist. In *Rescue Archaeology*, edited by P. Rahtz, pp. 235–240. Penguin Books, Harmondsworth.

Weinstein-Evron, M.
1998   *Early Natufian el-Wad revisited.* Etudes et Recherches Archéologiques de l'Université de Liège 77.

Welbourn, A.
1984   Endo Ceramics and Power Strategies. In *Ideology, Power and Prehistory*, edited by D. Miller and C. Tilley, pp. 17–24. Cambridge University Press, Cambridge.

Wheeler, R.E.M.
1954   *Archaeology from the Earth.* Clarendon Press, Oxford.

White Deer, G.
1997   Return of the Sacred: Spirituality and the Scientific Imperative. In *Native Americans and Archaeologists: Stepping Stones to Common Ground*, edited by N. Swidler, K. F. Dongoske, R. Anyon, and A. S. Downer, pp. 37–43. Altamira Press, Walnut Creek, California.

Whitley, J.
2002   Too Many Ancestors. *Antiquity* 76:119–126.

Whittle, A.
1996   *Europe in the Neolithic. The Creation of New Worlds.* Cambridge University Press, Cambridge.

Wilson, M.
2001   Tales from the Trenches. The People, Policies, and Procedures of Cultural Resource Management, pts. 1 and 2. *SAA Archaeological Record* 1(2):30–33; 1(3):37–38, 44.

Woodburn, J.
1980   Hunters and Gatherers Today and Reconstruction of the Past. In *Soviet and Western Anthropology*, edited by E. Gellner, pp. 95–118. Duckworth, London.

Wright, G. A.
1978   Social Differentiation in the Early Natufian. In *Social Archaeology,*

Beyond Subsistence and Dating, edited by C. Redman, M. J. Berman, E. V. Curtin, W. T. Langhorne Jr., N. M. Versaggi, and J. C. Wanser, pp. 201–223. Academic Press, New York.

Wright, H. T. (ed.)
1984   *On the Evolution of Complex Societies.* Undeena Publications, Malibu, California.

Wylie, A.
1989   Archaeological Cables and Tacking: The Implications of Practice for Bernstein's 'Options Beyond Objectivism and Relativism.' *Philosophy of the Social Sciences* 19:1–18.
1994   On 'Capturing Facts Alive in the Past' (Or Present): Response to Fotiadis and to Little. *American Antiquity* 59:556–560.

Wylie, A., and M. J. Lynott (eds.)
1995   *Ethics in American Archaeology: Challenges for the 1990s.* Society for American Archaeology.

Yates, T.
1993   Frameworks for an Archaeology of the Body. In *Interpretative Archaeology*, edited by C. Tilley, pp. 31–72. Berg, London, Providence.

Yentsch, A.
1991   The Symbolic Dimensions of Pottery: Sex-Related Attributes of English and Anglo-American Household Pots. In *The Archaeology of Inequality*, edited by R. H. McGuire and R. Paynter, pp.192–230. Blackwell, Oxford.

Yoffee, N., and A. Sherratt (eds.)
1993   *Archaeological Theory: Who Sets the Agenda?* Cambridge University Press, Cambridge.

Zeder, M.
1997   *The American Archaeologist. A Profile.* AltaMira Press, Walnut Creek, California. Zvelebil, M.
1995   Indo-European Origins and the Agricultural Transition in Europe. *Journal of European Archaeology* 3:33–70.

Acknowledgments

The following chapters have been previously published as indicated. Parts of Chapter 1 have been published as "Archaeological Reflexivity and the 'Local' Voice," in *Anthropological Quarterly*, 2003. Chapter 2 is from *Archaeology under Fire*, edited by L. Meskell, pp. 124–139, Routledge, 1998. Chapter 3 is a previously unpublished paper delivered at the SAA meetings in Denver in 2002. Chapter 4 is from *Antiquity* 71:691–700, 1997. Chapter 5 is from *Antiquity* 72:21–27, 1998. Chapter 6 is from *Journal of Mediterranean Archaeology* 12(1):83–85, 1999. Chapter 7 has been accepted for publication by *American Antiquity* 68(3) © 2003 by Society for American Archaeology, and is reprinted by permission of *American Antiquity*. Chapter 8 is to be published in *Social Archaeology*, edited by L. Meskell and R. Preucel, Blackwell. Chapter 9 is from *Agency in Archaeology*, edited by M.-A. Dobres and J. Robb, pp. 21–33, Routledge, London, 2000. Chaper 10 is to be published in *Unwrapping the Sacred Bundle*, edited by S. Yanagisako and D. Segal, Duke University Press. Chapter 11 is from *Understanding the Neolithic of NW Europe*, edited by E. Edmonds and C. Richards, pp. 84–101, Cruithne Press, 1998. Chapter 12 is from *Ancient Lakes, Their Cultural and Biological Diversity*, edited by H. Kawanane, G. W. Coulter, and A. C. Roosevelt, pp. 61–73, Kenobi Productions, 1999. Chapter 13 is a book review published in *Cambridge Archaeological Journal* 10(2):376–380, 1999. Chapter 14 will appear in *American Antiquity* 68(4) © 2003 by Society for American Archaeology, and is reprinted by permission of *American Antiquity*. Chapter 15 is to be published in *Papers in Honor of Ufuk Esin*, edited by M. Özdoğan, Istanbul. Chapter 16 is a revised version of a lecture delivered at the W. F. Albright Institute of Archaeological Research in Jerusalem in March 2002, when the author was the third Trude Dothan Lecturer in Ancient Near Eastern Studies. This series, which also includes lectures at Al-Quds and the Hebrew Universities, was sponsored by the Albright Institute and endowed by the Dorot Foundation. It will be published in *Near Eastern Archaeology*.

About the Author

Ian Hodder received his B.A. at the Institute of Archaeology in London in 1971. He then went on to do his Ph.D. (1975) at Cambridge University. He first taught at Leeds University before returning to teach at Cambridge from 1977 to 1999 where he became Professor of Archaeology, Fellow of Darwin College, and Fellow of the British Academy. In 1999 he moved to Stanford University where he is now Dunlevie Family Professor in the Department of Cultural and Social Anthropology. His main books include *Spatial Analysis in Archaeology* (1976, Cambridge, with C. Orton), *Symbols in Action* (1982, Cambridge), *Reading the Past* (1986, Cambridge), *The Domestication of Europe* (1990, Blackwell), and *The Archaeological Process* (1999, Blackwell).

Index

abandonment: and closure at wetlands sites in eastern England, 119, 122; processes of at Çatalhöyük, 27, 90, 148; of settlements and building of megaliths in northern Europe, 107–108. *See also* settlement history

agency: and post-structuralist interpretations of material culture, 76–78; and roles of individuals in long-term processes, 83–92

agriculture: Anatolia and origins of, 133–34; Çatalhöyük and discourse on origins of, 45; causality and origins of, 98; concept of *domus* and origins of, 99–109; role of women in early, 155–61

American Anthropologist (journal), 3

Anatolia: and archaeological discourse on Near East, 12; architectural change in Neolithic, 152; Çatalhöyük and prehistory of, 20, 167; and origins of agriculture, 133–34; and repetitive practices in Neolithic, 147. *See also* Çatalhöyük; Turkey

Ancestral Geographies of the Neolithic: Landscapes, Monuments and Memory (Edmonds, 1999), 97–98, 125–29

Andrén, A., 108–109

Andrews, P., 62–63

animals. *See* faunal artifacts

anthropology: and four-field approach, 93–96; implications of location of archaeology within, 7; reflexive discussion in, 5. *See also* social anthropology

Anyon, R., 72

Appadurai, Arjun, 72

Approaches to Social Archaeology (Renfrew, 1984), 71

archaeology: critique of idea of autonomous intellectual in, 49–51; and discourse on Near East, 11–13; and distinction between dialogue and debate, 2; idea of confession in, 23–24, 28; implications of academic location within anthropology, 7; implications of shift in definition of, 2; and international charters for management of sites, 1; and new forms of writing, 4–5. *See also* Çatalhöyük; contract archaeology; dialogue; field methods; interpretation; New Archaeology; post-processual archaeology; reflexivity and reflexive archaeology; social archaeology; theory

Archaeology and Society (Clark, 1939), 69–70

archaeometry, and universities in U.S., 94–95

art and artists: and depictions of women and men at Çatalhöyük, 171; function of at Çatalhöyük, 91; and houses at Çatalhöyük, 100, 136, 138, 142; industrial revolution and rural images in, 159; and multivocality at Çatalhöyük, 171–75; wild resources and symbolism at Çatalhöyük, 98, 157, 160, 161. *See also* paintings; sculpture

Aşikli Höyük (Turkey): and distinct characteristics of sites in Anatolia, 133–34; and houses, 99, 100, 102, 105, 109, 148

Australia, and public outreach in archaeology, 61

autonomy, and image of archaeologist as intellectual, 49–50

Bailey, D., 100

Barker, Philip, 32, 33, 37

Barrett, J., 76, 85, 126

Bartu, Ayfer, 25, 165, 169

behaviorism, and views of agency, 84

Belfer-Cohen, A., 131

belief, influence of on archaeological science, 44

Bell, C., 108

Bender, B., 102, 126, 129

Bhabha, Homi, 24